About Island Press

■■

Island Press, a nonprofit organization, publishes, markets, and distributes the most advanced thinking on the conservation of our natural resources—books about soil, land, water, forests, wildlife, and hazardous and toxic wastes. These books are practical tools used by public officials, business and industry leaders, natural resource managers, and concerned citizens working to solve both local and global resource problems.

Founded in 1978, Island Press reorganized in 1984 to meet the increasing demand for substantive books on all resource-related issues. Island Press publishes and distributes under its own imprint and offers these services to other nonprofit organizations.

Support for Island Press is provided by The Geraldine R. Dodge Foundation, The Energy Foundation, The Charles Engelhard Foundation, The Ford Foundation, Glen Eagles Foundation, The George Gund Foundation, William and Flora Hewlett Foundation, The James Irvine Foundation, The John D. and Catherine T. MacArthur Foundation, The Andrew W. Mellon Foundation, The Joyce Mertz-Gilmore Foundation, The New-Land Foundation, The Pew Charitable Trusts, The Rockefeller Brothers Fund, The Tides Foundation, and individual donors.

Environmental Leadership

Environmental
Leadership

DEVELOPING EFFECTIVE
SKILLS AND STYLES

■■

*Edited by Joyce K. Berry
and John C. Gordon*

FOREWORD BY WHITNEY TILT,
NATIONAL FISH AND
WILDLIFE FOUNDATION

ISLAND PRESS

Washington, D.C. ❑ *Covelo, California*

Library of Congress Cataloging-in-Publication Data

Environmental Leadership: Developing Effective Skills and Styles
   edited by Joyce K. Berry and John C. Gordon.
       p.   cm.
   Includes bibliographical references and index.
   ISBN 1-55963-243-7.—ISBN 1-55963-244-5 (pbk.)
   1. Conservation leadership.   2. Conservationists.
   3. Environmentalists   I. Berry, Joyce K.   II. Gordon, J. C.
   (John C.), 1939–
   S944.5.L42L43   1993   93-6542
   333.7'2'0684—dc20   CIP

Printed on recycled, acid-free paper.

Manufactured in the United States of America

10 9 8 7 6 5 4 3 2 1

Dedicated to the Editors' leadership role models:
the alumni of the Yale University
School of Forestry and Environmental Studies

Contents

III. LEADERSHIP STYLES AND EXPERIENCE

Foreword

■■■

I have often wondered when I went over the edge. Was it explaining the sex life of a lobster freshly plucked from Long Island Sound to an inner-city kid from Bridgeport? Perhaps it was Ornithology 101, which introduced me to the wonders of spring migration at Horicon Marsh in Wisconsin. Or maybe those hours of crouching half-frozen in a duck blind on Maryland's Eastern Shore had more lasting effects than the frostbite. Whatever the reasons, I count myself among the fortunate few that can claim a career in natural resource conservation. Put another way, I get paid for what I love to do.

Like many in the broad field of conservation, I have been successful in converting an early interest in all things natural into a full-time position as a *conservationist*. Many factors played a role in this career choice including education, mentors, persistence, and luck. Of this list, I would say that mentors and luck played the biggest role.

Welcome to a career where the career path is meandering and often without signposts. Welcome to a profession where positions are few, the hours are long, and salaries are a pittance compared to positions in other fields. On the other hand, welcome to a career that allows mixing career with vocation. You get to work with a lot of people just as dedicated and quixotic as you are, and if you do it right, in the words of Edward Abbey, you'll outlive the bastards.

Working to forge a balance between the environment and human needs is a challenging and demanding job. A want ad for such a task should read:

WANTED: Individual with strong scientific background to save the world. Demonstrated knowledge of politics, negotiation, finance, and people management a must. Experience in managing overworked and underpaid staff, working long hours, and ability to work miracles desirable. Salary negotiable, but less than you deserve.

Obviously, few mortals have the credentials to apply for such a position. Yet every day, conservation organizations, large and small, government or private, seek recruits to fill job descriptions that are larger than life.

The qualifications for a successful and effective career in natural resource conservation, however, are not overstated. To find personal and professional rewards in this field, a wealth of skills must be added to one's professional arsenal. A strong scientific background must be grounded with an ability to communicate and understand the political arena in which our game is only one of many. In short, it is not enough to be a good biologist. An effective conservationist must go beyond a single discipline to become a good communicator, people manager, and politician. If you are successful in that, you will likely find that others are looking to you as a leader.

Once, after presenting a lecture on conservation challenges and leadership at the Yale School of Forestry, I was asked by a student, "Do you consider yourself a leader?" My immediate reply: "No, I still consider myself a student." Afterwards, John Gordon, Joyce Berry, and I returned to the question of who are the leaders of the conservation profession. Recognizing that we lacked a useful definition of what constitutes an effective leader, we were hard pressed to define conservation leadership. This book is our answer.

Recently, as a sort of introductory primer on conservation, I assembled a small collection of books and articles that I now press on new staff and interns. Alongside the well-known volumes of Aldo Leopold's *Sand County Almanac*, Stephen Fox's *John Muir and His Legacy*, and other stalwarts, I have Edward Abbey's *Monkey Wrench Gang* (my radical side) and Norman Maclean's *A River Runs Through It* (my literary side). When it comes to explaining what it is to be a professional, I turn to Jack Ward Thomas. Addressing a conference on the present challenges, Jack concludes:

These are indeed interesting times, a time of testing. It is useless to look back for the good old days—they are gone. It is pointless to look around for others to lead—they aren't there. For better or worse, we're it. Whether we recognize it or not, we are agents of change in how natural resources are treated, considered, and used. If we succeed there will be accolades from historians. If we fail historians will, doubtless, take little notice—but history will be much different.

If we as natural resource professionals are not willing to take on the leadership responsibilities and the onerous duties entailed in management, administration, budgeting, popular communication, and politics, who will? Who will shape the conservation agenda in your absence? Failure to master the multiple disciplines of natural resources management will not only limit your work as a professional; it will likely lead to personal frustration and lack of career advancement as well.

To use a baseball metaphor, you get to first base largely with your formal education. But as you advance along the base paths, exposed all the while to an increasingly political world, you will have difficulty scoring a run if you continue to rely solely on your skills in biology. You may get thrown out stealing second, may rarely even see third base, and may never get the satisfaction of sliding home. Like it or not the buzzwords—*politics, communications, conflict resolution,* and *balanced budget*—are here to stay. Mastering your profession will require attention to these disciplines of Biopolitics. It is the only game in town. You can either play it well as a leader, or you can sit on the sidelines.

It is no fun being a loser. Winning is a different story, however, and makes the game worthwhile. We are told that leaders are formed by education, experience, and challenges. Winston Churchill is quoted as stating, "Play for more than you can afford to lose and you will learn the game." The problem is we can't *afford* to lose. It remains to be seen what the final score will be. Personally, I am looking forward to playing the next inning. Remember, conservation is among those rare opportunities where we can combine a profession with a vocation and hobby. If we get paid for doing something we love to do, we should do it well.

—Whitney Tilt
Project Director,
National Fish and Wildlife Foundation

Acknowledgments

■■

The editors thank the National Fish and Wildlife Foundation for support of this book as well as our first leadership class. The foundation has become an innovator and strong advocate of leadership programs, and we have learned and benefited greatly from their work and our association with them. We extend a special thank you to Whitney Tilt, Foundation Project Director, for his professional and personal dedication to leadership education.

We appreciate also the sponsorship provided by the Pew Charitable Trusts for the Career-Long Education Program at the Yale University School of Forestry and Environmental Studies.

We cannot imagine a more cooperative group of contributors. We thank them for their serious work, their openness, and their good cheer. It was our pleasure and good fortune to work with each one.

Thanks also to Carol Ziegler who handled the long job of putting together all the pieces of the manuscript.

At Island Press, we thank former Vice President Sumner Pingree who started us on our journey and Editor in Chief Joe Ingram who provided encouragement all along the way. Most especially, we thank Executive Editor Barbara Dean. Barbara has worked with us continually throughout this project and we cannot thank her enough for her support and wise counsel.

I

Leadership
Characteristics

1 Environmental Leadership:

WHO AND WHY

■■■

John C. Gordon and Joyce K. Berry

THE NEED FOR environmental leadership has never been greater. Government, business and industry, and not-for-profit organizations are all seeking solutions to environmental problems that are increasingly visible to all. All agree that a key element in improving the environment is leadership—the ability of an individual or a group to guide positive change toward a vision of an environmentally better future. We believe that environmental problems—or opportunities—are different enough from other human contexts to need a special kind of leadership.

Traditional leadership models have been drawn most frequently from the worlds of politics, the military, and religion; the current leadership literature is heavily biased toward leadership in business and industry. These traditional views of leadership have much to offer the environmental leader, but they can be misleading too. Many traditional leaders are given high marks for accomplishing much in a short time, for example, regardless of the ultimate sustainability of what they and their followers achieve. Rapid accomplishment and change are often important goals for environmental leaders, but they are rarely sufficient criteria for judging environmentally effective leadership. Indeed, it may be that the traditional practice of leadership, drawn from and based on these traditional sources and methods, has created many of the environmental difficulties we face today. Moreover, traditional leaders have been first and foremost effective *adversaries* of competing causes; slaying dragons has always been a sure route to leadership success. Now we are beginning to see that environ-

3

mental problems are not most effectively and sustainably solved through adversarial processes; seeking common ground, negotiation, and cooperation are better suited to most of the complex, long-term problems facing environmental leaders.

We think, therefore, that we can define this difference between traditional leadership and environmental leadership by relating environmental leadership to the key characteristics of environmental problems: long times to solutions; complex systems; an emotion-charged context; a relatively weak and scattered science base; and an absolute need for integration across a wide array of areas of knowledge and human attitudes and concerns. In aggregate, these five characteristics demonstrate why environmental leadership may require special effort and attention. Environmental challenges inevitably arise from complex systems of natural history and human desire and capability. This in turn dictates that responses are almost always complex and long-term; it may take decades to know whether a problem has been solved. Almost always, the science and the technological basis for a response are inadequate at the time the problem is identified. Integrated environmental science is young and small with respect to the entire scientific establishment, and information is scattered among diverse discipline-bound sources. This inherently weak science base will probably be a major constraint on environmental leaders for a long time. Almost all environmental challenges are subject to strong human emotions; environment and human health are firmly connected in the public's perception, and few are uninterested in their own body. Similarly, strong and often conflicting feelings about nature are inherent in our culture. Thus, environmental leaders are rarely confronted with a human context bathed in cool, detached rationality. And finally, all these characteristics dictate that lasting solutions must carefully integrate knowledge from many sources as well as human attitudes and feelings as well as sensitive treatment of economic and physical constraints and boundary conditions.

At the same time, the environmental and natural resources professions are changing; their values, perceived clients, incoming members are different than they were and indeed show signs of continued rapid change. Formerly, resource managers most often saw their clients as special-interest groups of resource users. Today a much larger fraction of the public is interested in resources. Leaders of environmental interest groups used to see themselves as saving specific resources or defeating specific polluters. Today global issues, often involving everyone as both "culprit" and "victim," have emerged. Global change, human population increase, and regional air pollution are but three examples.

The people who become environmental professionals today are increasingly different from those of the recent past. The resource management professions were, only a decade ago, almost entirely filled by white males with a technocratic turn of mind. Today women and people of color are increasingly represented. Environmental advocacy groups used to be upper middle class with predominately suburban values. Today the range of participation is broader, and urban people and urban issues are rising in importance. Federal agencies with environmental responsibilities, such as the USDA Forest Service, are finding that the public's changing perceptions of forests and forestry and their role in preserving biological diversity (for example) conflict with their past approaches to managing the national forests. As old values and practices conflict with new, and external pressures increase, terms like "gridlock" and "burnout" are used more frequently to describe the agency's condition. Painful change is obviously under way. Industries that formerly viewed environmental regulations as constraints are increasingly striving to view them as sources of competitive advantage, and the "environmental manager" is beginning to replace the "environmental lawyer" in corporate culture.

All leadership seems to be changing toward a more participatory and open model. Public involvement in environmental and natural resource decisions is often formally or informally mandated and it is increasing—a new development that is becoming especially important to environmental leaders. Similarly, all leadership is particularly visible and necessary in times of rapid change; thus, it is an important time to understand the who and why of environmental leadership.

This book assembles a series of personal accounts of leadership by a diverse array of environmental leaders who discuss their path to leadership, the skills they have found useful, and the characteristics and contexts of leadership as they see it. A substantial number of these contributors we know from their participation with the Yale School of Forestry and Environmental Studies. In selecting the authors, we used only two criteria: first, success in environmental leadership; second, diversity of organizational experience, career stage, and geographic location. The book is aimed at all Americans who aspire to environmental leadership—or are already practicing it—in order to achieve better stewardship of our environment and natural resources. We particularly hope to reach those at an early stage of an environmental career and those who see themselves as potential leaders. Our belief, based on many years of professional experience, is that leadership can be learned. Indeed, we think that all of us will find ourselves leading others at some time and place in our career, and that overt preparation for leadership should be an integral part of professional education and experience.

LEARNING LEADERSHIP

Three general notions, not entirely compatible with each other, are commonly held about the human quality called leadership. Some maintain that leaders are born not made—and thus that attempting to teach leadership is futile. A second notion is that theories of leadership, as developed by academic or business people, constitute the only true foundation for teaching people to lead. The third notion is that leadership, at least in the sense of environmental leadership, is not yet sufficiently congruent with *any* theory for it to provide a reliable basis for thought and action. In this view, experience, observation, and individual thinking must substitute for theory as a basis for teaching. We subscribe to the third view—without denying the importance of so-called innate qualities (intelligence, courage, compassion) or the utility of theories in certain situations.

Our approach to teaching leadership in the classroom thus has included four elements, all found in the personal vignettes of leadership presented in this book. "Leadership in Natural Resource Science and Management," a course taught for masters and doctoral students at Yale, is taken predominantly by students in the School of Forestry and Environmental Studies. This is a diverse group—with approximately one-fifth from overseas and a great variety of undergraduate backgrounds and professional experience. Many have held leadership positions in government, nonprofit organizations, and business.

In the class, we first examine the characteristics of leaders as observed in contemporary environmental and natural resources organizations. We begin by asking students to describe the characteristics of those they consider leaders and then to discuss these traits in the context of leadership characteristics drawn from the literature. From this, we distill and prioritize a list of characteristics that seem to fit most environmental leaders, and we examine those that seem to be particularly useful in specific organizational settings. At first glance, these always seem to be slippery abstractions; on closer examination they reveal content that can indeed be taught. Vision, for example, always appears high on the list (along with knowledge, strength of character and purpose, ability to communicate, and empathy with those who are led). Vision, upon examination, can be described as the ability to look usefully ahead and assess where an organization should go in order to achieve its purposes and best serve its clients and society. Thus, a step is taken toward teaching "vision." Examining organizational and social trends, thinking about where these may lead in one, five, or ten years, and synthesizing the implications is a relatively straightforward mental process. That it is subject to great uncertainty should not be a deterrent; vision is not clairvoyance (and is more rarely luck than supposed). Rather, effective vision is the product of practice—practice in thinking ahead, using all available data, and testing predictions and insights. Thus it becomes learnable and, by inference, teachable.

The second topic we analyze in the class is leadership skills. Certain common threads of capability run through the environmental leadership banner. These skills are highly developed in most environmental leaders: ethics and personal values; communication; management; conflict assessment and resolution; influencing legislation and policy— and, inevitably, "fiscal development" or fundraising. These skills are applied differently, of course, in different organizations and sectors. (A corporate environmental leader may be more concerned with the fundraising activities of other organizations than with, for example, raising funds from private foundations for corporate activities, while a not-for-profit leader may find the ability to secure external gifts and grants for the organization a precondition for effective leadership.) Nevertheless, all are important for environmental leaders.

Our third element is the observation of leaders themselves. All environmental leadership depends on the context: organizational culture, geographic location, variability in the natural environment—all affect leadership, and leaders respond in an enormous variety of effective ways. Only by studying examples of this variety, we think, can one begin to assemble a mental picture of effectiveness in environmental leadership. An effective corporate environmental leader for a forests products company in the Pacific Northwest will likely be a quite different package of skills, knowledge, and persona than an effective leader of an environmental advocacy group based in New York. Allowing students directly to observe leaders' similarities and differences leads them to think very specifically about the ingredients of leadership. Therefore, we select environmental leaders and bring them to the class, telling them frankly that they are being critically observed as well as presenting their view of leadership.

Finally, we ask our students to construct leadership prescriptions for real organizations and real situations. Each prescription is developed for an organization with which the student is familiar, often through working with them or for them in the past. The prescriptions are presented, both in writing and orally to the class, in four parts: the current status (with a brief history); the leadership challenge or problem (most often a need for change); the student's options for solving the problem; and, finally, the indicators that could be monitored to see whether the problem is actually solved.

OUR THEME AND OBJECTIVE

Our teaching experience led us to assemble the book; we wished to capture our approach and to illustrate our four teaching elements with the lives of real environmental leaders. Thus, we have encouraged the contributors to be personal and to describe their experiences in their own language. We have tried to impose a minimum of structure on their accounts of leadership; it was less important to us to foster similarity among chapters than to present a sample of the true breadth of response to challenge—which is, to us, the soul of environmental leadership. We invite readers to observe our sample of leaders and use their observations as tools to fashion their own leadership skills and style. We have deliberately avoided the criteria of fame and charisma in our selection of leaders, although our authors certainly exhibit those qualities variously and in abundance. Rather, we have focused on variety and success in the hope that readers from all parts of the environmental and natural resources community can identify with and learn from as many of these leaders as possible. Some of our chosen leaders are near the beginning of their career; others have led successfully for decades.

Often, given its complexity and variety of challenges, it seems amazing that environmental leadership happens at all. But it does, as can be seen in the following chapters. Our objective is that readers will, after reading, thinking, and discussing this book, say "I can do that" and feel empowered to develop their environmental leadership skills.

A PREVIEW

We have organized this book into three parts. In Part I, we set the boundary conditions for our view of leadership. Part II reviews leadership skills that we think are important, and Part III presents a variety of leadership experiences. Here we discuss the attributes of each chapter and explain why we think it is particularly important for readers to note and ponder. In the final chapter, we offer a synthesis that highlights common themes and constructs a picture of environmental leadership based on this sample.

In Chapter 2, Charles H. W. Foster, an environmental leader with past and present roles in state government, national nonprofit groups, and academia, examines the definition and acquisition of leadership characteristics. He argues that leaders are made, often by organizational circumstances, not born. He further discusses what is "different" about environmental leadership and emphasizes the importance of the transsocial and transregional nature of environmental issues.

In Chapter 3, Jack Ward Thomas—a government scientist who has been a leader in wildlife biology and management through a time of enormous professional change as well as a central figure in controversies over the conservation of threatened and endangered species—discusses the role ethics plays in environmental leadership. He emphasizes the importance of individual and professional ethics and the particular significance of a strong land ethic for natural resource leaders.

In Chapter 4, Carol Rosenblum Perry—a technical writer and editor who has worked on a huge variety of technical and popular environmental subjects and has written a book on technical writing—examines the nature of communication and its importance to environmental leaders. She argues that communication is much more than the transmission of information and that environmental subjects, in their complexity and contentiousness, require exceptional care and skill in communication. She offers numerous explicit examples of the application of communication skills in environmental leadership.

In Chapter 5, Ty Tice—an environmental mediator and "advocate for consensus" who has been in the middle of numerous acrimonious environmental disputes—reminds us that conflict presents opportunity as well as danger and should be neither feared nor avoided by environmental leaders. Leaders should not, he argues, be mediators, but they should selectively apply mediation skills.

In Chapter 6, James Lyons presents the "real" as opposed to the "textbook" view of legislative processes. Lyons has been involved in environmental policymaking in Washington, D.C., as the policy leader for a professional society and in a variety of congressional staff roles and has most recently been a principal in drafting legislation about old-growth forests on public lands. He notes that environmental leadership in the United States has been pretty much congruent with the ability to understand and influence federal legislation. After discussing leadership characteristics effective in policy and legislative action, Lyons stresses the need for leaders to take advantage of special times and situations to achieve their goals.

In Chapter 7, Henry H. Webster—who has led a large state forestry agency and two academic departments and has been an economics researcher with the USDA Forest Service—discusses the degree of congruence between "management" and "leadership" and presents examples in which sensitive management *is* effective leadership. He emphasizes the importance of "management through thinking and cooperation" in situations where no organization alone possesses the power or resources to solve large environmental problems.

In Chapter 8, W. Kent Olson—who has been the CEO of two nonprofit organizations—discusses how CEOs and boards of directors can work together to lead and how leaders can accomplish philanthropic goals. He also examines relationships between boards and staff members.

In Chapter 9, Leslie Carothers—an environmental attorney who has filled leadership roles in federal and state government and is now in a Fortune 500 corporation—emphasizes that many leadership skills that appear innate are in fact learned and that demonstrating commitment is a signal leadership characteristic. She emphasizes that a leader's *basic* talent is to be able to grasp enough of complex and specialized information from a huge array of disciplines to spot weaknesses and uncertainties.

In Chapter 10, Jeff Sirmon argues that new societal values are calling forth a new model of public agency leadership characterized by focus on processes, networks, and a "community of interest." Sirmon now leads International Programs for the USDA Forest Service and has held a variety of leadership positions in that organization, including that of regional forester in the budgetarily largest Forest Service region, the Pacific Northwest, although he is not a professional forester by education. He points out that demands on environmental leaders—as well as their rewards—don't mesh well with the long time it takes to resolve environmental problems.

In Chapter 11, Ralph Schmidt—who is senior advisor on forests and biodiversity for the United Nations Development Program and has been the leader of a commonwealth agency in Puerto Rico—provides a penetrating account of ways that the international community has addressed the problem of tropical deforestation. Schmidt explains why institutional weaknesses—not individuals—have prevented effective leadership in international forestry.

In Chapter 12, Jay Espy—CEO of the Maine Coast Heritage Trust and an example of a rising young environmental leader—argues, like others, that leaders are created, not born, and that any organization, even a small one, has many leaders. He says this is particularly true in environmental organizations because of the variety of problems encountered and the diversity of expertise needed to attack them. Unless staff and board members feel they own the organization, no amount of "leadership" will accomplish its goals.

In Chapter 13, William Brown—who has served in leadership roles with both nonprofit organizations and large industry (and began his professional career as an ornithologist)—points out that environmental excellence is now routinely demanded of companies by their customers and the society around them, a demand that creates many leadership opportunities. He describes the principles of corporate environmentalism and emphasizes the need for education within the company to change attitudes and practices.

In Chapter 14, James Crowfoot—who has been dean of a major natural resources school and has done seminal research on the nature of conflicts and conflict resolution as a social psychologist—argues that given the major social changes now under way, academic leadership of environmental units is changing and will be vastly different in the near future. He sees environmental leadership as a circle of interdependent values and behavior: being compassionate; knowing what is and what could be; acting interdependently; sharing power; honoring and conserving resources; and promoting change.

In Chapter 15, Jon Jensen—a program officer for one of the largest U.S. charitable foundations who has also led a nonprofit conservation organization—describes the special nature of the charitable foundation and its need to strive for great breadth of understanding. He discusses reactive versus proactive grant making, as well as the opportunities for leadership that both modes present.

Each chapter thus contains at least one, and usually several, retrospective analyses of specific leadership challenges faced by its author. These, in our view, should not be applied to the reader's situation as guiding cases; rather, they should be analyzed in relation to the characteristics and skills an aspiring leader needs to develop. They can be guides, therefore, to what we need to know. In the concluding chapter we draw together all these individual insights about leadership to suggest the major themes that emerge.

2 What Makes a Leader?

....

Charles H. W. Foster

FEW SUBJECTS have had more written about them than leadership. The observations range from the profound to the profane. They extend over the range of recorded history. In Matthew 15:14, for example, we are advised of the perils of lack of leadership: "If the blind lead the blind, both shall fall into the ditch." As for what constitutes a leader, the Roman historian Tacitus's observation that reason and judgment are the qualities of a leader still holds true today. Ralph Waldo Emerson's celebrated epigram about an institution being simply the lengthened shadow of one man has validity for many successful environmental organizations, particularly during their formative stages. And there is the modern bumper sticker with its wry reminder: If you're not the lead dog, the view never changes.

This chapter intends to look more closely at how leadership characteristics are defined. The focus will be on environmental leadership. The scholarly references used are admittedly selective. Where possible, I have illustrated the points with examples drawn from my own professional experience and exposure. When it comes to the bottom line, be reassured that given the right inclinations and circumstances, virtually *anyone* can be a leader.

ESSENTIALS OF LEADERSHIP

The term leadership seems to have come from the Anglo-Saxon term *laedon*, which means to travel, to go, to move in some way, to set a direction (Langton 1984). Extending this concept of motion to the human dimension, Abraham Zaleznik (1966) has defined leadership as the capacity of an individual to alter the thoughts and actions of others. Similarly, James MacGregor Burns (1978) talks about leaders being persons with certain motives or purposes mobilizing resources in order to arouse, engage, and satisfy the needs of followers. Judging by these selected definitions, then, leadership seems to display several distinct characteristics.

First: *Leaders tend to be individuals.* One hears occasionally about organizational leadership—the Izaak Walton League's fight for national water pollution control legislation in the 1950s, for example—but the organizational mantle usually cloaks one or more people who provide the real energy and drive. As John Gardner (1990) has observed, people have a tendency to aggrandize the role of a leader.

Second: *In order to have leaders there must be followers.* As an example, I can recall listening to Harvard professor Charles W. Eliot address the Massachusetts Joint Legislative Committee on Natural Resources during the early 1950s on behalf of the Bay Circuit, a proposed greenbelt of public and private open spaces that would surround Boston's urban core. Rarely did another person testify in support of the idea. Eliot was a prospective leader, but one still in need of followers.

Third: *There cannot be successful leadership without some kind of end results.* These are usually expressed in material terms—for example, Director Conrad Wirth's successful espousal of Mission 66, the National Park Service's ten-year program to upgrade visitor facilities within the national park system. But there can be important *thought* leaders as well. Aldo Leopold's writings, for example, have had a profound effect on successive generations of conservationists.

Fourth: *The thought or action, whatever it may be, must be deemed useful.* Those judging the utility need to be independent of the proponent. If not impressive in number, they must at least be recognized opinion shapers. Usefulness need not be instantaneous. Often an idea takes time to root and flower. In fact, there are some (Strozier and Offer 1985) who contend that appreciable time must elapse before an act of true leadership can be validated. Henry David Thoreau is the classic example here. His recognition did not occur for well over a half-century after his death.

TYPOLOGY OF LEADERSHIP

There are many ways to classify leadership. First and foremost is the distinction made by James MacGregor Burns (1978) between *transformational* and *transactional* leadership. In the case of the former, leaders seek to satisfy the higher needs of followers. The latter approach is concerned more with exchanges of actions and services between leaders and followers. Stewart Udall's leadership as secretary of the Department of the Interior in 1961, for example, had the objective of transforming a pedestrian and rather moribund department into the nation's premier conservation agency. In the case of William Ruckelshaus (Anne Gorsuch's replacement in 1983 as administrator of the Environmental Protection Agency), his principal task was to make a demoralized governmental department work properly again after the trying, early years of the first Reagan administration.

Second, one may identify distinct *categories* of leadership (Bailey 1988). Pure leadership, for example, is based on the singular devotion of followers. Value-induced leadership arises from agreement on common values. Instrumental leadership occurs when action is advanced by rewards or penalties. Environmental illustrations of all three categories abound. Ralph Nader's initial engagement with the auto industry over safety and air quality standards, for example, was fueled by the efforts of a devoted band of followers. Antivivisectionists derive much of their solidarity from a strongly shared sense of concern for the well-being of animals. Progress in water pollution abatement has emerged from a mixture of governmental sanctions and grant programs.

Third, leadership often displays characteristic *styles* (Bailey 1988). The so-called numinous (godlike) style of leadership is less common in the western world than in other cultures. An environmental example here would be the Agha Khan Foundation and its efforts worldwide to improve energy use and efficiency in Muslim villages. Familial leadership is predicated on a bond between equals. This brings to mind the grassroots congresses of bioregionalists, now held biennially on a continental scale with the encouragement of San Francisco's Planet Drum Foundation. Expert leadership depends primarily on what the leader knows or can do. The expertise of Douglas Foy's Conservation

Law Foundation, for example, as well as its legal clout, has helped persuade the New England utility industry to make a major commitment to energy conservation.

There are also distinct *manifestations* of leadership. It can be flamboyant, for example, as were the environmental representations of Barry Commoner and Paul Ehrlich during the 1970s. Robert Moses, legendary developer of New York's far-flung system of parks, parkways, beaches, and bridges, with his retinue of aides and his elaborate headquarters facilities at Randall's Island, Belmont State Park, and Jones Beach, is a prototypical example of imperial leadership. All leaders are somewhat manipulative. The late California congressman Phillip Burton, for example, originator of the omnibus "park barrel" (park authorization) bills of the late 1970s, was renowned for his use of influence as chairman of the House Interior Subcommittee on National Parks and Recreation. There are also consensual leaders who possess the stature and skill to forge agreement on needed actions. Frank Gregg, the first chairman of the New England River Basins Commission and the director of Interior's Bureau of Land Management during the Carter administration, was a master of consensuality. Americans also have a proclivity for symbolic leaders. These are figures whose lives take on meaning even beyond their own accomplishments. Rachael Carson was one such person. Modest and retiring by nature, and an unlikely candidate for deification, she nonetheless became a symbol of the national environmental quality movement that swept the country in the late 1960s and early 1970s.

CHARACTERISTICS OF LEADERSHIP

Regardless of how leadership is categorized, it tends to possess certain characteristics. Despite popular references to single-handed action, for example, leadership is more typically *collective* in nature. It takes a lot of people to ensure a successful outcome. Good examples of successful, collective behavior are the coalition of national conservation organizations that waged a ten-year battle to win passage of the 1980 Alaska National Interest Lands Conservation Act and the similar lengthy fight by the Clean Air Coalition to have Congress enact the Clean Air Act Amendments of 1990.

Leadership is also *dissensual* in practice. The very dynamic of leadership can be expected to generate conflict, sharpen demands, strengthen values, and enhance motives. In my own case, the leadership required to bring into being a reorganized, cabinet-level, Massachusetts Executive Office of Environmental Affairs during the early 1970s generated four years of intense conflict and dissent but culminated in an organizational structure that is still functioning today. The positive role of dissent is often overlooked and underappreciated in the normal human tendency to avoid trouble.

Leadership, by definition, is always *causative*—that is, something happens. I can recall two particular illustrations of this observation. One was the national leadership provided by Senator Robert S. Kerr (OK), the chairman of the Senate Select Committee on National Water Resources, in bringing about long-needed reforms in water resources planning, coordination, research, and management. Without Senator Kerr's seniority, knowledge of history and procedure, and personal stature, none of this would have happened. Similarly, Representative Wayne Aspinall (CO) had no equal in his ability to deliver once he was convinced of a need. As chairman of the congressionally authorized Public Land Law Review Commission and the long-time chairman of the House Interior and Insular Affairs Committee, Aspinall was perhaps the only person who could have achieved passage of the Federal Land Management and Protection Act of 1970, the organic act that set aside for all time the historic policy of wholesale disposition of the public domain.

At its best, leadership is *morally purposeful*. And in the case of transforming leadership, it is often elevating. Few of us have not encountered leaders who have heightened our sense of purpose and commitment. I can recall a poignant moment in November 1980 when René Dubos traveled to the Yale School of Forestry and Environmental Studies to offer the annual Charles Lathrop Pack lecture. Then nearly eighty years of age, Dubos elected to come to New Haven from New York by train and stand in venerable Sage Hall for nearly two hours, addressing a packed audience and answering questions. Afterward he was thronged by students who were well aware that the moment was at hand to meet a rare blend of scientist, philosopher, and environmentalist.

INGREDIENTS OF LEADERSHIP

Can we summarize the ingredients necessary for successful leadership? There seem to be four.

First: *An individual must be present with the personal capacity to lead.* He or she must be knowledgeable. But beyond sheer knowledge, the person must be able to grasp information readily. Added to these intellectual qualities should be intuitive capabilities, good judgment, and sound reasoning. Interpersonal skills are also critical. The ability to empathize, for example, is absolutely vital. Our prototypical leader must also enjoy inner security and the confidence derived therefrom.

I can recall serving on the first Environmental Advisory Board of the Corps of Engineers from 1970 to 1972 and watching Lieutenant General Frederick Clarke, the chief of engineers, begin to redirect an entrenched, traditional, development agency into more environmentally responsive actions. Clarke sensibly began working at both ends. He first saw to it that the board held the bulk of its meetings at the district level so that persuasion could be applied from the bottom up. But he also insisted on having all of his top staff present at every Advisory Board meeting. Clarke demonstrated how important it is for an agency leader to be secure in his own organization before attempting to bring about change.

Second: *The individual so identified should be able to attract and hold a significant followership.* Followers normally occur in some numbers. It is helpful if their ranks include representatives of groups with established credibility. If possible, followers should be distributed across the full spectrum of issues. They should be of a caliber to follow through with or without the leader.

Of the eight governors I have worked for in Massachusetts, Francis W. Sargent comes the closest to illustrating this leadership model. The Sargent cabinet in 1971 was comprised of accomplished but strong-willed individuals. The governor deliberately encouraged them to operate forthrightly and independently. Yet, in the case of major inter-agency disagreements, such as the decision to take Interstate 95 around rather than across the environmentally sensitive Fowl Meadows tract in Canton and Milton, it was the governor's own public credibility and personal popularity that were called upon to carry the day. Although the cabinet officers appeared to come up with and execute the policy decisions, we were only reflections of Sargent's particular style of decentralized leadership.

Contrary to prevailing opinion, leaders do not have to be prominent to be successful. A forest supervisor I worked for on a summer fire crew in Oregon's Fremont National Forest forty years ago gave me a bit of advice I have never forgotten. There are two ways to get ahead in an organization, he said. One is to do a good job, get recognized, and take over your superior's position. But the better way is to do a good job, give him credit for it, and then succeed him when he gets promoted. You will then have a friend in high places for life.

Third: *A situation should be at hand that is amenable to leadership action.* For example, there should be a tangible problem, need, or opportunity. No other competing leadership element should stand in the way. The cause must be validated by fact or informed opinion, and the timing must be opportune in social, economic, and political terms.

For an illustration, let me return to the case of Professor Eliot. During the 1980s, a vigorous young state deputy commissioner of environmental management, Robert L. Yaro, rediscovered the Bay Circuit and saw to it that funds for implementation of a state trails program were included in a 1984 Massachusetts environmental bond issue. A public/private Bay Circuit Alliance has now been formed to take operating responsibility for the 160-mile regional trail system. All of this, I might add, has occurred under the watchful and approving eyes of octogenarian Charles Eliot, now a leader *with* followers.

Fourth: *Something needs to happen in a recognizable way*—an expression, thought, or explicit action. This must occur within a reasonable time frame. To be considered a case of successful leadership, the outcome must always be meritorious and, preferably, socially useful. It should also endure.

Many of these descriptions remind me of Russell E. Train, now chairman of the board of the World Wildlife Fund/Conservation Foundation and the recipient of a 1991 Presidential Medal of Freedom. Confidant of presidents and world leaders, administrator of important environmental programs in the Council on Environmental Quality, the Department of the Interior, and the Environmental Protection Agency, as well as one of the nation's most accomplished private conservation leaders, Train possesses a personal record of leadership results that is virtually unrivaled.

THE CHARISMATIC LEADER

At this point, we should comment on the special case of the charismatic leader. European philosopher Max Weber appears to have brought the concept into use (Spinrad 1991), borrowing the Greek term *charisma* (gift) to describe the special personal appeal enjoyed by certain figures. In common parlance, leadership and charisma are believed to go hand in hand. One imagines a self-confident, assured, insightful person, operating outside and even counter to the traditional institutional setting, with the capacity to induce others to his or her views. Yet, in modern times, charismatic leaders are more frequently the product of mass persuasion techniques. They tend to arise in times of crisis and fade away when conditions moderate. As Weber himself observed, a leader cannot be truly charismatic without a perceived ability to deliver.

Environment has certainly had its share of charismatic leaders. The epitome is perhaps David Brower, long-time leader of the Sierra Club and founder of Friends of the Earth. Now approaching eighty years of age, this rangy six-footer, with his shock of white hair and engaging way of advocating the need to save the world, is still a commanding presence at the lectern. But the term charisma would also apply to Dr. Thomas Lovejoy, the Smithsonian Institution's assistant secretary for external affairs and an architect of the imaginative concept of "debt-for-nature" swaps. Lovejoy's persistence, his grace and charm, coupled with his solid credentials in science, have made him uniquely able to enlist the rich, famous, and powerful in his special cause of tropical rain forest conservation.

WHAT LEADERSHIP IS NOT

It is especially important to understand what leadership is *not*. Leaders are not dependent on status or office, for example. They need not have or exercise authority. Leadership is not simply a manifestation of long and faithful service. Nor is it necessarily a mark of recognition or popularity. Is leadership merely an alternative form of force or dominance? The experts say no. True leadership seems to be based on intrinsically motivated relationships. It depends on a high degree of mutual understanding between leader and follower. In some cases, the attachment to the leader turns out to be the follower's principal reward.

Gifford Pinchot seems to have enjoyed those relationships with the men of the fledgling USDA Forest Service. "GP," as he was known to his foresters, could ride and shoot with the best of them. He was a romantic, evangelical mix of hero and role model at a time when his agency most needed those leadership qualities.

But the leaders, too, will have certain obligations of their own. They must preserve the quality and sustain the vitality of their group, not sap it through self-serving actions. They must ensure fairness and equity at all times between leader and follower. They must use their position to set challenging goals and objectives for their group, yet try to minimize any ambiguity of expectations. And they must seek permanent, not temporary, outcomes. Pinchot seemed to do all of that and more in the course of an extraordinary career.

ENVIRONMENTAL LEADERSHIP

With the general characteristics of leadership now in mind, what then are the particular dimensions of environmental leadership? Environmental leadership, I contend, is a distinct category of leadership even though the field is still in its infancy. Here the term encompasses any activity involving the management, use, or protection of natural resources. One needs to look first at what is different about environmental leadership; then, who the nation's environmental leaders are; and finally, what we know about them and the way they work.

Leadership Differences

The first difference between environmental and other leadership organizations is the strong tradition of amateurs, volunteers, and part-timers inherent from the very start of the conservation movement. In stark contrast with most business or governmental institutions, the bulk of environmental leadership operates within loosely structured organizations. The implications here are twofold. First, conventional environmental organizations frequently lack a distinguishable hierarchy or authority structure. For a large organization, this can make it unwieldy or even unmanageable. One simply cannot tell environmentalists what to do and when to do it. But, conversely, it is the loose grassroots character of the typical environmental organization that gives the movement much of its credibility. It cannot be captured easily by a special constituency nor, indeed, by its own managers. When I joined The Nature Conservancy in 1966 as its first professional president, for example, the tension between the volunteer chapter structure and the central staff was almost palpable. The five-million-member National Wildlife Federation has experienced similar problems.

The second distinguishing characteristic of an environmental organization is the scope of its subject matter. Environmental leaders must deal with issues that are frequently transsocietal in nature and often without limits of scale or geography. This makes program focusing difficult and program continuity next to impossible. The result is constantly shifting priorities, applications, and activities. Consider the case of New England's respected Appalachian Mountain Club, formed in 1876 to advance "geographical exploration." Today, the AMC is a full-fledged, general conservation organization offering a broad range of research, educational, and recreational services.

The third difference is that environmental leadership occurs in a wide variety of contexts. There are, for example, environmental leaders who hold responsible positions in official natural resource agencies. These people are blessed with a sizable staff and abundant funding and wield substantial regulatory powers. Not infrequently, however, governmental leaders find themselves constrained by the terms of their statutory empowerment. At the other extreme are informal organizations like the campus-based Public Interest Research Groups. Largely because of their freedom to innovate, PIRGs have managed to compile an enviable record in conducting research and advancing environmental compliance.

A fourth characteristic of environmental leadership is its appeal to a limited spectrum of human society. Despite many efforts to the contrary, the movement has remained largely a middle to upper-class phenomenon. It has yet to make a plausible connection with the victims of race, hunger, poverty, inferior housing, and poor health. In fact, one of the dilemmas facing environmentalists today is that so many environmentally degrading factors, at least on the surface, appear to improve the material aspects of human well-being.

If you should visit Aberdare National Park in Kenya (the site of the famed Treetops Hotel), for example, the small subsistence farms on the fringes bespeak the inevitable conflicts occurring between the needs of people and those of animals. Similarly, the spotted owl controversy in the U.S. Pacific Northwest seems to pit the forest products industry and its dependent communities against advocates of endangered species preservation. The coming of age of environmental mediation and other conflict resolution devices is reflective of the growing realization that environmentalism will have to become more consensual and less confrontational if it is to retain the depth of support it enjoys today among the American public.

National Leaders

Just who are the nation's environmental leaders? The question was first raised in 1971 by the Natural Resources Council of America (NRCA), an association representing more than seventy of the leading national, regional, and scientific organizations in the United States. The directory of leaders published at that time was supplanted by a second edition, *National Leaders of American Conservation*, issued in 1985. To ensure continuity, the same criteria were utilized for both books. Individuals could be living or deceased and could be active in a variety of categories of service. But each had to have made a distinctive contribution, and that contribution had to be of at least regional significance. Eligible activities were those concerned with the preservation or wise use of one or more natural resources.

The NRCA went out of its way to emphasize what would *not* be recognized. Political figures or officeholders per se were not eligible for inclusion. Part-time enthusiasts or those seeking recognition were not to be selected. Designations would not be accorded to persons displaying merely a sincere and dedicated interest in conservation or as a mark of their recognition or popularity. Despite these caveats, the final roster swelled to nearly five hundred figures proposed by over two hundred nominators.

Nongovernmental Leaders

In 1989, another attempt was made to assess the state of environmental leadership. The Virginia-based Conservation Fund organized the Conservation Leadership Project and undertook a national study of private environmental leaders (Snow 1992). The survey was limited to the leaders of nongovernmental organizations and to a sampling of their related academic and volunteer communities. The purposes were to develop a profile of the top ranks of modern environmental leaders and to identify their status, needs, and aspirations. Completed questionnaires were received from more than five hundred participants. The responses underscored many problems encountered today in environmental leadership.

The researchers found, for example, that most nongovernmental organizations, despite their high public acclaim, suffered from chronic undersupport. Their leaders were often poorly prepared and trained, isolated from their peers, and substantially disconnected from their grassroots constituencies. The typical leader seemed to practice a trial-by-error style of management. Elitism often prevailed. The governance of such organizations seemed to be lacking in diversity and expertise. Most regrettable of all, the staff of the typical nongovernmental environmental organization seemed ill-equipped to accomplish the underlying objective of their profession—to convert the conservation ethic into a true national ethos. Steps to improve environmental leadership could be summarized in six strategies, the Conservation Fund advised.

Leadership Strategies

First, current leaders should be provided opportunities for development through in-service and other training programs. Second, every effort should be made to enlarge the pool of leaders. Scholarship assistance, internships, mentorships, and recruitment of successful professionals from other fields were among the approaches suggested. Third, academia should be utilized more extensively for leadership development and training, particularly at the graduate level of study. Fourth, volunteerism should be revitalized at all levels, both by creating new opportunities and by better defining volunteer roles and responsibilities. As a fifth strategy, the leadership experts recommended expanded participation by minorities and other nontraditional groups in order to resolve the problem of limited representation. And sixth, in order to build a national environmental ethos, there must be more effective outreach to other key sectors of society, especially church, school, business, labor, and the media.

Leadership Initiatives

In addition to the six basic strategies just outlined, the Conservation Fund's Leadership Project cited twenty-three specific initiatives that would help improve environmental leadership. They fell generally into four categories: movement-wide recommendations, organizational recommendations, recommendations to funders, and recommendations to academia. Among them was a new institutional entity to design and carry out a development program for conservationists and environmentalists emphasizing such areas as organizational development, communications, and interorganizational ("common ground") approaches. Given an improved "culture of leadership" among staff professionals and a supportive institutional environment, it was felt that future leaders could be developed within their own organizations. Funders were encouraged to favor general support over project support and to lend a sympathetic ear to requests for grants specific to leadership training and development. An overhaul of academic programs concerned with environment was also recommended. It was thought that prospective professionals would profit from receiving as much training in the human dimension as in the technical and scientific aspects of natural resources.

SUMMING IT UP

How, then, can we summarize environmental leadership? As a prescription for success, those of you who are (or would be) leaders should always try to pick issues that are timely and doable. Strive to be factually correct in all your assertions. Be reasonable in your positions, but do not hesitate to stretch the limits of the possible. It is also important to be more than a single-issue leader. Having done all of the above, you should then work persistently to accomplish your objectives by enlisting the full support, confidence, loyalty, and, indeed, enthusiasm of your followers. Above all, listen carefully to their views and don't be afraid to select a cadre of followers to help, even those who may outstrip you in ability and ultimately outshine you in accomplishment.

Apart from honing the edges of your own organization, you should be sensitive to a number of outside factors that may be crucial to successful action. One is to identify those in a position to decide the outcome and strive to be credible with them. Another is to develop an outer zone of informed neutrals who can be counted upon not to take sides. Finally, you must understand the value of symbolic behavior. If you really want to be a leader, you should look and act like one at all times.

REFERENCES

Bailey, F. G. 1988. *Humbuggery and Manipulation: The Art of Leadership*. Ithaca: Cornell University Press.

Bass, B. M. 1985. *Leadership and Performance Beyond Expectations*. New York. Free Press.

Bersi, R. 1980. In H. Moore, P. Diamandoupolis, J. L. Fisher, and L. H. Smith, eds., *Defining Leadership*. AASCU Study 3. Washington: American Association of State Colleges and Universities.

Bleedorn, B.D.B. 1988. *Creative Leadership for a Global Future: Studies and Speculations*. American University Study Series XIV (Education) 12. New York: Peter Lang.

Brooks, P. 1972. *The House of Life: Rachael Carson at Work*. Boston: Houghton Mifflin.

Burford, A. M. 1986. *Are You Tough Enough?* New York: McGraw-Hill.

Burns, J. M. 1978. *Leadership*. New York: Harper & Row.

Cahn, R. 1978. *Footprints on the Planet: A Search for an Environmental Ethic*. New York: Universe Books.

Caro, R. A. 1974. *The Power Broker: Robert Moses and the Fall of New York*. New York: Knopf.

Chandler, J. A. 1991. "Public Administration and Private Management: Is There a Difference?" *Public Administration* 69 (3):385–392.

Chase, G. 1980. *Bromides for Public Managers*. (Adapted by M. V. Kurkjian.) Case Study Series N-16-84-586. Cambridge: Kennedy School of Government, Harvard University.

Clawson, M. 1971. *The Bureau of Land Management*. New York: Praeger.

Cooper, J. M., Jr. 1987. "Gifford Pinchot Creates a Forest Service." In J. W. Doig and E. C. Hargrove, eds., *Leadership and Innovation*. Baltimore: Johns Hopkins University Press.

Flader, S. L. 1974. *Thinking Like a Mountain: Aldo Leopold and the Evolution of an Ecological Attitude Toward Deer, Wolves, and Forests*. Columbia: University of Missouri Press.

Fox, S. 1981. *John Muir and His Legacy: The American Conservation Movement.* Boston: Little, Brown.

Gardner, J. W. 1990. *On Leadership.* New York: Free Press.

Hays, S. P. 1987. *Beauty, Health, and Permanence: Environmental Politics in the United States, 1955–85.* New York: Cambridge University Press.

House, R. J., W. D. Spangler, and J. Woycke. 1991. "Personality and Charisma in the U.S. Presidency: A Psychological Theory of Leader Effectiveness." *Administrative Science Quarterly 36(3):364–396.*

Kotter, J. P. 1990. *A Force for Change: How Leadership Differs from Management.* New York: Free Press.

Langton, S. 1984. *Environmental Leadership.* Lexington, MA: Lexington Books.

McPhee, J. 1971. *Encounters with the Archdruid.* New York: Farrar, Straus & Giroux.

Morgan, A. H. 1977. *Robert S. Kerr: The Senate Years.* Norman: University of Oklahoma Press.

Reuss, M. 1983. *Shaping Environmental Awareness: The United States Army Corps of Engineers Environmental Advisory Board, 1970–1980.* Environmental History Series EP-870-1-10. Washington: U.S. Army Corps of Engineers.

Snow, Donald. 1992. *Inside the Environmental Movement: Meeting the Leadership Challenge.* Washington: Island Press.

Spinrad, W. 1991. "Charisma: A Blighted Concept and an Alternative Formula." *Political Science Quarterly* 106(2):295–312.

Stogdill, R. M. 1974. *Handbook of Leadership: A Survey of Theory and Research.* New York: Free Press.

Stroud, R. H., ed. 1985. *National Leaders of American Conservation.* Washington: Smithsonian Institute Press.

Strozier, C. B., and D. Offer, eds. 1985. *The Leader: Psychohistorical Essays.* New York: Plenum Press.

Sun, M. 1990. "How Do You Measure the Lovejoy Effect?" *Science* 247:1174–1176.

Udall, S. L. 1963. *The Quiet Crisis.* New York: Holt, Rinehart & Winston.

Zaleznik, A. 1966. *Human Dimensions of Leadership.* New York: Harper & Row.

II

Leadership
Skills

3 Ethics for Leaders

■■■

Jack Ward Thomas

I WAS BORN in Fort Worth, Texas, on 7 September 1934 and raised in the small town of Handley. Though my high school was small, there was a full science/math curriculum and an opportunity for full participation in athletics. My grandfather's nearby farm offered hunting, fishing, camping, and riding.

I entered the Agricultural and Mechanical College of Texas in 1953—at that time, it was all-male and all-military in makeup. My intent was to become a veterinarian. As soon as I discovered it was possible to obtain a degree in wildlife management, however, I switched majors. Graduation came in 1957 along with a regular Air Force commission.

The Texas Game and Fish Commission offered me a job at Sonora handling "wildlife management" (which really meant regulation of hunting activities and census efforts) for an area bigger than the State of Massachusetts for the princely sum of $300 a month. Two years later, in 1960, I was transferred to become project leader for Edwards Plateau, an area containing the biggest deer herd in North America— all on private land. Handling such responsibility and a staff of some twenty to twenty-five people at age twenty-four was both a maturing and a learning experience.

Dealing with hundreds of private landowners, politicians, and commissioners during the decade of the "doe wars" sharpened my skills in dealing with all kinds of people and tough political situations and led to a certain expertise in applying what has become known as biopolitics. Though it was not part of my job, we conducted research activities in our "spare time" that led to a number of publications. By 1966, it became evident to me that it was time to move on to a position where the remuneration was closer to a living wage. I applied for federal service and, because of my "spare time" research publications, was rated as eligible for both management and research positions.

The U.S. Forest Service, after offering the position to several other candidates with advanced degrees, contacted me about a research job in a new research unit at Morgantown, West Virginia. I accepted in late 1966. For the next three years, while going to school part time, I was part of a research team working on the effects of even-aged timber management on deer, turkeys, grouse, and hunters. My study areas were in the Monongahela National Forest, and this was the period when the controversy over clearcutting led to the National Forest Management Act. So now I was viewing biopolitics at the national level.

In 1969, I was granted an M.S. degree from West Virginia University in wildlife ecology and offered the position of project leader. I was to begin the nation's first research unit in what was called urban forestry at Amherst, Massachusetts, with an interdisciplinary staff of scientists. This move also offered me the opportunity to become a part-time student at the University of Massachusetts in pursuit of a Ph.D. degree in forestry.

My three and a half years at Amherst provided not only experience with a new culture and a new view of wildlife management and forestry but also experience with interdisciplinary and interinstitutional research efforts. In my university work I was allowed maximum freedom to pursue coursework that was broad and diverse, ranging from regional planning to advanced economics to ecology. My dissertation involved determining habitat requirements of songbirds in suburban areas—quite a change for a big game biologist.

In 1973, opportunity came to return to the west as project leader for range and wildlife habitat research at La Grande, Oregon. This was one job in the Forest Service that I truly coveted. And I was not disappointed, having now spent nineteen years in that job. Exciting things have happened in that twenty years since 1973.

Shortly after arriving in Oregon, I led a team charged with developing a system to manage for the 379 species of vertebrates in the Blue Mountains—all at the same time. The result was *Wildlife Habitats in Managed Forests—The Blue Mountains of Oregon and Washington*, which led to the Wildlife Habitat Relationships Program of the Forest Service. This effort was followed by the job of compiling and editing *Elk of North America—Ecology and Management* and *Wildlife Habitats in Managed Rangelands—the Great Basin of Oregon.* Other work continued and by 1992 my publication list comprised over 275 items.

In 1989, the heads of the Forest Service, Bureau of Land Management, National Park Service, and Fish and Wildlife Service tendered an offer that could not be refused: leadership of the Interagency Scientific Committee to develop a scientifically credible strategy to manage the northern spotted owl. The committee's report, *A Conservation Strategy for the Northern Spotted Owl,* has been at the center of the biggest flaps over natural resource management in the United States in the last half of the twentieth century. But in spite of every attack the committee's work has remained unshaken and has come to form the basis of the recovery plan for the species. This has been the ultimate lesson in biopolitics—a lesson involving numerous appearances before House and Senate committees as well as appearances in federal courts and before the "God Squad."

In short, my career has been, by choice, that of a field biologist. I have held no positions of power but, perhaps, my career illustrates that one can have influence without position. If there is any secret to this it is in constant learning, seizing opportunity, being flexible, and pursuing one's own vision of a career.

What comes next? Who knows? I can hardly wait to find out.

WHERE "ETHICS" COMES IN

The word "ethics" is commonly used in connection with natural resource leadership but often with little understanding of its meaning and implications in that context. Webster's Collegiate Dictionary defines ethics as the discipline dealing with what is good and bad and with moral duty and obligations; a set of moral principles and values; a theory or system of moral values; the principles of conduct governing an individual or group.

Ethics as a philosophical discipline, the first definition, appears to have very little influence on how natural resource leaders carry out their day-to-day activities. The other three definitions, however, encompass the principles of conduct and values that describe the ethical relationships between individuals and in professional behavior and in natural resource management. I believe these activities can be divided into three basic categories: personal ethics, professional ethics, and land ethics. Natural resource professionals today must exert leadership in all three categories.

PERSONAL ETHICS

Whether personal, group, or societal, ethics is based on some concept of what conduct is right and what conduct is wrong. But who makes the rules? Although perceptions of ethical behavior differ from one society to another, perceptions *within* a society tend to be remarkably similar. In the western world, the general code of ethical behavior governing person-to-person interactions is contained in five of the Ten Commandments: "Thou shalt not . . . kill, commit adultery, steal, bear false witness, nor covet . . . anything that is thy neighbor's."

These commandments—commonsense rules that allow a human society to function in a relatively stable, sustainable state—are unequivocal statements of right and wrong. From this underlying bedrock arose a multitude of customs, rules, and laws applicable to a myriad of circumstances. In nearly all western societies, most of these five commandments have been codified into civil law. In the beginning, adherence to these increasingly complex laws equaled ethical behavior.

Reliance on an evolving and ever more complex set of rules to govern every conceivable situation produced rigid responses to ethical questions that inevitably arose in widely and continuously varying circumstances. Applying rigid standards of ethical behavior in all circumstances inevitably leads to some lessening of rigidity in the individual and societal concept of what is right and wrong. This flexibility comes with the recognition that what constitutes ethical behavior depends on the particular circumstances of the situation and the moment. This is called "situational ethics." In person-to-person behavior, the concept is commonly simplified to the "golden rule" common to many religions: Behave toward others as you would have them behave toward you.

Persons who adhere to these commandments or the overarching golden rule or both in their daily lives are usually considered ethical. But one can also act unethically by acquiescing in a wrong activity, by looking the other way to avoid confronting an ethical issue, by re-maining silent in the face of unethical activity, or by carrying out orders that are in themselves unethical. Everyone must make decisions that are replete with ethical overtones every day. The cumulative result of these decisions defines the ethical person. Questions about ethical behavior do not ordinarily come in the form of a clear-cut challenge to honor and courage. More commonly, such tests come in small pack-ages and quiet ways—and they do come often. For most professionals, it is these small personal tests that determine a person's reputation for integrity and ethical behavior . . . or the lack of same.

A frequent complaint among young people in natural resource man-agement is that they are pressured by superiors to modify reports inappropriately or, at least, acquiesce in courses of action they consider unethical. But coercion—like the tango—requires two: one to coerce and one to accede. Individuals must base their actions first on their personal values and only then rely on the values of their society and profession. (Judging the conduct of others is another matter and should be approached differently—and more leniently—because one seldom has complete knowledge of the circumstances surrounding an action.)

PROFESSIONAL ETHICS

Ethics relates to professional behavior as well. Here the underlying principles of ethical behavior are modified or expanded to deal with individual performance according to standards set by a professional group. People who consider themselves "professionals," and, for whatever reason, in a different guild from other professionals, com-monly form organizations that further the aims and welfare of their group.

The Wildlife Society, American Fisheries Society, Society for Range Management, and Society of American Foresters are all well-established professional organizations. Most such groups formulate codes of ethics to guide their professional activities and to demonstrate to their members and to society at large that the group's members—individually and collectively—are worthy of society's recognition and respect. The Wildlife Society (1978), for example, has produced a code of ethics to guide the activities of certified wildlife biologists. Another example is the code of ethics for the Society of American Foresters (1992b). When the fancy words of The Wildlife Society's code are stripped away and the statements reduced to their essence, they say:

1. Tell folks that your prime responsibility is to the public interest, the wildlife resource, and the environment.
2. Don't perform professional services for anybody whose role or primary intent is to damage the wildlife resource.
3. Work hard.
4. Don't agree to perform tasks for which you are not qualified.
5. Don't reveal confidential information about your employer's business.
6. Don't brag about your abilities.
7. Don't take or offer bribes.
8. Uphold the dignity and integrity of your profession.
9. Respect the competence, judgment, and authority of other professionals. [Thomas 1986:35]

One simple but essential admonition seems to be missing from these codes. Tell the truth! Telling the truth is so basic to ethical behavior that it should be the unspoken foundation supporting all other statements governing professional conduct. Even so, the need to tell the truth should be clearly stated and stand above all other admonitions to professionals. As I have stated elsewhere (Thomas 1986:36):

More and more, lately, I seem to find myself advising troubled colleagues to tell the truth. It seems so simple. Yet it can be so liberating. We live in an age of euphemisms, half-truths, obfuscations, double-talk, and double-think. This atmosphere has closed in on us so gradually, so cloaked in the camouflage of the committee or team report, so justified by the need to get the job done, that we have come to consider such things the norm. Tell the truth, all the truth, all the time. It is the right thing, the healthy thing, the professional thing to do.

Another component of professional ethics is acceptance and respect for diversity in viewpoint and philosophy among professional colleagues. For example, there are many different philosophies among natural resource management professionals concerning how they relate to the natural world. Remember, there are no inherent rights or wrongs in these philosophical positions—they merely *are*. Some tend to be anthropocentric and take a utilitarian view of land—that is, land exists for people and is to be managed to satisfy people's needs (DeVall and Sessions 1984; Leopold 1949). Others are mainly biocentric in their philosophy (Kennedy and Mincolla 1985), view humans as part of nature (Leopold 1949), and subscribe to the admonition voiced by Sessions (1977:450) to be concerned with organic wholeness, and to love that and not man apart from that.

When professionals of the biocentric and anthropocentric persuasions serve together on various teams in land management agencies—particularly those agencies that are essentially anthropocentric in mission and tradition—discord is likely. Before participants judge the ethics of their coworkers, they should consider the differences between biocentric and anthropocentric philosophies and how they might influence individual behavior.

More and more commonly, teams of professionals from different disciplines work together to derive approaches to natural resource management objectives. In the USDA Forest Service, these teams provide information to decision makers on how projects deemed necessary to implement forest plans can be achieved within constraints of the laws and approved standards and guidelines. The teams are often pressed to reach a collective position on which all members can agree. Those who are difficult to bring into the fold quickly attain the reputation for not being "team players." As Lichatowich (1992) points out, the word "team" in team player is misleading. A team is a group of individuals with different points of view, different skills, or different experience brought together to achieve a common goal—a goal whose achievement needs the individual contributions of the team members. The *different* contributions of the team members are important. Contrast that notion with "team players"—people who wait until decisions are made and then conform their thinking to fit.

A reputation as a non–team-player is not ordinarily conducive to career advancement. So the question of ethical compromise arises, as well as the question of when compromise—which after all is the art of political achievement—grades into unethical behavior. Natural resource management professionals need to recognize that teams will often be unable to derive a course of action without negative effects on certain natural resource attributes. These negative effects must be fully revealed along with the plan's positive aspects. Bella (1992) describes what happens when well-meaning employees filter out such negative information in organizational systems. Among the common properties of such organizational systems is the increased likelihood of selectively producing and perpetuating information favorable to these systems. Favorable assessments that don't disrupt organizations can perpetuate those systems while contrary assessments tend to be systematically filtered. Occupants of the highest positions in the organization are the members most dependent on such a diet and as a result their perceptions are highly vulnerable to this risk.

The ethical responsibility for administrators and other decision makers thus seems clear: Guard against such distortion by consciously working toward a professional working environment where diversity of viewpoint is accepted, where bad news can be safely delivered, and where honesty is consistently rewarded. Decision makers are paid to make the hard decisions. The reliability of the information on which these decisions depend is partly a product of the willingness of administrators to seek out and listen to the truth, however disappointing or disconcerting it may be.

Some purists may question the ethics of even entertaining the notion that biopolitics in natural resource management might be handled ethically. But without skilled and ethical practitioners of biopolitics, natural resources cannot be managed. Biological information is not derived through immaculate conception, and politics can as readily be ennobling as corrupting. After all, experiments are designed, data collected, analyses performed, and management conclusions drawn by human beings conditioned by culture, education, and experience. Further, all management decisions are made within the context of laws, court opinions, social and political acceptability, policies, customs, and the availability of resources.

The ethical practice of biopolitics can be complicated by the recognition that, for most endeavors in natural resource management in a democracy, goals are set through some political process or combination of processes. The democratic process thrives on compromise and, as a result, the guidance provided in law and regulations is frequently confusing, unclear, and intentionally vague or ambiguous. These goals and directives are not guaranteed to be well stated, appropriate, well founded, or even achievable. Yet natural resource management professionals must attempt to achieve the goals, change the direction, or—if the conflict with conscience is too great—to refuse to participate or even resign. For those professionals who are concerned with ethical behavior, these conditions produce a constantly shifting melee of combatants and petitioners who create crises that must be continually faced.

Even then, assuming professional competence and hard work, following personal and professional ethical standards can be relatively easy. After all, in most cases one must only *refrain* from some action—don't bear false witness, don't take or offer bribes, and so on. Evaluating the ethical consequences of omission—such as less than full disclosure of the consequences of proposed management actions, acquiescence in deceptive euphemisms, and silence on issues when a clearly expressed statement might have influenced the outcome—is far more difficult.

Although professional societies are frequently conceived of and advertised as watchdogs of professional standards, in reality that role usually begins and ends with formulating a set of ethical standards. Rarely do professional associations deal with charges that a member has violated the profession's ethical standards. Punishment normally lies in the lowered status and respect accorded by fellow professionals. Such can be a formidable deterrent to unethical behavior. Conversely, rewards for maintaining and practicing good ethical standards are accorded through the good opinion of colleagues, a primary motivating force governing professional behavior.

The degree of trust that the public and elected officials accord to professional groups likewise derives from experience gained over years of listening to what professionals say and comparing what they say to what they do. In natural resource management, as Aldo Leopold noted, the "signature" of the actions of professionals is clearly written, year by year and activity by activity, on the land itself. Loss of public confidence in the ethical behavior of a profession can be quickly discerned when laws are passed that constrain professional prerogatives in management action. Shifts in confidence can also be seen by observing who is consulted by elected or appointed officials in time of crisis.

Recent crises in dealing with threatened and endangered species, allocation of remaining old-growth forests in the Pacific Northwest, and declining forest health in the Intermountain West have been marked by elected officials turning for help more and more to professionals, especially scientists, both inside and outside government agencies. The role of natural resource professionals, depending on the position occupied, lies not only in making resource decisions but more commonly in defining options and the likely outcomes of implementing them. The professional's foremost obligation is to ensure an open, honest discussion of the risks and trade-offs of alternative management actions in the best traditions of good science and in the best interest of society both present and future. Today, the circumstances surrounding such questions as the appropriate allocation of the remaining old-growth forests are recognized, at least by some, as matters of ethics as well as of economics (Booth 1992).

The test of a person's ethical standards is said to be how they act when no one else will ever know what they do. The only person to judge morality in such circumstances is the individual. Superficially, then, consideration of ethics might seem to amount to nothing when no one will ever know. Not so. For as Thoreau observed: "Public opinion is a weak tyrant compared with our own private opinion. What a man thinks of himself, that it is which determines, or rather indicates, his fate."

Thoreau's observation is particularly instructive to those whose profession is also their vocation and not merely a job. I believe that natural resource management professionals do, indeed, have a vocation. Vocation has been defined as work one is called to by the gods. Two criteria have been put forward (Buechner 1973) by which vocation can be determined: It is work the person most *needs* to do, and work the world *needs* to have done. A sense of professionalism lies solely with the individual. Professionalism does not depend on professional societies or organizations, nor on employers. Professionalism is a reflection, through behavior, of vocation with its commitment and sharply focused will. Those with these attributes will find a way—or make a way—to express their sense of professionalism. Once the individual has defined "professional" in his or her own mind and seared these standards into the soul, a standard for the conduct of a career has been established.

LAND ETHICS

We have discussed the evolution of ethics from relations between individuals to its application in guiding professional conduct. Now we will consider the revolutionary concept put forth decades ago by Aldo Leopold (1949:204). According to Leopold, ethics should be enlarged so that

> the boundaries of the community . . . include soils, waters, plants and animals, collectively, the land. . . . In short, a land ethic changes the role of *Homo sapiens* from conqueror of the land-community to plain member and citizen of it. It implies respect for his fellow-members, and also respect for the community as such.

Earlier Leopold (1933:634) had argued:

> Economic criteria did not suffice to adjust men to society; they do not suffice to adjust society to its environment. If our present evolutionary impetus is an upward one, it is ecologically probable that ethics will eventually be extended to the land. The present conservation movement may constitute the beginning of such an extension. If and when it takes place, it may radically modify what now appears as insuperable economic obstacles to better land use.

In 1947, Leopold, with only a vision of the possibilities of land-use ethics, stated that such ethics were determined entirely by economic self-interest. He cited as proof of that statement the observation that philosophy and religion had not yet heard of it. Writing forty-five years later, his son Starker Leopold (1978:119) commented: "Unfortunately, I see little indication that this pious hope expressed by my father is being realized."

But the situation has changed dramatically in the fourteen years since Starker Leopold's observation. Both philosophy and religion have become increasingly concerned with the evolution of a land-use ethic. This evolving concern can be seen in the emergence of such journals as *Environmental Ethics* in 1979; in the serious discourse about the ethical relation of humans to other animals and to the land (for example, Callicott 1989); and in such meetings as the "Joint Appeal by Religion and Science for the Environment," which emphasized the linkage of social justice and environmental preservation (Moehlmann 1992). Leopold's land-use ethic can be summarized as:

> The "key-log" which must be moved to release the evolutionary process for our ethic is simply this: quit thinking about decent land-use as solely an economic problem. Examine each question in terms of what is ethically

and esthetically right, as well as what is economically expedient. A thing is right when it tends to preserve the integrity, stability, and beauty of the biotic community. It is wrong when it tends otherwise. . . . The mechanism of operation is the same for any ethic: social approbation for right actions: social disapproval for wrong actions. [Leopold 1949:224–225]

In brief, then, a land ethic is nothing more than the acceptance of constraints on human treatment of land in the short term to ensure long-term preservation of the integrity, stability, and beauty of the biotic community. Building on that conceptual foundation, professional societies have moved toward adoption of a land-ethic canon. The Society of American Foresters is currently developing such a canon (Linnartz et al. 1991; Craig et al. 1992) and has already adopted a position statement on retaining biodiversity in ecosystems (Society of American Foresters 1992a). Recent issues of the *Journal of Forestry* have included articles on a broadened view of professional responsibilities (Thomas 1992), the social responsibilities of landownership (Weber 1991), and the development of a land ethic (Gregg 1991; Chapman 1992).

Such interest in a land ethic on the part of land management professionals has, for whatever reason, trailed behind the demands of a highly vocal segment of the public around the world (Maser 1991; Barton 1992). "New Forestry," "Ecosystem Management," and "Sustainable Forestry" are the result of a growing swell of public, professional, and political concern that is insistently producing a land ethic.

One clear sign is that the phrase "such and such a course should be followed because it's right" (or should be avoided because it's wrong) is being heard more and more frequently in debates over the appropriateness of land management activities. The recent decision of the chief of the Forest Service and the director of the Bureau of Land Management—to dramatically reduce clearcutting in the forests of the United States and to adopt "ecosystem management"—seems unlikely to be a response to new technical information. More likely, the decision was made because the public—as well as many agency personnel—has come to believe that clearcutting is not always in keeping with the land-use ethic of preserving "the integrity, stability, and beauty of the biotic community."

The challenge facing leaders of the natural resource management professions in the next several decades will be to continue developing and instituting a land-use ethic. In their leadership lie the seeds of renewed public respect and trust. In their resistance, or their reluctant acquiescence, lies a continued erosion of public trust.

THE FUTURE OF ETHICS

Traditionally, ethics operates at two levels of conduct—person-to-person relations and individual/society interactions. But as we have seen, another level of ethics is now emerging rapidly, nearly sixty years after it was first proposed—the extension of ethics to the treatment of land. This rapidly developing extension of ethics is particularly significant to those engaged in managing renewable natural resources. H. W. Rockwell (1991:3) has made an observation about the profession of forestry that serves well as the endpoint for this discussion of ethics as applied to natural resource management:

> Finally, we have missed the fact that leadership involves moral choice. It is not just the ethical balancing of established precepts, but the courage and humility to divine, weigh, and balance "first principles" in the face of tremendous uncertainty. It is this responsibility that reveals leadership as not a right or a privilege but an awesome duty, and one not necessarily to be sought. Are foresters [or natural resource management professionals] really up to the task?

REFERENCES

Barton, W. J. 1992. "Responsibility and Credibility." *Journal of Forestry* 90(4):3.

Bella, D. A. 1992. "Ethics and the Credibility of Applied Science." In *Ethical Questions for Resource Managers*, edited by G. H. Reeves, D. L. Bottom, and M. H. Brookes. General Technical Report PNW-GTR-288. Portland, OR: U.S. Department of Agriculture, Forest Service, Pacific Northwest Research Station.

Booth, D. E. 1992. "The Economics and Ethics of Old-Growth Forests." *Environmental Ethics* 14(1):43–62.

Buechner, F. 1973. *Wishful Thinking*. New York: Harper & Row.

Callicott, J. B. 1989. *In Defense of the Land Ethic—Essays in Environmental Philosophy*. Albany: State University of New York Press.

Chapman, H. H. 1992. "The Profession of Forestry and Professional Ethics." *Journal of Forestry* 90(4):14–17, 34.

Craig, R., Z. Carnett, J. Difley, J. E. Force, E. W. Frazer, and N. E. Linnartz. 1992. "Land Ethic Canon Proposal: A Report from the Task Force." *Journal of Forestry* 90(8):40–41.

DeVall, B., and G. Sessions. 1984. "The Development of Natural Resources and the Integrity of Nature." *Environmental Ethics* 6(4):293–322.

Greenly, J. C. 1971. "The Effects of Biopolitics on Proper Game Management." *Proceedings of Western Associates of State Game and Fish Commissioners* 51:505–509.

Gregg, N. T. 1991. "Can Foresters Romance a Land Ethic?" *Journal of Forestry* 89(4):11.

Kennedy, J. J., and J. A. Mincolla. 1985. "Early Career Development of Fisheries and Wildlife Biologists in Two Forest Service Regions." *Transactions of the 50th North American Wildlife and Natural Resources Conference.*

Leopold, A. 1933. "The Conservation Ethic." *Journal of Forestry* 31:634.

———. 1949. *A Sand County Almanac and Sketches Here and There.* New York: Oxford University Press.

Leopold, A. S. 1978. "Wildlife and Forest Practice." In *Wildlife in America.* Washington: Council on Environmental Quality.

Lichatowich, J. 1992. "Managing for Sustainable Fisheries: Some Social, Economic, and Ethical Considerations." In *Ethical Questions for Resource Managers,* edited by G. H. Reeves, D. L. Bottom, and M. H. Brookes. General Technical Report PNW-GTR-288. Portland, OR: U.S. Department of Agriculture, Forest Service, Pacific Northwest Research Station.

Linnartz, N. E., R. S. Craig, and M. B. Dickerman. 1991. "Land Ethic Canon—Recommended by the Committee." *Journal of Forestry* 89(2):30, 38.

Livingston, J. A. 1981. *The Fallacy of Wildlife Conservation.* Toronto: McClellan & Stewart.

Maser, C. 1991. "Authenticity in the Forestry Profession." *Journal of Forestry* 89(2):30, 38.

Moehlmann, J. 1992. "The Religious Community and the Environment." *BioScience* 42(8):627.

Peek, J. M., R. J. Pedersen, and J. W. Thomas 1982. "The Future of Elk and Elk Hunting." In *Elk of North America—Ecology and Management,* edited by J. W. Thomas and D. E. Torveill. Harrisburg, PA: Stackpole Books.

Perschel, R. T. 1991. "Pioneering a New Human/Nature Relationship." *Journal of Forestry* 89(4):18–21, 28.

Rockwell, H. W., Jr. 1991. "Leadership." *Journal of Forestry* 89(2):3.

Sessions, G. 1977. "Spinoza and Jeffers on Man in Nature." *Inquiry* 20:481–528.

Society of American Foresters. 1992a. "Biological Diversity in Forest Ecosystems—a Position of the Society of American Foresters." *Journal of Forestry* 90(2):42–43.

_____. 1992b. "Code of Ethics for Members of the Society of American Foresters." *Journal of Forestry* 90(4):16.

Thomas, J. W. 1985. "Towards the Managed Forest—Going Places We've Never Been." *For. Chron.* 61(2):168–172.

_____. 1986. "Effectiveness—the Hallmark of the Natural Resource Management Professional." *Transactions of the 51st North American Wildlife and Natural Resources Conference.*

_____. 1992. "On Being Professional—the Responsibilities of a Worthy Profession." *Journal of Forestry* 90 (2):12–16.

Weber, L. J. 1991. "The Social Responsibility of Land Ownership." *Journal of Forestry* 89 (4):12–17, 25.

4 The Environment of Words

A COMMUNICATIONS PRIMER
FOR LEADERS

●●●

Carol Rosenblum Perry

If you cannot—in the long run—tell everyone what you have been
doing, your doing has been worthless.
　　—ERWIN SCHRÖDINGER

Muddiness is not merely a disturber of prose, it is also a destroyer of
life, of hope: death on the highway caused by a badly worded road
sign, . . . anguish of a traveler . . . not being met because of a slipshod
telegram . . .
　　—WILLIAM STRUNK, JR., AND E. B. WHITE

A LEADER'S ABILITY to communicate—to tell what's going on and be
clear about it—is both medicine chest and arsenal: Well-chosen words
and pictures have the power to remedy, bond, persuade, catalyze,
demolish. A leader with poor communication skills is, at best, a
passable manager and, at worst, a contradiction in terms.

In this chapter, I distill my observations about communicating with
words, drawing from my fifteen years' experience as a technical
writer-editor and, through that work, my associations with people I
consider leaders. Both freelance and at Oregon State University, I have
edited over four hundred research papers and several books on forestry; produced a regional computer newsletter and edited locally
written documentation; lectured to students and professionals about
writing; and published a book, *The Fine Art of Technical Writing*,

46

which sets forth a philosophy and key points to help authors think their way through everything from letters to major reports.

Here I focus not so much on skills for improving technique—other books already do that—but on the *environment within which words operate* because you cannot communicate with words unless you understand their context (the philosophical framework that surrounds them) and subtext (the motives and feelings that underlie them). I assume that most readers of this book are specialists addressing a broad audience because this is where the need is and where the challenge lies. Though my examples, couched as hypothetical situations but based on real events, come largely from Pacific Northwest forestry issues, the underlying principles apply broadly and to all media.

PRESENTER AND RECEIVER: AN INTIMATE PARTNERSHIP

The need to communicate—from *communicare*, the Latin root meaning, literally, "to make common"—stretches back tens of thousands of years to images of bulls, bison, and horses, to curious spray-painted outlines of human hands, decorating cave walls. The embedded messages are lost to us, but then they weren't meant for us. Unfortunately, the messages that *are* meant for us often are as cryptic as Ice Age cave art, and for good reason. They masquerade as communiqués. The message senders seem to lack either the skills or, worse, the intent to communicate. Or they fail to recognize that, to be true to its root, communication takes two.

Humans have a strong search image (mental image sensitizing people to the manifestation of that image in the world around them) for twosomes, perhaps because the most fundamental relationship we know—male and female—is a dyad. Whatever the reason, duality is the template we unconsciously apply to everything we encounter. Most societies see the world, at one level, as twosomes: life and death, light and dark, day and night, good and evil, sick and well, feast and famine, war and peace, and so on.

The communications dyad is *presenter* (writer, speaker, visual artist including video or film maker) and *receiver* (the audience—reader, listener, viewer). In any given situation the dynamic between presenter and receiver may be fixed or fluid. When a public speaker addresses an audience, for example, the dynamic is fixed because the participants' "labels" define who is presenting (the speaker) and who is receiving (the assembled listeners). Even if listeners ask questions during a question and answer session after the talk, the dynamic doesn't materially change. But when a roundtable of specialists convenes to solve a common problem or when school chums assemble at a class reunion, the dynamic is fluid because the participants are alternately presenters and receivers. Perhaps less obvious, though, is how presenters and receivers fundamentally relate.

Examine your preconceptions about this relationship. If they characterize the presenter as actively proffering information to a passive receiver, trash them and begin again. The receiver, far from being an empty vessel waiting to be filled, comes to the communications arena—the designated sphere for "making common"—with a brain loaded with past conversations and contexts:

> You [the receiver] begin to create a "mental space" of what the other person is talking about, a space that is richly furnished with meanings and allusions. While this space is partly built out of what you are hearing, *a large part of it is actually created out of what you already know* [emphasis mine]. . . . It is no longer possible to give any objective external account of the "information content." [Peat 1991:116–117]

So if the receiver is active and of equal stature with the presenter, if the act of imparting information is a creative one and not a simple transfer, and if the information content is subjective because it's customized by how the receiver sieves it, then you can begin to see how intimate the partnership between presenter and receiver is—and why the first order of business for writers, speakers, and visual artists is to define in their own minds the intended (primary) and unintended (peripheral) audiences for a given presentation.

Let's say you're an atmospheric scientist writing up pollution-control recommendations for a special task force appointed by the governor. Your intended audience is the task force and, by association, the governor's office. But your unintended audience includes other scientists in your field or related fields, environmental or other special-interest groups, personnel in the industries targeted for control, regulatory agencies charged with monitoring, and the environmentally conscious public.

If you're part of a scientific panel formulating an array of forest-management alternatives at the behest of two congressional committees, your intended audience is the members of those committees and, by association, others in Congress. But your unintended audience includes other scientists in your field or related fields, public resource-management agencies, private industrial and nonindustrial forest land-owners, other politicians whose constituencies stand to be affected by legislation or regulation, environmental or other special-interest groups, and the general public.

If you're an independent producer making a video about the basics of ecology for fifth and sixth graders, your intended audience is the students. But your unintended audience includes teachers who show the video, teachers who hear about the video from those showing it, school administrators who approve the video for viewing, and possibly students' parents or others in the community interested in educating young citizens.

Thus the format you choose, the length and complexity of your material, the words you use, the tone you take, all form a filter that, by its nature, includes some receivers and excludes others. If you fail to define your audience, the shape of your presentation will define it for you—and you may miss the mark. That is, you may fail to "make common."

THE POLARIZATION OF THE PARTNERSHIP

Partners in a dyad may be opposites or complements. Take, for example, the dyad "good and evil." Technoculture sees these partners as opposites: Beatific "good" and reprehensible "evil" vie for dominance in a cosmic street fight until (à la survival of the fittest) one partner prevails. Wholistic cultures see these partners as complements, two sides of the same coin: "Good" and "evil," accepted without judgment, engage in an open-ended cosmic dance. Worldview, then, shapes individual point of view—which is further refined by attitude. And in the communications arena, *regardless of the words*, attitude can strongly influence whether there's a polarization of the partnership or a meeting of the minds.

An adversarial attitude will polarize an existing dyad or create a dyad if one doesn't already exist and then polarize it—and, either way, perpetuate the rift. Where polarization is historical or inherent, the partners expect to have trouble communicating, and inevitably do. Imagine a meeting in which archenemies "management and labor" nominally assemble to come to agreement on contract issues during collective bargaining. Despite the meeting's objective (agreement on issues), the partners create a working environment so antagonistic as to virtually ensure that they'll (in the long term) propagate their historical enmity and (in the short term) fail to communicate. They arrange the meeting room, a spacious rectangle, such that two long parallel tables are separated by a large gap; management representatives sit at one table, labor reps at the other, talking to one another across the gap. The physical setup of the room—two sides separated by a "no man's land"—reflects and reinforces the adversarial attitude brought to bargaining. If the attitude were, say, one of determination to compromise despite admitted differences, you would expect a different physical setup, perhaps one large table centered in a cozier room—and a different *outcome* because the psychological gap would have been closed along with the physical one.

But a conciliatory attitude doesn't guarantee good communications because the search image for duality is so strong that a dyad can materialize where none seemed likely, and then polarize despite one's attitude. Where polarization is inadvertent, whether the partners ultimately communicate is unpredictable and probably depends on how closely they were allied before they polarized. Imagine a multidisciplinary team of scientists convened to brainstorm on approaches for restoring cutover public forests to old-growth conditions that support old-growth-associated wildlife. There is nothing historically or inherently adversarial about this group, as there is for management and labor. Quite the contrary: The participants, many of whom frequently collaborate on research projects, come together around a common cause with a common goal. Yet not long into the meeting, several "foresters" disrupt the equilibrium by dominating discussion; disequilibrium splits the group into a dyad—"foresters and wildlifers"—that no one foresaw; the newly created partners become increasingly polarized as each marks territory and scrambles to control the proceedings. Group dynamics become stranger and stranger, more and more chaotic, until the partners achieve a new equilibrium—in which case communication is reestablished. Had the partners deadlocked, communication would have been hamstrung indefinitely.

But the attitude of an "outside player" also can polarize a dyad or create one and then polarize it because dyads don't exist in a vacuum. Where polarization is caused by a third party, the partners will have extreme difficulty communicating because the outside player queers the relationship between them. In the Pacific Northwest, for example, where a hot debate centers on appropriate allocation of forests, particularly old-growth forests and the status of the associated endangered northern spotted owl, battle lines are drawn between a polarized dyad—"loggers and environmentalists"—fostered by the press, an outside player who, theoretically, should be observer-recorder only and no player at all. The press manipulates the partnership, deepens the rift, by vilifying each partner to the other and reinforcing the drama to the news-consuming public through such filters as headlines, sound bites, and photo opportunities. As a result, "loggers" become land rapers who want to cut as many trees as possible in the shortest time for maximum profit, the owl and the future resource be damned; "environmentalists" become preservationists who want to lock up old-growth forests to save the owl, local economies be damned. In reality, except for a few radicals, true "loggers" and "environmentalists" are not as previously characterized, nor is either group monolithic. Moreover, other groups—including public agencies (like the Forest Service and Bureau of Land Management), private timber companies, and university scientists researching the biology that underlies natural resource management—are involved and do not accurately fit either label. By *creating*, not just reporting, the news, the press becomes a presenter. By fueling controversy, which sells newspapers and air time, it becomes a presenter *polarizing*, not informing, the public.

The biggest dangers of polarization, whatever its genesis, are that an array of solutions is never examined (because duality appears to offer the possibility of only two) and that the real issue, the one that stirred the controversy in the first place, becomes so distorted or oversimplified as to be lost. With regard to the latter danger, in the Northwest forestry debate the real issue is limits: How much timber can we cut in the short term and still in the long term have timber, other "forest values" (scenic beauty, recreation, species habitat), and economic stability? The issue is not "jobs versus owls." Indeed, if all spotted owls were to disappear tomorrow, timber jobs would still be jeopardized because current harvest volumes cannot be sustained (that is, the limit of the resource has been reached). So how to sidestep, roadblock, or at least minimize polarization?

Come to the communications arena prepared. Communication takes preparation—and not only of notes, visual aids, or verbal strategy.

- Realize that humans find comfort in their biases, that old programming dies hard, and that the smell of battle may at times be irresistible.
- Recognize the strong penchant for groups to form dyads and for dyads to polarize, and sensitize yourself to the signs of the "first cracks."
- Because attitude usually does make a difference, adopt a positive attitude through which you convey your desire to communicate—not spar—and monitor that attitude to be sure it doesn't quietly erode. People who have a mind to "make common" are far more likely to do so than those who either have not been so deliberate as to analyze the subtext of their words or, having done so, admit to other agendas.

Work to elevate discussion to "common ground." Common ground is the shared basis from which we must think and then act to resolve complex issues such as those in the environmental arena. But determining what constitutes common ground may be problematic; after all, partnerships would not tend to polarize so readily if partners weren't more inclined to rally around their differences than their similarities.

- Highlight (verbally point to) the fact that the issues involved are complex. Sometimes what seems obvious isn't to everyone. Underscore that resolutions to complex problems will themselves be complex.
- Ask questions, rather than make statements. Questions are open, statements closed. And formulate questions that address the "big picture," that stretch for "something larger," for a whole greater than the sum of its parts. Questions that address only day-to-day concerns, immediate needs, are necessary but insufficient: Their answers alone will lead, logical step by logical step, through a tyranny of small decisions to the wrong outcome. In the Northwest forestry debate, the key questions are two, and they aim for

the skies: "What do we want our forests to provide over the short and long term?" and "How do we get there?" The quality of such questions elevates discussion from the isolated valleys in which we see only ourselves, our own narrow interests, to a plateau from which we see the entire landscape and all elements in it. The view unites, rather than polarizes, us—and helps us focus on the real issue.

Approach the communications arena as "ritual space." The poet Robert Bly (1990:194–5) suggests that "change or transformation can happen only . . . in ritual space . . . [where] a turn of phrase or a turn of a symbol replaces the turn of the sword." Approaching the communications arena as ritual space, then, may be a clever device through which to eradicate the closed-circuit thinking that feeds polarization.

Ritual space is an environment we consecrate through a deliberate symbolic act or protocol which signals that the usual modes of thought or operation must be left outside so that Bly's "change or transformation" can take place within. Any place could be ritual space if appropriately consecrated: a grassy knoll, someone's living room, a corporate conference room. The act of consecration might be sitting in a circle (King Arthur's Knights of the Round Table), wearing a certain item (a scientist's white lab coat, a judge's long black robe and even wig) or removing it (shoes shed before entering the home), or invoking an intricate set of rules within a special structure (any professional sport). The town hall in the New England town meeting, a model of raw democracy in action, is a classic example of ritual space; therein, citizens are able to take action on community problems because they vest the process and, by association, the place with power.

Vesting power is the key. Other places you might recognize as ritual space—a classroom, a doctor's office, the floor of the U.S. Congress—don't always function like it because the power they once held has been eroded or abused. In theory, for example, a classroom is ritual space: a place consecrated for learning in which students gain knowledge (are "changed"). But students are "changed" only when knowledge is clearly viewed and valued. If society mistakes facts or good grades for knowledge, fails to understand that knowledge is more than analysis, sees the classroom as the vector to jobs but not responsibility, then knowledge is divested of its power, and the classroom ceases to be ritual space.

If empowering an environment can empower the words or images presented there, and the acts that follow, then:

- The communications arena should always be consecrated as ritual space so that participants can leave dogma at the door and enter with a mindset to "make common." The creative leader might light a candle in each corner of the room, or give everyone a blue armband to wear, or lay out a simple set of ground rules for interacting, much as a marriage counselor might do. This approach gains everyone the broadest view, gives best access to common ground—and minimizes the likelihood of polarization.
- Dyads already polarized should convene only in ritual space so that partners can—without losing face—call a halt to hostilities.

The onerous tasks of elevating discussion to common ground, keeping it focused on the real issue, and creating ritual space are made even more so because, as the next section elaborates, the new ideas born of Bly's "change or transformation" are infuriatingly slow to sink in.

THE IMPENETRABILITY OF NEW IDEAS

The way that new ideas fail to penetrate our understanding gives added meaning to the term "hardheaded." Even when a presenter speaks or writes plainly, even when the material presented is targeted to the right audience, even when the material's form and content are ideally matched, new ideas tend to roll off like water off a duck's back.

Suppose you're an ecologist addressing an open public meeting in southwest Oregon about the value of old-growth forest to humans and other animals. You know, going in, that the participants and the issue have been polarized. Undaunted, you propose a broad range of management scenarios ensuring both "jobs" and "owls," including the *new* idea of "managing for old growth"—that is, as you explain, the idea of managing at least part of the second-growth forest with silvicultural practices that actually create old-growth forest structure and habitat. But your proposal elicits a sea of blank looks, and the questions you later field from the audience confirm your failure to communicate. Reflecting, you realize too late that your listeners—"loggers" and "environmentalists" alike—probably never heard the emotionally loaded words "manage" and "old growth" wedded in a phrase. No matter how plainly stated, the union seems a paradox, simply doesn't compute. But why?

Recall that the receiver comes to the communications arena (in this case, the public meeting) with a richly furnished mental space. More often than not, however, the furnishings first act as a barricade to the hail of information—which is why the brain initially repels a new idea. It has to get used to it. It has to test the water, so to speak; to try a bite or two. Like a hunter examining spoor, the brain must assess quality, quantity, texture, consistency, especially if the information is not what the receiver anticipated. That is, the brain needs to dovetail expectations (what the receiver expected to hear or see) with reality (what was actually presented). Such processing takes time and the will to be open-minded. Unfortunately, time is of the essence with environmental issues, and the will to be open-minded is always hard to come by. So how to end-run these difficulties to help new ideas penetrate?

Repeat new ideas. Present your new idea in as many communications arenas as possible—in articles in scientific, other technical, or popular outlets; in newspaper editorials, interviews, or letters to the editor; in talks to professional societies, public agencies, special-interest groups, or the public at large; via slide tapes or videotapes for clubs, schools, or other organizations; in interviews and feature programs on commercial and public radio and television. The more different arenas, the more different audiences, the better the chance for saturation. But repetition takes time and, even then, holds only part of the solution.

Highlight new ideas. Verbally point to the fact that your idea is new, and then repeat it for emphasis. For instance, the ecologist proposing to "manage for old growth" might pause after introducing this new idea, tell the audience he's going to repeat what he just said and then repeat it slowly and deliberately, word for word, and drive the point home by elaborating: "I know this sounds strange to you, talking about 'management' and 'old growth' in one breath. But the idea's not really all that strange. We can tailor existing practices and stretch out the time frame for applying them to mimic what, up till now, only nature has produced . . ." The speaker's self-interruption jolts listeners, focuses their attention, forces them to grapple at least momentarily with the new idea—which begins their longer-term mental processing.

Package new ideas. Cloak your new idea in familiar wrappings so it doesn't seem so alien. To illustrate the power of packaging: In my community, which considers itself environmentally conscious, residents have been able to recycle conveniently (in front of their residences) for some years. But recycling was spotty until the local disposal company began handing out labeled red plastic bins in which to "package" recyclables. The bins went like hotcakes (the company ran out and had to order more), and now red bins dot the curbside on garbage day in each neighborhood. More than just recyclable garbage was packaged here: Once sanctified through a standard, recognizable container, recycling became the right thing to do. But how to package and promote ideas that have no concrete expression?

Invoke metaphor. Metaphor—a figure of speech that packages something alien or out of context in something familiar and therefore relevant—may be the most powerful verbal tool a presenter has for helping new ideas penetrate.

Whatever metaphor you use must be geared to your intended audience. If you're a scientist trying to educate a broad audience about the importance of maintaining biological diversity in the face of changing global climate, you might invoke an "insurance" metaphor, something everyone would relate to: "Life is uncertain. So you buy health insurance to protect against the costs of catastrophic illness. You buy life insurance to provide financial security for your survivors. Likewise, you should buy 'environment insurance'—by maintaining and reclaiming as many different habitats and associated species as possible—to protect against the unknown consequences of climate change. In an uncertain world, you need to keep all your options open . . ." Heads nod. Any gap between speaker and listeners disappears. You've gained your listeners' full attention—and they've understood a concept that might otherwise have eluded them—through metaphor.

Or suppose you're a naturalist conducting a walk in the woods for participants of an Elderhostel workshop, all environmentally active senior citizens from urban areas. You stop by a large standing dead tree peppered with holes and describe its ecological role by invoking a "condo" metaphor—"a snag functions something like a time-share condo"—and elaborate on how primary cavity-nesting birds, the snag's first tenants, create "apartments" that are shared over time by other birds and small mammals. A little farther on, you tell the seniors that roots form an elaborate network in the soil, transporting water and nutrients from plant to plant with the aid of various biochemical helpers, microbes, and fungus/root associations called mycorrhizae. You liken this belowground network to a subway system with its many interconnecting routes and myriad passengers needing to go uptown or down. Again, you've made your point through metaphor.

Go visual. You may need to go beyond words—to images—in order to help new ideas penetrate, especially where matters of scale are involved, where the item of interest is normally hidden from view, or where an unfamiliar process or technology is introduced.

The first astronauts to behold Earth from space were tongue-tied describing its awesome beauty, its tranquillity; but the color photos they returned to us spoke volumes. A minister of agriculture may remain skeptical about the range and pace of deforestation in his country until he's presented with Landsat photos showing the extensive smoke of slash and burn. A soil biologist might have difficulty communicating how the plants we see as individuals aboveground are networked belowground until she projects a slide showing, in cross section from an experimental soil box, the massive, fanlike web of fine roots that physically link spindly young conifers. A forest engineer may be unable to fully convey the ecological benefits of helicopter logging over traditional methods that mar the landscape with roads and compact soils until he shows a video comparing on-site operations using helicopters and older approaches.

Whether you choose still or moving pictures, photos or drawings, depends on your objectives. Where action is the key to communicating a new idea, as for helicopter logging, use video. Where outcome is the key, as for the unexpectedly rapid biological recovery of the area devastated by the 1980 eruption of Mount St. Helens, use still photos or slides. Where an abstraction (like a concept or projection) is the key, as for the anticipated migration patterns of habitat types due to global climate change, use drawings.

Communicating new ideas will continue to try the patience of those introducing them. You as presenter must recognize that an idea *is* new—this is not always obvious. You must persist in promoting it through whatever technique or combination of techniques works, fully anticipating penetration to be slow. And you must pay special attention to the words you use because, as the poet Walt Whitman admonishes, "there are no two words the same any more than there are two persons the same."

THE MEANING OF WORDS

Culture shapes what we say, and are able to say. The Native American writer Jamake Highwater (1982:5–6) laments the way in which the dominant culture expresses some ideas:

> When an English word is descriptive—like the word "wilderness"—I am often appalled by what is implied. . . . After all, the forest is not "wild" in the sense that it is something needing to be tamed or controlled or harnessed. For Blackfeet Indians, the forest is the natural state of the world. It is the cities that are wild and seem to need "taming."

Primal peoples, who live close to nature, avoid generalization in language because they avoid generalization in life (Leonard 1981). For example, tribal farmers of the Trobriand Islands, east of New Guinea, use many different words to describe the food staple that non-Trobrianders would call a yam, depending on its degree of ripeness, shape, color, size, or time of harvest. To the Trobriander, each word is rich with meaning.

Our culture, too, is mirrored by our language. We generalize to buffer ourselves from nature and the demands of a complex everyday life; craft sentences whose elements are as ambiguously related to one another as we are; hide behind passive constructions that make it difficult to determine just who or what is responsible for the stated action. We suffer not only economic, but linguistic, inflation, using more and more words to say less and less. We spout jargons that distinguish subcultures—whose members still fail to communicate with the words they thought they had in common. Take, for example, the subculture "scientists." Imagine a multidisciplinary group of university scientists pooling expertise about how to sustain adequate timber harvest levels, biological diversity, and socioeconomic stability in the Pacific Northwest. After protracted discussion, the group agrees that additional research is needed before they can crystallize proposals for action. But as participants begin to spell out research specifics, discussion becomes muddled—until participants realize that the economists among them understand "research" to mean doing computer modeling, the biologists understand it to mean installing replicated experiments, the sociologists to mean conducting surveys.

What words mean, then, goes beyond their dictionary definitions because their environment further delineates them. So how to become more respectful of words?

Be sensitive to "trigger" words. Trigger words, as the term implies, carry an emotional load and spark an emotional response. In the Pacific Northwest forestry debate, for example, many environmentalists see red when they hear the word "clearcutting" because they view this practice as threatening the forest resource. Many loggers see red when they hear the word "preservation" because they view this practice as threatening their livelihood.

Triggers can be used deliberately (say, to exacerbate polarization) or inadvertently. For instance, the word "manage" is relatively neutral when used by a university professor lecturing to students about "managing resources" or by a district ranger discussing "management options" with staff. But when a timber-industry spokesperson writes about "managing forests" in an op-ed piece for the *Portland Oregonian*, the word "managing" may carry an emotional load for some readers (say, members of a conservation group) that it might not for others (say, members of a downtown business association) because all readers will interpret the word in light of who's talking.

Even with the best intentions, it's not always easy to recognize potential triggers. So ponder these guidelines:

- Carefully consider all possible audiences for your material. Remember that each receiver hears creatively—unconsciously matching what you say with what he or she already believes—and that words exist not in isolation but in an environment that shapes meaning.
- Prefer specifics to generalities so that receivers' expectations can't as easily color the presenter's remarks. Generalizations like "managing forests" virtually beg readers or listeners to supply their own interpretations, to infer what was meant. And if inference is not what the presenter intended, then meaning is—however inadvertently—altered. Had the timber spokesperson instead written about "managing forests by selectively thinning 80- to 100-year-old stands, leaving six green trees, four to six snags, and two logs per acre, and maintaining a thousand-foot buffer around riparian zones"—the triggering effect of "manage" for some readers might have been damped or even nullified.

Use jargon judiciously. Jargon—the technical vocabulary of specialists—is inherently neither good nor bad. Many technical fields could not function without new terms denoting new concepts or procedures; moreover, some freshly coined or bootlegged expressions are self-explanatory and immensely useful. Jargon is only a problem when the presenter forgets who the receivers are. So if you intend to communicate to a broader audience than specialists, define your technical terms as plainly as possible or translate them into language your audience will understand. Otherwise, you'll either alienate receivers or leave them in the dust.

Don't abuse words. As a culture, we abuse not only children, drugs, food, and credit; we abuse words. Some words are bandied about too liberally: The more common their usage, the less power they carry. Others are spoken carelessly: Their boundaries indistinct, they flop this way and that, vulnerable to manipulation.

"Soft" words are words used—mistakenly—to show sensitivity, to force a bond with the receiver. Take, for example, a current favorite: "share." True sharing requires implicit prior assent. You "share" a life with your mate by both agreeing, ritually or informally, to do so; you "share" a piece of chocolate cheesecake only with someone who wants a few bites. You don't "share" information. That is presumptuous, even arrogant, because it invokes false intimacy with a receiver who has assented to nothing. "I want to share these thoughts with you" means "I want to tell you something . . ." If you "tell" information, listeners are free to respond, positively or negatively; but if you "share" it, they feel trapped into complicity. Leave soft words to the New Age Manager's Lexicon. Realize that you don't have to use soft words to be sensitive any more than you have to use abstract words to convey concepts or big words to make an impression.

"Gutted" words are words used to elevate the commonplace—which eviscerates them. Take the word "vision," in the sense of a supernatural revelation, something seen with exceptional mental acuity—a powerful word evoking a powerful, and uncommon, experience. The founding fathers of the United States may well have tried to crystallize their "vision" of what this nation should be by drafting the Constitution and Bill of Rights. But an agency manager's "vision" is likely to be little more than a set of "goals" or "objectives" inappropriately exalted beyond the prosaic.

"Puffed" words are words used to aggrandize language—"as if bigger

words and more expansive sentences imply bigger, more expansive thinking" (Perry 1991:98). Take, for example, the word "opportunity." A youngster from a poor family might properly talk about her "opportunity" to better herself by attending college now that she's been awarded a full-tuition scholarship. But a company president's "fiscal opportunities" are really only "good ways to make money"; a politician's "photo opportunity" is little more than a brief picture-taking session with the press; a backpacker's "recreation opportunity" may simply be hiking and camping in a wilderness area. When puffed words combine to make puffed sentences, the damage is compounded. For as more words are inflated, the "signal-to-noise" ratio drops dramatically, and the text comes to resemble cotton candy—big, fluffy, and entirely lacking in substance.

Recognize the power of words to define, or alter, reality. Realize that there may be no more ignorant remark than "It's just a semantic difference."

THE BEST USE OF RESOURCES

Most professionals seem to have too little money, and even less time, to optimize the task at hand. And this is no less true in communications. So how to make the best use of limited resources?

Exploit "unproductive" time. There are books and seminars galore on time management—that is, the management of scheduled time, of time intended to be "productive." But what about "unproductive" time?

Clear presentation requires clear thinking. And clear thinking requires gestation—the mental composting of ideas that proceeds undaunted when you're not consciously thinking about anything, when your mind is freewheeling, unfocused. So make the best use of unproductive time—when you're taking a shower, commuting to work, mowing the lawn, vacuuming the living room, chopping wood, walking the dog—by keeping a little notebook or pocket tape recorder handy so that as ideas sprout unexpectedly, and they will, you can capture them while they're fresh for later elaboration (Perry 1991).

Clear thinking also requires reflection, the conscious processing of gestated ideas—virtually a lost art in technoculture because we're all so busy working through our lists. What's more, there's important feedback between gestation and reflection: Reflecting on gestated ideas will prompt yet more ideas to gestate and sprout, for later reflection. So use unproductive time for reflection as well.

Size up graphics. As supports in the environment of words, graphics—tables; line art such as charts, graphs, and illustrations; photographs and slides—can be powerful storytellers. But they can also be superfluous, redundant, costly.

When writing, use tables and figures (line art or photographs) to streamline text or highlight comparisons: Tables provide greater detail in a visually organized way, and figures show what words can't tell as succinctly or effectively. Minimize repetition among text, tables, and figures. And where either a table or a figure could display the same information, prefer the figure; your readers will. Consult a professional technical writer or editor for tips on graphics for documents.

Where written words don't require images, as in this chapter, don't feel compelled to conjure any up. To provide visual relief for the reader, break up text with appropriate heads and subheads, displayed listings, sidebars (related text printed beside the main text, often boxed or shaded), rules (horizontal lines), and white space. Use type face and size as graphic elements if you're desktop-publishing your material. But consult an artist or desktop professional first: The technology, alas, allows you to run rampant, possibly compromising good design.

When speaking, use slides or overheads only when they advance your point: Too often, this speaker's crutch is the listener's bane. Keep graphics simple; the visual clutter of too many numbers or too many words distracts listeners and may cause them to space out on your message. Prefer figures to tables, especially when speaking to non-specialists. Indeed, think carefully about who your audience is as you decide which kinds of images to show. Consult an audiovisual media specialist for tips on graphics for talks.

Be a stickler for high quality. Poorly prepared visuals detract from a verbal presentation and may be worse than no visuals at all. If you can afford it, have line art professionally drafted by hand or computer. If you have more time than money, are computer friendly, *and know the basics of good design*, try generating line art yourself with a graphics package. Use only photographs that have sharp images and are well composed (or well cropped). Because the color slides you use for talks convert poorly to the black and white prints you'll usually need for documents (color is far more expensive to reproduce in printed matter than black and white), consider keeping two cameras loaded with film—one with color, the other with black and white—and taking duplicate shots.

Buy others' skills to extend your own. It's false economy to try to do everything yourself. If you can afford it, it's well worth the money to periodically hire skilled contractors whom you can rely on to "stretch" your time—and your ability to communicate. You might occasionally barter or bootleg services, but don't count on these for the long haul: To barter, you'll have to find just the right match; and when bootlegging, you'll have to settle for whatever you get, if you don't wear out your welcome first.

Look for people whose skills complement yours, which demands honest self-assessment. If you're a "big picture" person, get help with the detail work; if you're a great starter but a poor finisher, find someone else to carry through what you initiate; if you're a dynamic public speaker but a weak writer, seek a coauthor or ghostwriter; if you're a scientist compiling technical contributions for a reference manual, arrange for a project manager to oversee editing and production.

For example, any team of specialists preparing a multiply authored book, a research compendium, an environmental impact statement, or similar large or complex documents should include an editor and a graphic artist. An editor scrutinizes the document for clarity, organization, consistency, conciseness, grammatical accuracy, word usage, and format and ensures that a "paper by committee" doesn't read like one. A graphic artist ensures professional-quality drafting, illustration, and camera copy for the printer and (recall the importance of packaging) gives report design its due; the fact that you have the latest desktop-publishing software does *not* make you an artist or layout expert. The editor's and artist's contributions begin early—long before hands-on work—through consultation. The key information they offer at the outset—about, for example, how revisions should flow among coauthors and editor, how rough artwork should be prepared, or how typists should format word-processed text for conversion to the artist's layout software—will save time, money, and headaches later on and maximize product quality.

Compile a listing (maybe on your computer, for easy updating) of qualified contractors you've used or who've been recommended by reliable colleagues so that, when the need arises, you have names at your fingertips. If you're considering an unknown, ask for work samples and references. Whenever possible, arrange for contractors far in advance; they may not be available at the last minute. And don't hire strictly on the basis of low bid unless you have no other choice: The cheapest help may well be the least experienced, which will cost you in the end.

Set priorities for allocating resources to stretch your budget. Consider, say, using contractors only on the most critical or visible projects or on the most sensitive aspect of a project. If the 500-page environmental impact statement you're preparing will be accompanied by a 25-page "reader's digest" that synthesizes and translates for laypersons, use your editor and artist on the digest—your public face—and let the specialists who'll be reading the larger document fend for themselves.

Realize that some projects should be undertaken only if you can afford to hire professionals. Do-it-yourself video looks like it and puts audiences off: Television and the cinema have made all of us highly sophisticated viewers with little tolerance for home-movie quality. As a conceptually and technically complex marriage of words, pictures, and sound, video takes months and thousands of dollars to produce. If you don't have the resources, try another approach, maybe a slide-tape presentation.

Plan! It's also false economy not to plan. Time and money will inevitably be squandered if you don't plan and saved if you do. Suppose you're coordinating preparation of a large, multiply authored document with a hard deadline. You should plan the project from start to finish, realizing of course that nothing ever goes exactly as planned. As part of planning, you'll need to:

- Select the working team (authors, contractors, other technical and clerical support staff), and brainstorm with them to outline objectives, assign tasks, and anticipate needs and potential hangups. Be sure you include support staff—they're the mechanics who know the nuts and bolts of getting the job done.
- Create a set of guidelines for both text and artwork to standardize contributions that ultimately have to mesh, and give everyone a copy. The guidelines should be substantive enough to provide key information and appropriate detail (favor examples, which are

worth many words of explanation), but brief enough that contributors will actually use them.

- Put together a *realistic* timeline that accounts for "unexpected problems," give everyone a copy, and, within reason, stick to it. Zealously monitor the project's progress by keeping a constant eye on time; realize, for example, that when writers miss due dates for drafts, editing and production get squeezed, and overall publication quality suffers. Update the timeline as needed, and circulate revised copies.
- Periodically, touch base with key people, and meet briefly and informally, in subgroups and as a whole team, to be sure everyone's still headed in the same direction and to air whatever might be lurking unexpressed. Again, don't forget to include support staff. Contact and feedback boost morale, which boosts product quality.

INFORMATION: TOO MUCH BUT NOT ENOUGH

The speed at which information can be electronically transmitted is far greater than the speed at which human brains can process it—which puts us all in a state of permanent information overload. One danger of overload is that a presenter's thoughts may be at best "half processed" because there's too much information to assimilate; and half-processed thoughts, by their nature riddled with ambiguities, can lead to wrong inference and hence altered meaning. A second danger is that there's too little signal and too much noise—and confusion over which is which. A third danger is that, as the futurist Arthur C. Clark warns, too much knowledge "can clog the wheels of imagination." A fourth danger is that specialization—a mechanism we use to cope with overload, to gain control—may *isolate* us from one another in the "global village" in which electronic circuitry was forecast to profoundly *connect* everyone (McLuhan and Fiore 1967).

Paradoxically, the environmental arena suffers from too much information and not enough. That is, the demand for knowledge about complex interactions and feedbacks in natural systems may outstrip a presenter's ability to provide that knowledge because—information overload notwithstanding—"all the facts aren't in." The catch is, of course, that all the facts will *never* be in. A crucial part of the presenter's task, then, is to communicate that there are, and will continue to be, limits on knowledge as well as other resources, and that limits on knowledge and the associated uncertainty about "what we don't know" cannot paralyze reasonable people into inaction for fear of doing the wrong thing. For the environmental leader, this may be the ultimate communiqué.

ACKNOWLEDGMENT

This chapter owes a large debt to the cosmological ecologist David A. Perry, one of the best presenters and receivers I know, who, through a decade-long conversation, has helped me forge many of the ideas expressed here.

REFERENCES

Bly, R. 1990. *Iron John*. Reading, MA: Addison-Wesley.

Highwater, J. 1982. *The Primal Mind: Vision and Reality in Indian America*. New York: Meridian.

Leonard, G. 1981. *The Transformation: A Guide to the Inevitable Changes in Humankind*. Los Angeles: Tarcher.

McLuhan, M., and Q. Fiore. 1967. *The Medium Is the Massage*. New York: Bantam Books.

Peat, F. D. 1991. *The Philosopher's Stone*. New York: Bantam Books.

Perry, C. R. 1991. *The Fine Art of Technical Writing*. Hillsboro, OR: Blue Heron.

5 Managing Conflict

■■■

Ty Tice

ANYONE WITH AN APTITUDE for leadership and an iota of entrepreneurial spirit will ask the question, "Why do I do what I do?" as a kind
of mid-career reality check. For me this occurred fifteen years after
college when a change in the tax code dashed the prospects of my
promising business venture based on a tax avoidance scheme for
amassing wealth. The answer to my self-query was a decision to quit
investing time, money, and psychic capital in what I considered du-
bious ventures and to "recycle" my career to make it more consistent
with my personal values.

Aided by lessons learned through experience in the for-profit business and nonprofit conservation worlds, I sought to identify some new
criteria for personal success. Instead of investing energy in ventures
that had little utility other than making a living, I resolved that the first
criterion for my new career be that it generate a good or service that is
useful in a broad social context. Second, I wanted the intellectual
content of my new career to address important and challenging issues, not the deadly repetitive pap that characterized my business
experience. Third, I needed my new career path to lead to a place of
professional independence where the risks and rewards for making
good decisions would be direct and measurable. These three career
criteria—social utility, intellectual significance, and professional
independence—led me to the threshold of the Yale School of Forestry
and Environmental Studies (FES) and the first step along a new career
path in environmental mediation. The challenge was to match my
fifteen years of business experience with the skills expected of an environmental resource manager or policymaker.

Following graduation while in a FES temporary staff position administering special programs, my search for a career path seemed to produce many more questions than I had answers. Why, it dawned, were trained resource professionals so often ineffectual in their management of natural resources? From my vantage point, it appeared that the really important natural resource decisions were either hopelessly deadlocked or were being dealt with piecemeal by bureaucrats, politicians, and judges in highly adversarial and usually adjudicatory forums.

The environmental policy formulation "game" relegated resource managers to a secondary role of expert witness for competing interest groups. In this capacity, resource managers readily became cannon fodder for lawyers adept at questioning their credentials and scientific credibility. Environmental policymaking seemed to be on a merry-go-round of legislate, promulgate, regulate, and litigate with little opportunity for resource managers to exercise their scientific and professional skills. Nowhere was there a safe place for scientists and resource managers to collaborate and solve problems.

Somewhere, it seemed, there must be a better method of resolving complex conflicts over natural resource and environmental issues than the win-lose-draw paradigm still so much in evidence. In business, when objectives are competing, ground rules vague, and outcomes uncertain, a skillful broker can sometimes enter the scene and help parties reach a conclusion that meets their needs. If such a negotiation-based process can perform well in the private sector, why not, I reasoned, apply something like it in the environmental public policy arena as well?

Fortunately for my new career, a network of Yale contacts put me in touch with Dr. Gerald W. Cormick and his Institute for Environmental Mediation based at the University of Washington in Seattle. Cormick, whose background includes labor and social dispute mediation, had obtained private foundation funding to experiment with adapting the familiar two-party labor/management mediation model to complex multiparty environmental disputes. Cormick and a small staff of research assistant/mediators were successfully mediating environmental conflicts, and the results were characterized by state-of-the-art agreements containing elements that no single party had thought of before. This was the organization I joined in 1979.

Cormick's experiment showed how the mediation of environmental conflicts differs from labor/management bargaining. Environmental mediation characteristically involves many more than two interested parties with no previous experience in collective bargaining negotiations. Moreover, parties to environmental conflicts are unlikely to negotiate again over the same site-specific issues. Therefore, anything missing in a one-time settlement package cannot be held over to the next round of contract negotiations. And, unlike labor/management mediation, there was no institutional framework for environmental mediation except an ad hoc structure of our own making. On the positive side, the consensus requirement encourages synergy since no party has a corner on environmental facts.

The process of environmental mediation has been documented and assessed by Gail Bingham in *Resolving Environmental Disputes: A Decade of Experience*. The nonprofit organizations around at the inception of environmental mediation have, for the most part, reorganized or vanished. A wide variety of public and private organizations, as well as partnerships that provide environmental mediation services to communities, states, regions, and nations, have replaced them. Initial training for the specialty is now available on many campuses, including the School of Forestry and Environmental Studies at Yale University, the School of Natural Resources at the University of Michigan, the Graduate School of Public Affairs at the University of Washington, and Harvard–MIT's Public Disputes Program. To advance the field, the Ford Foundation created the National Institute for Dispute Resolution (NIDR), which has successfully spawned mediation groups in six state governments. The Society for Professionals in Dispute Resolution (SPIDR) lobbies to prevent bar associations from having mediation become the exclusive domain of lawyers.

You can see that my career path is not without its twists, turns, dead ends, and uncertainties. I've been on my present career path for a dozen years, more than half as long as environmental mediation has been practiced. What I do now in private practice continues to measure up to my original criteria. There is something special about being witness to truly synergistic conflict resolutions that result from mediation. As long as the satisfaction of being an advocate for consensus holds, I keep at it. Being forever in the middle has a down side, though. It is with some envy that I see the satisfaction some leaders derive from total commitment to a cause.

LEADERSHIP AND CONFLICT MANAGEMENT

The ability to accurately assess and resolve conflict is an important leadership skill and may prove decisive at various points in a leader's career. But it is not necessary nor is it advisable that a leader become a mediator in the sense of taking on a mediator's unique set of responsibilities in conflict situations. A leader's role is to exert influence and precipitate action. Leaders are first and foremost advocates for causes whom others come to rely on and follow. Mediators may possess some of these traits, but in a single-dimensional sense. Mediators are advocates for settling things through a process of consensus-based negotiations. They must remain neutral on the *substance* of the conflict. Even the perception of a substantive bias will render a mediator useless as a process manager. Furthermore, as outsiders with no direct stake in the conflict, mediators have little of substantive value to bring to the table. If they did, they would doubtless become unacceptable to one or more of the parties.

Leaders who try to assume a mediator's procedural role will tend to confuse and perhaps alienate their followers. They may also lose their effectiveness as advocates for their cause since it simply isn't possible to simultaneously perform both mediator and leader roles with credibility. Leaders can, however, benefit both their organizations and their careers by rethinking their attitude about conflict and then becoming skilled at assessing conflict's dangers and opportunities.

Conflict is not something to be feared or avoided by leaders. It is not a symptom of failure. Instead it is a phenomenon containing elements of both danger and opportunity whose time has come in terms of need for change. Indeed, our western culture can learn much from an older Chinese culture that continues to use two discrete language symbols to convey the meaning of conflict: Individually their symbols represent danger and opportunity; when used in combination, however, they represent conflict or crisis.

CRISIS AS OPPORTUNITY

Leaders too frequently overplay the macho side of conflict, forcing it to become a one-dimensional, dangerous, win/lose game. Other leaders less inclined to fight ("let's sue the bastards") may try flight ("let's find a way to avoid this conflict and maybe it will go away"). Either way the likely outcome is that conflict only becomes more one-sidedly dangerous. The opportunity for creative collaboration is forgone.

Far better that new generations of leaders resist taking the bait. While respecting conflict's dangerous downside, they should also assess its opportunities for positive change. The important message for leaders is that conflict becomes more manageable following a timely and accurate assessment. In the hands of a skillful leader, conflict can provide the opportunity to initiate change for the better, or it can become a dangerous excuse for going to war. Since conflict is inevitable and neutral in character, it is largely up to leadership to assess how it will be managed. It is leadership, or lack thereof, that puts the positive or negative spin onto conflict. In my experience, success at conflict assessment and management ultimately becomes the measure of a leader's success or failure.

I don't wish to imply that every conflict can or even should be negotiated. I do, however, encourage assessment of every conflict for its negotiation potential. Conflicts resulting from a real or perceived violation of a civil or treaty right, for example, are probably not appropriate for negotiation. Only a foolish leader would allow an inalienable right to hit the negotiation table. Cultural conflicts and battles over values are nearly as nonnegotiable as civil rights issues, but certain elements of such conflicts can sometimes be defined for negotiation without compromising the broader interests of the parties involved. The bottom line is that many opportunities for creative dispute resolution are being squandered by unmindful leadership—especially where environmental issues are concerned. Missed or flawed conflict assessments by leaders result in closing windows of opportunity for negotiation and allowing the conflict to escalate dangerously beyond control.

If successful conflict management is the essence of leadership, then leaders must consistently make correct strategic and tactical determinations about how to manage based on an accurate assessment. For example, there might be overriding organizational benefits to litigating rather than settling a particular issue. Highly visible conflicts possess exceptional strategic value to an organization in terms of membership development, fundraising, and media attention. A leader needs to factor in these and other organizational imperatives when determining the appropriate conflict management strategy.

Perhaps it's helpful to display the alternative strategies available to leaders for managing conflict as levels in a conflict management staircase (Figure 1). Following conflict assessment, leaders may choose the appropriate step to land on. Collectively, the steps constitute what has come to be termed alternative dispute resolution (ADR)—that is, alternative ways to manage conflict. Displayed in steps, the diagram shows how they change in nature: from informal to formal, from

FIGURE 1. Conflict Management Staircase

WAR   the last recourse in conflict management: everyone usually loses

STRIKE   the balance of power is actively tested; can lead to violence

BOYCOTT   market forces are employed to decide the conflict; you ride with the economic tide

LITIGATION   a judge or jury decides whether you win or lose; a lawyer customarily plays your hand

ARBITRATION   an arbitrator decides the conflict; frequently the decision is binding on you

———————————————*

FACT FINDING   you turn to an expert fact finder for an opinion about your conflict, but not to decide it

MEDIATION   you focus on the substance of your conflict while allowing a mediator to manage the settlement process

NEGOTIATION   you manage both the substance and the process of conflict resolution by playing the hand you've been dealt

CONCILIATION   you are made to feel better about being embroiled in conflict; seldon conclusive

CAPITULATION   you give up your conflict; you lose

* This line marks an important landing for manager consideration. Below the landing managers directly control the outcome of their conflict. Above the landing the outcome of their conflict is relegated to other, more powerful authorities and/or potentially violent events.

self-determining to adjudicatory, from voluntary to coercive, from consensus-driven to power-driven, at escalating levels.

The solid horizontal line between fact finding (advisory) and arbitration (binding) is the landing at which leaders hand over direct control of their conflict and its outcome to an adjudicatory authority or powerful events. Below the landing, leaders retain control over how conflict is resolved and the nature of its resolution. These steps tend to emphasize informality and creativity and serve to maintain relationships. Above the landing, the steps tend to emphasize procedural rules. These steps are coercive and tend to do great harm to ongoing relationships.

Experienced leaders recognize that they can keep more of their conflict management options open by starting low on the staircase with conflict management strategies that emphasize informal negotiations. It is relatively easy to climb up the conflict resolution staircase, but relatively difficult to back down. Inexperienced leaders tend to favor movement up the steps rather than movement down them. While negotiation can be employed at any level, its use appears to be more fruitful when it is employed on a step *below* the landing, on a level where the power to resolve a conflict is given to a higher authority and is not left to the discretion of the leader.

Whether a first or last resort, the decision to negotiate should be based on a careful and accurate assessment of the conflict and the alternative forums for accomplishing resolution. In my experience, the biggest disasters suffered by leaders occur when they make an inaccurate assessment of their relative power in a conflict.

CONFLICT MANAGEMENT SKILLS

There are four basic skills inherent to being a mediator. How effectively a mediator performs the skills of *assessing, convening, facilitating*, and *brokering* are the measures of a mediator's success. Thus we'll look at these skills first. Later in this section I'll offer some "kitchen talk" about how these and other conflict management skills can be important to leaders. This arrangement, I think, will preserve the distinction between the roles of an independent mediator and the leader/ negotiator as player in the management of conflict.

Assessing the Nature of Conflict

Before taking on a mediation case I insist on doing a "walk-around" to meet each of the parties up-close-and-personal. This gives me a chance to understand where they are coming from and where they expect to go. It also gives them a chance to assess the mediation process and me. By listening to their recitations of "reality" and by asking probing questions about their needs, I can begin to get a fix on where the common ground lies and how their relative priorities may allow room for mediating subsequent trade-offs. Mostly, I want to assure myself that the parties are sufficiently uncertain about their chances of prevailing on other win/lose conflict resolution "steps" so that they will make a good faith effort in mediation. Parties turn to mediation only as a "lesser evil" for getting their needs met and putting the conflict behind them. If they think they can win-it-all through litigation, arbitration, resorting to the ballot box, or going to war, they are poor candidates for mediated negotiations. I'll have more to say about conflict assessing for leaders later on.

Convening the Parties

Everyone knows where to find their local courthouse and generally understands the nature of the high-stake conflict resolutions that occur there. But it's challenging for a mediator to find a neutral meeting place for the first mediation session and decide on the shape of a table to seat the parties comfortably. After finding an acceptable site, a mediator's next order of business is to help the parties adopt ground rules for their negotiations. Ground rules are intended to define the terms of engagement the negotiators agree to abide by; they also constitute the procedural framework for the mediation process. Ground rules attempt to anticipate all the procedural glitches that might surprise negotiators after they commence bargaining. Also, by successfully negotiating ground rules, the parties realize that they can agree on something and become invested in a process for reaching settlement. Without total ownership of both process and substance, the parties probably won't accept the result in a way that will assure its implementation. Basically, ground rules for mediation result from the parties agreeing to answers for the following questions:

- Whose knees belong under the negotiation table? (All parties holding potential veto power over a settlement must be present.)
- What's on the table for negotiation? (There must be agreement on the range of issues that are within bounds for negotiation.)
- When is it reasonable for negotiations to conclude? (A hard and fast deadline is important since delay serves party interests differentially.)
- What will the mediated agreement look like? (Try to define the form an agreement is likely to take: written contract, memorandum of understanding, consent decree, consensus recommendation, and so on.)
- How will sign-off by the parties and their constituent organizations be obtained? (Determine how the agreement will be ratified.)
- Who takes responsibility for implementing the agreement? (Consensus agreements are the beginning, not the end. Parties will need to develop mechanisms for executing, monitoring, and modifying their agreements.)

A slew of other procedural questions will need to be anticipated as well, such as:

- Are mediation sessions to be open or closed to the public?
- What constraints can be placed on communications with the media?
- How will proprietary information be protected?
- Is it back to square one in the event mediation fails? Or do they keep their gains and agree to disagree on the rest?

The overall objective of establishing ground rules up front in the convening phase is to have sufficiently thorough procedural guidelines in place so that the process of negotiation won't get in the way of substantive progress once the bargaining gets hot and heavy.

Facilitating Discussions

Contrary to popular perception, most negotiation breakthroughs occur when the parties are away from the table, either caucusing or doing their homework with constituents between mediation sessions.

Mediator-facilitated meetings serve to transmit and receive information, give parties an opportunity to try out positions, and acknowledge tentative "meetings of minds" often reached elsewhere. Progress in mediation results when a party makes an offer that addresses another party's need. Such an offer is frequently prefaced with "What if we did (thus and such) . . . could you do (this and that)?" This handy question conveys a readiness to deal. Skillful facilitation involves finding ways to prompt such offers and counteroffers, a process that leads to the mediator's brokering role. Simply being a meeting facilitator isn't sufficient unless the meetings actually do something to produce movement toward a possible settlement. To meet for the sake of meeting is a waste of everyone's time.

When negotiations bog down, a mediator's artfulness must come into play. My favorite strategy is to become an "agent of reality" with one or more of the parties during caucus. Basically I ask them if they are prepared to walk away from all the progress they have made and return to the dangerous, uncertain side of the conflict. (The standard mediation ground rule is: In lieu of consensus it's all bets off, back to square one.) Should "agent of reality" fail, another tactic is to become a "prophet of doom" and remind a recalcitrant party, again during caucus, about the worst-case scenario that is likely to be visited upon them if mediation fails.

Brokering a Consensus

The moment of truth for negotiators comes when they are ready to jointly announce their consensus package and begin its implementation. As with earlier constituent ratification, it is imperative that key politicians, administrators, bureaucrats, and others be kept informed about the nature of the agreement that negotiators are likely to bring their way. What I term a "red flag" check is primarily a mediator's responsibility. It gives early notice about a possible mediated agreement to political, economic, and administrative interests that are integral to its subsequent implementation. If any of these interests "red flags" a problem, there is still time for negotiators to heed the warning and make adjustments in their package. Finally, a mediator should clue negotiators that even the most skilled crafters of agreement language cannot possibly anticipate every future problem. Therefore, the signing of a settlement agreement concluding mediation should be viewed not as an ending but as a start. Implementation of the consensus package is the first day of a new paradigm for ongoing collaboration. To succeed in implementation, negotiating parties must redeploy themselves to support, monitor, and carry out the fruits of their negotiations.

The conflict management skills considered thus far are generic to the mediator's success. Excepting conflict assessment, the skills of convening, facilitating, and brokering negotiations are of secondary importance to leadership success. This then is a good place to offer some "kitchen talk" about conflict management that has broad application for leaders.

Developing a Sense of Timing

Mediators need to develop a sense for when to intervene in conflict. Leaders need to become equally adept at seeing windows of opportunity as well as the pitfalls of failing to act. A military commander, for example, will understand the tactical advantage of a first strike versus the delay created by a holding action or scorched earth strategy. Either may prove decisive in warfare; both are instrumental to a sense of timing. Similarly, a mediator who intervenes in conflict too early may sap one party's ability to organize forces and marshal resources, leaving them in an inferior power position. Conversely, intervening too late may find parties so locked into win/lose strategies that they have no resources or patience left to take up negotiations, mediated or otherwise. As mentioned earlier, the classic time for the mediator to intervene is when leaders are sufficiently uncertain about their options that they perceive mediation to be the lesser evil for getting their conflict resolved. Leaders likewise must develop a sense for knowing when to hold them and when to fold them.

Understanding the BATNA Concept

Roger Fischer and William Ury conceived a very handy conflict assessment tool for anyone interested in becoming skilled at conflict management. They termed it BATNA—better alternative to a negotiated agreement. In essence, BATNA reminds a party to conflict that the power to prevail outright rarely stands aside for a negotiated compromise. If a leader's conflict assessment indicates there is a better alternative to negotiations, that alternative will be pursued regardless of protestations to the contrary. Statements of a "willingness to negotiate" serve only as a cover.

It's a leader's responsibility to assess BATNA before, during, and approaching the end of negotiations—in other words, *continually*. Negotiations don't occur in a vacuum. Outside events can often precipitate BATNA changes for better or worse. By keeping a watchful eye on the BATNA, leaders and mediators alike can maneuver to avoid the "train wrecks" that occur when inappropriate conflict management strategies are blindly pursued oblivious to power balance changes.

Developing Better Forums

A resource management model deserving of another chance is the now defunct Federal Regional Council (FRC) and its coordinating mission. Before falling victim to the "less government is better" policy, the FRC in the Pacific Northwest provided a valuable forum for resource managers in federal agencies to meet regularly and discuss interjurisdictional conflicts. FRC leadership used its positive influence, sometimes with professional mediators present, to convene leaders from various agencies in order to discuss their interagency conflicts. This opportunity for high-level "kitchen talk" frequently resulted in agencies making more accurate assessments of conflict and allowed for more timely convening of parties to negotiate consensually. Even when leadership chose not to negotiate, they did so with their perceptions checked out and a better understanding of the upside and downside risks associated with the alternatives.

To conclude this section on conflict management skills, readers are reminded that when seeking to manage conflict they should bear in mind that:

- Parties cannot be made to negotiate . . . they may only find it in their best self-interest to do so.
- Efforts to institutionalize frameworks to encourage negotiation-based conflict management should stress incentives over coercion and allow plenty of room for informal "kitchen talk."
- Skill in alternative dispute resolution (ADR) is more art than science, but an understanding of the nature of conflict and its alternatives is important to leadership careers.

CONFLICT MANAGEMENT AND SCIENCE

Mediated negotiations, under consensus ground rules, improve the opportunities for scientific and technical input into environmental policymaking. Elsewhere I have advanced five hypotheses to explain why scientific input into environmental policymaking is so often a painful and frustrating experience for the scientist and an inconclusive and divisive experience for the policymaker:

1. Parties engaged in conflicts over environmental issues frequently employ science and technology as proxies for attaining other objectives.
2. Scientists who venture into public policymaking or adjudicatory conflict settlement tend to be used as cannon fodder or attack dogs.
3. Technological quick fixes for complex public policy issues are rare and illusory. Nonetheless, the quest for such Holy Grail solutions preoccupies our hearts, our minds, and our pocketbooks.
4. Science is of such pervasive importance to scientists that they tend to ignore needs and values beyond the boundaries of their particular disciplines.
5. Public policy choices involving natural resource and environmental trade-offs are full of uncertainty and risk. Therefore, those involved in policymaking can allow for incomplete information and an uncertain future by implementing their policies as though they are "experiments."

My purpose in developing these hypotheses is to stimulate both scientists and policymakers to find better ways to interact. Scientists need to become less equivocal in providing qualified expert advice despite less than scientific certainty. Policymakers need to become more tolerant and respectful of equivocal expert advice when sufficient data and peer review simply aren't available to allow for scientific certainty. A conflict management forum based on negotiation using consensus ground rules offers the "safe ground" necessary for a scientist/policymaker interaction to occur when conditions of uncertainty prevail.

Here is a case study illustrating how scientific input from an unexpected source provided the key to resolving a highly charged national forest plan appeal when no single party had complete information:

Shawnee National Forest Plan Appeal: Ornithological research indicated that populations of neotropical (migratory songbird) species were crashing as their midwestern native forest habitat diminished. Many culprits were alleged by environmental appellants of the Shawnee National Forest Management Plan (southern Illinois)—including timber clearcuts, unauthorized motorized recreation use, adverse selection by forest management practices favoring propagation of game species, and others. Theories abounded and simply inflamed how parties perceived one another's motives and objectives. Through mediation it became possible for all the parties with a stake in Illinois' only national forest to get their needs on the table and gain an understanding about the needs of others. Interestingly, the resource management concept that was key to addressing the needs of the songbird advocates originated with a person who was at the table representing mining interests. By adapting a concept familiar to deep-pit miners, the Shawnee Forest Plan was amended by consensus to incorporate the concept of Forest Interior Management Units (FIMUs). These experimental land management areas contain undisturbed 100-acre core units surrounded by 1000 acres of wedge-shaped units that are managed. A key provision of FIMU is that at least 60 percent of the forest canopy always remains intact. This, ornithologists believe, will discourage songbird nest parasitization by cowbirds that gain access through openings in the forest canopy created by clearcuts and motorized trail expansions. This settlement of a complex resource management conflict became possible when scientists and policymakers, protected by consensus ground rules, negotiated.

DEVELOPING AND APPLYING CONFLICT MANAGEMENT SKILLS

Certain principles are vital to mediation skills and apply as well to leadership development in general. Recall what was stated earlier about how the interests of leaders and mediators diverge. Leaders have a proprietary interest in substantive issues embodied in a conflict. In a word, leaders are stakeholders. Mediators, on the other hand, must not hold (nor even be perceived to hold) the slightest stake in the substance of a conflict lest they become disqualified to run the process. The mediator's "stake" in a conflict is limited to the processes for resolving the conflict and then only to those alternatives that feature negotiations.

Despite this caveat, there are still significant benefits for the leader who is willing to study, understand, and develop some of the skills used by mediators in the course of doing their thing. The following principles highlight the skills integral to becoming a competent manager of conflict.

Principle 1: Patient Listening

In order to become an accurate assessor and resolver of conflict, it is first necessary to become a keen and intuitive listener. I'm not talking about allowing breaks in the conversation so you can think about what to say next. I'm talking about really *hearing* what the other party is saying and then asking questions to gain a better understanding of the needs expressed.

While assessing a conflict over road system expansion in the San Juan National Forest, for example, a colleague and I interviewed a dozen or more leaders of interest groups both for and against the project. It quickly became apparent that some of the parties were dead wrong about the other parties' position. Because they were relying on flawed preconceived notions, they were embarked on strategies that were totally divisive and would lead nowhere.

Leaders opposed to expanding the forest road system were preoccupied about being outnumbered at the negotiation table. They persistently challenged the participation of parties on the other side—especially the cattle grazers, who they perceived would join with timber, mining, and motorized recreation to outvote them. Even though voting plays no part in mediation, it became clear that certain parties would boycott mediation if certain other parties were seated at the table.

We mediators knew from our initial "walkabout" meetings with all the leaders that they were relying on mistaken perceptions about each other's needs and objectives. The trick was how to get all the parties to the table when some were threatening to walk if others were allowed in. Our solution was to hold a "talk-about-talking" meeting to which each party could come without committing to stay. Each party was encouraged to describe, for all to hear, what they needed to get out of mediation. All were surprised by what they heard! In particular, when the lead grazer's turn came, he explained that the mile of Forest Service road on his present allotment "was sometimes a mile too much." When roading opponents asked for further explanation, he added that *access* to rangeland was what cattlemen needed—not roads through their allotments which made cattle rustling too easy when beef prices rose. Dumbfounded anti-road leaders immediately called for a caucus and committed to proceeding with mediation without another word uttered about what interest groups deserved to be seated. By creating an opportunity for serious listening, we started a deadlocked conflict moving toward resolution.

Principle 2: Artful Questioning

After keen listening comes artful questioning. The basic purpose of mediation is to help parties get their needs met through direct negotiation. This cannot happen until the needs of competing interests become mutually understood. Understanding is accomplished by means of questioning aimed at obtaining information about one another's needs, not by questioning to attack them. Mediators learn early to develop a respect for the differences, since negotiating the differences provides the impetus for creativity. Not only can artful questions glean vital information about the nature of competing needs, they can also convey respect in ways that tend to be reciprocated.

An example of the power of artful questioning occurred in one of the most polarized conflicts I've mediated. It involved the National Rifle Association (NRA) and their asserted "right" to discharge firearms on public land. The Angeles National Forest's new land management plan was the focus of such heated conflict that even such traditional foes as the Sierra Club and American Motorcycle Association were aligned against the NRA's position.

The NRA seemed headed for a Supreme Court settlement if necessary. Artful questioning of the NRA's negotiator, however, suggested that their underlying needs could be met short of a court showdown. Basically, the NRA wanted accessible "core shooting areas" designated within the forest for membership use. Instead of having the NRA holed up fighting off its adversaries awaiting its day in court, the challenge for all parties became clear: how to define the concept of "core shooting area" (CSA) for inclusion in a new Angeles Forest Plan.

The issue was not whether or not to shoot on public land, since the shooting was an established fact. The issue was where and how shooting could be accommodated by all the interests participating in forest planning.

As various interest-group leaders questioned the NRA negotiator about CSA siting criteria, the outline of a possible agreement began to take shape. The first criterion for siting CSAs was "road accessibility." This had the effect of narrowing the "rights" issue from shooting in the entire forest to shooting only in those portions accessible to vehicles. Follow-up questions about parking and site maintenance resulted in more CSA criteria that further defined the concept and reduced the amount of forest affected by CSAs. Recreationists, whether on foot or on wheels, were no more keen about falling victim to stray bullets than shooters were eager to defend themselves against liability claims. Eventually questioning identified box canyon sites as another siting criterion. Utility companies with power line rights-of-way in the forest were eager to reduce insulator replacement costs due to random "plinking," and a beyond-the-line-of-sight criterion evolved. Questioning, then, succeeded in transforming a nonnegotiable "rights" conflict into a resource allocation conflict far easier to manage. With the impacts of shooting mitigated to everyone's satisfaction, consensus was finally achieved on a specific number of CSA sites. Leaders who develop proficiency at asking "what if?" will improve their opportunities for success.

Principle 3: Thinking Consensus

The objective of managing conflict is to have it settled with the least danger (of loss) and the most opportunity (for gain). The term that best describes this outcome is *consensus*. The stage for consensus is set when conflicting parties voluntarily decide to participate in negotiation. Consensus happens when participating parties become satisfied that enough of their respective needs are met that they can settle and put the conflict behind them. The consensus agreement package contains what the parties need most. Opting for mediation is one method that has proved effective for reaching consensus.

Thinking about a consensus objective totally changes the way parties negotiate with each other. If one party "has a problem," so do *all* the parties if they are committed to reaching consensus. Instead of using experience, information, and power to bludgeon the aggrieved party into submission, consensus thinking encourages everyone to bring their resources to bear on behalf of an aggrieved party. Without collaboration there cannot be consensus. The principle of managing by consensus is not as good as having it all every time, but it's certainly better than winding up with nothing but an escalating conflict.

Bellevue City, Washington, provides a good example of progress using consensus. When the Bellevue city council was presented with citizen petitions demanding reduced traffic congestion signed by more constituents than had voted in the last general election, they responded by passing an emergency interim traffic ordinance that satisfied no one. To their credit, the city council simultaneously offered the petition organizers and local business leaders an opportunity to engage in mediated negotiations and come back to them with a consensus recommendation for a permanent traffic solution. Citizen organizers met with business leaders and city officials in mediation with a deadline set by the council. They succeeded at conceiving a "red-amber-green" early warning system that linked future city growth to the actual performance of planned traffic mitigation measures. Developers could go ahead, pause, or be stopped in a technically predictable manner. Furthermore, they could spend private funds to effect traffic mitigation measures more rapidly if their self-interest so determined. A new traffic ordinance incorporating these measures was enacted by the city council with the support of the previously warring factions.

Principle 4: Experimenting

Implementing consensus agreements as though they were experiments is a principle that I strongly recommend to leaders concerned about sustaining their management decisions. Parties to conflicts involving natural resources rarely have all the necessary information at their disposal by the deadline for reaching agreement. The ability to consistently forge agreements, supported by consensus, is the mark of a true leader. In a perfect world, leaders could turn to scientists for the "right stuff" upon which agreements could be based. Sound science as a basis for environmental decision making is a goal few would argue with.

But what if scientists themselves disagree or are unable or unwilling to recommend the wise course when the time is ripe for leaders to decide? There comes a time—which is most of the time in the environmental arena—when leaders must decide what to do despite the uncertainty. It is then that it helps to view the decision or agreement as an experiment that will need vigilant monitoring and precise tuning as experience and data become available.

In mediation, I caution parties that their consensus agreement does not end their responsibilities. It only shifts the focus from agreeing to *implementing* their agreement. Unless parties to the settlement are prepared to accept their agreement as a beginning, not an end, they are setting themselves up for disappointment. Agreeing can be relatively easy, in fact, compared to the difficulty of implementing an agreement successfully.

Professor Kai Lee, formerly at the University of Washington and now director of the Department of Environmental Studies at Williams College, is doing some very interesting work on what is termed adaptive management. In brief, Lee recommends that leaders treat their agreements as controlled experiments that can accommodate feedback in the form of results, mistakes, better science, new data, and so forth. Such an implementation feedback mechanism allows leaders to make informed midcourse corrections to keep their agreement on the desired objective. Lee's insightful work matches my own observations over a decade of environmental mediation. If adaptive management isn't a chapter in this book, perhaps it should be the subject of one soon to follow.

The endangered spotted owl and its ancient forest habitat are a national cause célèbre competing for conservation and preservation interests. The outcome remains much in doubt. A microcosm of this conflict, again reflecting the importance of experimentation, was settled recently in the state of Washington at the behest of the commissioner of national resources (DNR). Public controversy about the future of Washington's remnant ancient forests on the remote Olympic Peninsula highlighted the interests needing to be part of any settlement that could hold. DNR leadership appointed a Commission on Old Growth to explore the issues and come up with consensus recommendations addressing the needs of environmentalists, timber companies, local communities, and school administrators.

The commission hired mediators to help develop a process to enable approximately thirty lay leaders, representative of affected interests, to engage each other in working groups and plenary sessions. The key issue focused on finding ways to manage state forest lands—including the remaining ancient forests—to derive both an economic benefit for Washington's schools and a sustainable ancient forest ecosystem for the greater public good. In making its consensus recommendations, the Commission on Old Growth acknowledged that much scientifically sound information about managing second-growth forests to replicate ancient forest characteristics was lacking. Consequently, a key recommendation was to "experiment" by selectively delaying ancient forest harvest while extending and monitoring second-growth rotations. While it's much too soon to tell whether Washington's Olympic Experimental Forest will achieve negotiated expectations, the important thing is that management, experimentation, and oversight are going forward collaboratively.

A CHECKLIST FOR LEADERS

In conclusion, here's a checklist that may be useful to leaders interested in acquiring or honing their negotiating/mediating skills:

- Read anything you can lay your hands on written by, in alphabetical order, Howard Bellman, Jon Brock, Gerald Cormack, Philip Harder, Kai Lee, Howard Raifa, and Arnold Zack. Both the Conservation Foundation and National Institute for Dispute Resolution are good sources of publication lists.
- Take a course offered by an experienced mediation expert. Be wary of courses offered by theorists who have not "done it."
- If you haven't actually organized as a party preparing for conflict, get involved in an advocacy role and learn firsthand what it's like to develop the power necessary to become an effective advocate.
- Try out mediation with conflict that is appropriate for negotiation. Discover what it's like to put your knees under the table with worthy adversaries.
- Get a feel for how your participation in a negotiation affects your various relationships with colleagues, constituents, adversaries, media, and the public. A willingness to negotiate is not without its consequences.
- Approach conflict with humility and understanding. Truth, wisdom, and virtue are rarely found on just one side of an issue.

- Attempts at reaching consensus may resemble grazing sheep until the needs get sorted out. Once accomplished, though, consensus takes on the force of a stampede.

Remember that successful conflict management begins with an understanding of conflict's dual nature: danger/opportunity. When conflict arises, a seasoned leader refrains from taking it personally or as a system failure. Conflict is evidence that interests are competing as inevitably they must in our pluralistic system of democracy. By accepting and respecting conflict as a powerful precursor to change, leaders can remain in personal control below the line on the conflict resolution staircase—that is, the conflict management alternatives emphasizing *negotiation*.

The key to successfully managing conflict is the ability to accurately assess the power balance driving the conflict. Here a leader's communication skills, experience, and sound judgment are all at a premium. Should the conflict assessment indicate there is no better alternative to negotiated agreement, negotiations may be convened with or without the assistance of an independent mediator. But it is essential that procedural ground rules be established before substantive bargaining begins. Observance of ground rules enables parties to engage in more creative, more productive, and less destructive conflicts.

Adopting ground rules also enhances the opportunities for synergy to occur. Instead of using closely held information or expertise to put down a negotiating partner, a consensus goal ensures that everyone at the table must use their information collaboratively. Information, science, and technology previously considered proprietary may become a shared resource when consensus is the objective. If one party is having a problem with getting a particular need met, under a consensus ground rule *all* parties share that problem. By bringing to bear the best that everyone at the table can offer, new options tend to surface that no party had thought of before. Thus the synergism stimulated by a consensus ground rule creates important new pieces for the dispute resolution "package," thereby taking advantage of the *opportunity* side of conflict. The environmental mediation process has proved capable of producing negotiated settlements that resolve long-deadlocked conflicts in unanticipated ways.

Mediators develop their own personal style for moving parties toward consensus. Some remain aloof from the parties. Others strive for familiarity. Some freely offer substantive suggestions as stalking horses to move deadlocked negotiations. Others never touch substance or do so only as a last resort. What matters is their capacity to earn—and hold—the confidence of the parties. Trust is achieved by insightful application of solid conflict management skills. Mediators must accurately assess conflicts, develop strategies of alternative dispute resolution, and guide the direction of the conflict to allow all parties to contribute to the decisions forming the agreement and its subsequent implementation.

No doubt there are as many styles of leadership as there are mediation styles. Nevertheless, a general understanding of the mediation process has something to offer leaders that can help them as conflict managers. Leaders can benefit from gaining an appreciation of the dual nature of conflict and an understanding of the alternative strategies for managing conflict. The use of mediation skills, where they fit, can complement any leadership style.

Adaptive management, as defined by Kai Lee, recommends that leaders implement their negotiated settlements as though they were experiments. The wisdom, understanding, and humility inherent in this approach are admirable. We humans—leaders included—are babes in our knowledge and appreciation of natural ecosystem function. To think that we can negotiate with imperfect information and produce outcomes that are certain is sheer arrogance and folly. Lee and others understand the difficulty of decision making under conditions of uncertainty and offer adaptive management as kind of a learn-as-we-go solution. By building monitoring and feedback mechanisms into the implementation of consensus agreements, leaders can assure the best use of the scientific method during and after the dispute resolution process. The ongoing experimental nature of implementation not only strengthens the bonds of agreement but improves the quality of future interactions as well.

REFERENCES

Bellman, H. S., C. Sampson, and G. W. Cormick. 1982. *Using Mediation When Siting Hazardous Waste Management Facilities: A Handbook.* U.S. Environmental Protection Agency (SW-944).

Bingham, G. 1986. *Resolving Environmental Disputes: A Decade of Experience.* Washington, DC: The Conservation Foundation.

Brock, J. 1982. *Bargaining Beyond Impasse.* Boston: Auburn House.

Cormick, G. W. 1982. "The Myth, the Reality and the Future of Environmental Mediation." *Environment,* 24 (7).

Danielson, L. J. and J. L. Watson. 1983. "Environmental Mediation." *Natural Resources Lawyer* (ABA). XV (4).

Fisher, R. with W. Ury. 1978. *International Mediation: A Working Guide.* New York: International Peace Academy.

Fisher, R. and W. Ury. 1981. *Getting to Yes.* Boston: Houghton Mifflin.

Harter, P. J. 1982. "Negotiating Regulations: A Cure for Malaise." *The Georgetown Law Journal.* 71 (1).

Lee, K. N. 1990. "Deliberately Seeking Sustainability." Unpublished paper.

Raiffa, H. 1982. *The Art and Science of Negotiations.* Cambridge, MA.: Belknap Press.

Sullivan, T. J. 1984. *Resolving Development Disputes Through Negotiations.* New York: Plenum Press.

Tice, O. M. 1989. "An Experiment in Applying Science to the Resolution of Environmental Conflict." Unpublished paper.

Zack, A. M. 1988. "Public Sector Mediation." Washington, DC: BNA Books.

RESOURCES

Here are some key organizations to contact for information about environmental dispute resolution:

Institute for Environmental Negotiation
Campbell Hall
University of Virginia
Charlottesville, VA 22903
(804-923-1970)

The Keystone Center
2033 M Street, N.W.
Washington, DC 20036
(202-872-0160)

The Mediation Institute
22231 Mulholland Highway, Suite 103
Woodland Hills, CA 91302
(818-591-9516)

RESOLVE
1250 24th Street, N.W., Suite 500
Washington, DC 20037
(202-778-9653)

Western Network
1215 Paseo de Peralta
Santa Fe, NM 87501
(505-982-9805)

6 Policy and Legislation

....

James R. Lyons

IT ISN'T OFTEN that I have the opportunity to sit back and reflect on my career and how I came to be where I am today. If someone were to ask me how I ended up working in legislation and policy, as happens quite often when people looking for work on Capitol Hill come by my office, my immediate response would be: luck.

In part, that is true. But the more I think about it, the more I realize that I am where I am because I *like* what I do. And, had I charted a course the day I left my graduate studies at Yale, this is not too far from where I would have wanted to be. But it hasn't been luck that got me here. There has been more direction, more drive and determination, and more calculating than that. But luck, or maybe fortunate timing, has played a significant role. With this said, I have attempted to reflect on my career and its development and have come to the following conclusions.

First, everything I have learned, all my experiences, and the people I have come to know, have in some way helped to influence my choice of career and my ability to achieve the goals I have set for myself.

Second, there are certain qualities and skills that have aided me in the field of policy and legislation. Improving upon these is critical, as I see it, to my ability to advance further in my chosen field.

Third, certain key events can have a significant impact on one's career. To some degree, one can control these events. In other instances, one cannot. The key, however, is to use one's experience and skills to deal with both the anticipated and the unexpected—and then try to turn such events to your advantage.

90

LIFE'S LESSONS

I never set out to work in the field of natural resources and the environment. I was born in northern New Jersey in 1955, not far from New York City. There were no forests, no picturesque mountains, no pristine streams. Terms like "environmental quality," "pollution," and "preservation" weren't a part of the vernacular of the time.

I was introduced to the outdoors by my father, who loved to fish and camp. My most important childhood memory of him was the way in which he would reward me for doing well in grade school. Provided my grades were up to standard, he would take me out of school on the first of April each year—the opening day of trout fishing season in nearby New York State—and take me fishing. At age five, that was quite a motivation. I would look forward the entire school year for the first day of April and the opportunity to go trout fishing with my father. There were other outdoor experiences we shared as a family. These provided me with an appreciation of the outdoors that is probably not unlike that of many people who have chosen a career in environment.

My father also set an example of public service that has clearly influenced my career choice. As a policeman and a volunteer fireman, my father worked revolving shifts (some days, some nights, many weekends) and could be called on to respond to a fire alarm or emergency at any time. This experience instilled in me a sense of the dedication that is inevitably part of such a lifestyle. It also made me painfully aware that the rewards of such a career are more personal than financial.

In fact, to supplement his family income, my father worked during his off hours as a carpenter. For my father, this meant many long hours and, often, little sleep. This, in turn, further limited the time he could spend with his wife and sons. So, in order to spend more time with him, I learned to take advantage of opportunities to help him in his work as a carpenter. At age six I began to learn the tools of the trade. I learned to anticipate what equipment was needed to perform a given task. If, for example, we were to hang a door, I would gather the tools needed to do the job. Anticipating the needs of the job and taking the initiative to get them together—both have proved to be valuable skills.

To give equal time, I should note that my mother—a dedicated homemaker and parent—was, and remains, an avid quilter and craft maker. This is a talent that she ingrained in me—especially the ability to visualize a project, to design it, to modify and refine it as the project progresses, and to complete it. Pride in her work and in sharing her skills with others, as a teacher of craft-making and quilting, were key elements of my early education.

Like many people who have chosen this career path, I did not plan to enter the field of environment and natural resources. I certainly had no preconceived goal to work in legislation and policy. I learned of natural resource management as a field through a chance encounter with an undergraduate student studying wildlife management at Rutgers University. I entered Rutgers with an interest, I thought, in biology and medicine. But a nearly disastrous freshman experience with chemistry—and the startling discovery that one could take courses in wildlife and forestry—set me on a completely different career path.

My chance interaction with that student, and my good fortune in meeting Jim Applegate, a professor at Cook College at Rutgers University, probably constitute the first critical fork in my career path. Jim Applegate (or "Doc") is one of those unique figures who has a passion for life and for learning and the ability to instill that passion in his students. There have been numerous times during my career where Doc's wise counsel has been invaluable.

Following my undergraduate studies at Rutgers, I entered the School of Forestry and Environmental Studies at Yale University. This, too, was a fortuitous decision. The alternatives I faced in choosing a graduate program came down to two options. One would have afforded me a grant covering tuition and expenses to study forestry in a more traditional vein. The other would have required me to pay a substantial part of the cost. I chose the second option. This investment, it turns out, has paid for itself many times over.

It was at Yale that I developed my interest in policy and in the "people part" of natural resource management. This I attribute to two things. First, Yale's natural resources program draws its richness from the diversity of its students and the experiences it offers. The graduate program emphasizes personal development and learning through personal challenge and experience. Second, I again had the good fortune of working closely with two people who helped to enrich my experience: Carl Reidel, a visiting professor from the University of Vermont, and Stephen Kellert, a professor of sociology. From Steve, in particular, I developed an appreciation for the human dimension in management—a fundamental element in natural resources policy and a critical element in understanding legislative process. It was Dr. Kellert who was also responsible for my first position as policy analyst for the U.S. Fish and Wildlife Service.

I have been in Washington, D.C., for thirteen years now. Like everyone I know with an interest in natural resources and environmental issues, I came in order to "put in my time." But, like many others, I never left. When I first came to Washington, I joined the staff of the U.S. Fish and Wildlife Service. As a policy analyst I was given opportunities to review and analyze current national issues. But my primary responsibility was to develop a new segment of a periodic national survey that the agency conducts to determine America's use of its fish and wildlife resources.

That assignment afforded me the opportunity to meet national leaders in the wildlife and natural resources profession. It also provided me with the chance to prove my ability to be innovative in designing a segment of the survey that had never been conducted previously. At the time, nonconsumptive users of fish and wildlife resources represented a new constituency for wildlife agencies and a potentially important ally. My role in leading this effort afforded me visibility and opportunities for professional growth that served as a springboard for my work in Washington.

Several years with the Fish and Wildlife Service increased my interest in policy and the legislative process. I found it frustrating to work in an agency that was continually given new legislative direction that it had limited ability to affect. I wanted to see firsthand how the legislative process worked. And I wanted to see if I could "get my hands dirty" as a participant in the process.

Politics, as well, played a role in my decision to leave the agency. A new administration with less than stellar environmental credentials had entered the White House. Life at the Department of the Interior was different under James Watt than it had been under the previous administration. Clearly, my political philosophy was not in tune with that of my new superiors. It was time for a change.

That change came in an interesting way. The decision to move on to head the policy program for the Society of American Foresters came at a time when I had just about given up on my career in Washington. I had spent nearly a year attempting to find employment with the

Congress. After repeated failures and false leads, I elected to return to Yale to pursue a Ph.D. in natural resources policy.

At another critical juncture in my career, I was notified on a Monday that I had been accepted as a Ph.D. candidate and my response was expected on Friday. That Friday, I received a phone call offering me the position of director of resource policy for the Society of American Foresters (SAF). Having to choose between learning about policy in academia or through "on-the-ground" experience, I chose the latter. I have never regretted this critical decision in my career.

My position at SAF offered me a chance, once again, to innovate and develop a program to bring professional foresters into the policy process. Working for a membership organization and reporting directly to its board of directors also helped me to understand the need to be responsive to a constituency—in this case foresters. My role was to bring professional expertise to bear on contemporary natural resource policy issues. In so doing, I was chief policy analyst, magazine columnist, spokesperson, and lobbyist.

I was a one-man policy program. Long hours and late nights were part of the job. And dealing with people—members of the organization, the staff, the board of directors, members of Congress and their staffs, agency administrators, interest groups, and my own limited staff—was a critical component to the success of the program.

The people I met in this position have become close friends, colleagues, mentors, and even adversaries to this day. It is an axiom of work in Washington that you should always treat people with respect and professional courtesy. Don't burn any bridges—because you never know where the people you work with today will end up tomorrow.

One of the clear benefits of my work with the SAF was the opportunity to work on the staff of the Committee on Agriculture. Congress, unlike other elements of the government, hires staff on a word-of-mouth, first-come, first-served basis. My first position—staff director for the Agriculture Subcommittee that deals with forestry issues—was the result of a friendship I developed with the departing staff director. Upon his promotion to associate counsel with the committee, he asked me if I would like to replace him on the subcommittee. I recall asking him how I should apply for the position. He told me not to worry—he would talk to the subcommittee chairman regarding my interest. The next day I received a phone call from the chairman asking me if I'd like the position and "how much it was going to cost him." Not the usual job interview. But not unusual for a position on Capitol Hill.

After approximately a year with the subcommittee, the chairman retired. I was planning to return to SAF when the staff director for the full Agriculture Committee asked me if I'd like to remain with the committee—to take responsibility for forestry and environmental issues for the committee chairman. This is the position I hold today.

In this position I've had the good fortune to deal with natural resource issues of national and international importance—old-growth forests, national forest management, below-cost timber sales, tropical deforestation, soil and water conservation, and pesticide regulation, to name a few. I developed the conservation and forestry titles of the 1990 Farm Bill for the House Agriculture Committee and negotiated these elements of the final law. Ironically, the staff person who led the Senate negotiations on the forestry title was a person I first hired as a summer intern at SAF, a man who later succeeded me as the organization's director of resource policy. As the saying goes, don't burn any bridges.

LEADERSHIP QUALITIES

There are many characteristics that I associate with being a sound policy analyst and a good legislative staff member. I offer the following in ascending order of importance.

Humility

Having provided staff support for a federal agency, a nonprofit organization, and a member of Congress, I feel confident in stating that gaining visibility and credit for one's work cannot be the factor that motivates one's participation in the field. In fact, as a policy analyst for the agency, I found it easier to be quietly effective by promoting ideas and positions that, if sound, were often grasped by my superiors as their own.

As staff to a congressional office, it is equally important to keep one's ego in check. Staff are often accused of running Congress. In some respects, this is true. But only if one has proved his or her capabilities to the member in question. Then one may hope of having the latitude to "speak for the member." The best of all worlds is to be considered "an informed source" in congressional circles. The worst of all worlds is to find yourself quoted in the *Washington Post*.

Patience

At times, you may see issues on the horizon yet feel helpless to address them before they become important enough to warrant congressional attention. A friend of mine on Capitol Hill likes to say, "Five problems coming down the road. Four of them will fall in a ditch before they get to you." These hardly sound like words of wisdom, I know. But the point of his comment, with the following interpretation, is well taken.

Members of Congress are very busy. They must deal with a wide range of issues and have little time to dwell on any one particular concern. It is therefore better to address an issue when it is significant enough to *demand* the members' attention. Such an approach has its failings. Of greatest concern, it makes Congress a reactive body— always responding to crises, seldom attempting to head them off. Nevertheless, in an environment where time is a valuable commodity, it is normally better to be patient and wait for an issue to ripen rather than attempting to force it into focus.

Tolerance

As one who is trained in natural resource issues, I admit that it is often frustrating to deal with staff and members of Congress who have no interest in matters that I believe should warrant congressional attention. There remain only a handful of staff, at least of those who deal with these issues on House and Senate committees, who have some training and experience in natural resource issues. Most often, staff are hired for their political experience and their affiliation with a member of Congress, either through a campaign or work in their congressional office. Hiring people for their experience and training in a particular field is the exception rather than the rule.

As a result, one responsibility of those who have such training is to promote an understanding of the technical side of natural resource issues. Another is to keep lobbyists—whether representing an agency, an industry, or an environmental point of view—honest in their factual presentations to members. Finally, issues are issues because of opposing, strongly held views. Tolerating the views of others is a necessary skill and a key element of the legislative process.

An Appreciation for Politics

Many people with an interest in policy view politics and policy as distinct. Some prefer to view policy as antiseptic: They analyze it, create models to explain it, and attempt to predict its behavior (as if it had a life of its own). I think the two are inseparable.

Policy formulation is a function of the substance of the issue and the politics of the time. A reluctance to deal with the political side of policy creates a false impression of how policy is formulated and false expectations of what one can hope to achieve in dealing with a policy issue. In fact, those who are skilled in dealing with policy have a strong appreciation for the people who make policy and their politics and the many factors that affect the decisions they make. Above all, they accept the dealing and compromise that are the essence of politics and policymaking.

Being a Good Listener

Politics, by definition, is the business of taking sides. To understand policy issues—particularly natural resource issues, which often tend to be emotionally charged—requires an ability to listen to all sides. Although the arguments made by some may not fit with your particular point of view, all sides want to be heard. More important, all sides must feel that their needs have been addressed if a compromise is to be reached.

A key to dealing with policy issues is ensuring that the affected parties have the opportunity to be a constructive part of the policy process and contribute to the eventual solution. If they are not heard, they may well attempt to disrupt the process. Rarely is a solution constructed that fails to include elements which satisfy all key sides of the issue.

An Ability to Juggle

Perhaps less a quality than a *necessity* is the ability to manage time and handle many issues at once. The skill involved here is the ability to juggle issues—moving from one to another without losing a sense of the substance or the politics.

Given the nature of natural resource issues, it is equally important that one be able to view the ideas, concerns, and desires of a variety of interests, as they pertain to a given issue, in context. Juggling may not be the appropriate analogy here. In fact, this skill is probably more akin to playing a revolving game of chess in which you try to play several opponents at the same time, keeping in mind the strategy of each game while attempting to anticipate the possible moves of each opponent.

People Skills

Policy and legislation are people-oriented. Issues don't become issues unless people with strongly held views—usually on opposite sides—make something an issue.

Working in an environment where your job is to deal with people with differing and sometimes polarized views is nothing if not challenging. Of course, it can also be rewarding when you can develop a solution that brings the sides together (or at least quiets their discord sufficiently to get a bill enacted into law).

Policy and legislation require every bit as much people skill as a foundation in natural resource management or environmental sciences. This is not to say that a foundation in the science of these issues isn't important. But to make policy requires a willingness to "mix it up" with people, to deal with the politics, and, at times, to accept an outcome that is politically correct even if it is not scientifically perfect.

Brevity

The ability to be concise is another key policy skill. Agency heads, members of Congress, and other policymakers are usually too busy and too disengaged from most issues to have the time to pour through pages of analysis. A concise summary of the issue—one that analyzes alternative solutions and offers a recommendation—is the key to getting your message to the person who will make the decision.

Ironically, this is the antithesis of the kind of writing that is encouraged in academia. It is certainly not a requirement in preparing one's graduate thesis. Yet this ability to "put it all on one page" is essential if one is to communicate effectively with policymakers.

This same skill applies to oral communication as well. When given the opportunity to follow up a memorandum or briefing paper with a personal briefing, you must be able to get to the point quickly and present it with a minimum of BS.

Tenacity

Being a tenacious advocate for one's position is another critical element in the policy process. This is particularly true if one is playing the role of an advocate for a particular interest group or cause but also applies to those representing a congressional office or committee. The legislative process hinges on compromise. You must be a strong spokesperson for your particular point of view to ensure that your concerns are addressed by compromise designed to resolve the issue.

Another reason why tenacity is such a valuable trait is that issues may take years to reach the point of national attention and even more years to be resolved. Debate over management of the Tongass National Forest, for example, continued for years before a legislative compromise was struck.

And the policy process does not end when a law is enacted. A strong influence in the implementation of most policies is the process of formulating regulations by the implementing agency. Of equal concern is obtaining funding for new programs and legislative initiatives. Failure to follow the process through the regulatory and funding processes may mean that good law never gets implemented—or is implemented in a way that fails to achieve its intended purpose. A clear failing of the conservation programs authorized by the 1990 Farm Bill was an inability—and concurrent lack of commitment—to funding them. Had interest groups continued to pressure for funding these programs, a different outcome might have resulted.

Imagination

Effective policy staff are good problem solvers. This requires both insight (to understand the problem) and imagination (to discover reasonable alternatives to solve it). As previously noted, part of this skill is listening. But, more important, understanding the motivations and needs of different parties and attempting to construct a solution that addresses their needs takes imagination.

Credibility

Credibility is one of the key ingredients of effective policy and legislative work. In Washington, information is a key to power and influence. Those who provide reliable information when it is needed, and in a manner in which it can be useful, find themselves called upon again and again.

In providing information you must ensure that it is accurate and reliable. Again, policymakers—be they congresspersons, agency administrators, or political candidates—need information quickly. Failing to provide accurate information, and an objective analysis of a situation when it is called for, can hurt your credibility and thus limit your access to the people you seek to influence.

Commitment

Commitment—to resolving an issue, to a particular cause, or to a particular member of Congress or political point of view—is critical if you wish to succeed in policy. One can have all the skills and attributes essential to being an effective participant in the policy process, but to be a leader requires commitment. Given the long hours, low pay, and lack of recognition that come with the position of legislative staff, personal commitment to dealing with the issues, is, at times, what it takes to make it through.

Commitment can take the form of dedication to a particular cause, such as the protection of ancient forests. Or it can reflect a commitment to a particular political perspective, such as defending private property rights. Regardless of the purpose, it is commitment that provides the drive and determination, the imagination and resourcefulness, and the patience to see an issue through from start to finish. The same is no doubt true for a successful athlete, artist, or business executive. Each differs only with respect to their interests and the nature of their trade or profession.

APPLYING LEADERSHIP SKILLS

The skills and qualities associated with leadership in policy and legislation are not synonymous with leadership. It takes more than these skills to provide leadership in dealing with current natural resource and environmental concerns. James MacGregor Burns, in his treatise *Leadership*, declared that: "Political leadership is a product of personal drives, social influences, political motivations, job skills, [and] the structure of career possibilities."

I agree, but I would state it more simply. Leadership happens when the right person is in the right place at the right time and seizes the opportunity to do something good. Of course, my simple characterization of leadership reflects my bias toward the virtues of public service and assumes that "good" means good in the context of the greater public purpose. But that simply reflects my own impression of what constitutes "good" policy.

It is probably fair to assume that certain qualities of leadership are inherent. Others are born of experience, both personal and professional. And while certain skills may be acquired through training and experience, some people may simply possess them naturally. What we cannot control, with rare exception, is timing and opportunities. It is the degree to which a person with the proper leadership qualities and skills can seize the opportunities that arise which determines whether that person can be a leader. Three brief examples apply.

During preparation of the 1990 Farm Bill, administration officials launched a national effort to promote tree planting and urban forestry. Staff of the House and Senate Agriculture Committees seized on this opportunity to draft the first ever forestry title for the Farm Bill. While the bill included measures to promote the president's tree planting initiative, the forestry title went beyond this to include measures to provide for improved private forestland stewardship and protection and to establish a national urban forestry program and a new office of international forestry in the USDA Forest Service.

Moreover, during development of the 1990 Farm Bill, the environmental community launched an initiative to require mandatory nutrient and pesticide management plans as a means of reducing the adverse effects of agriculture on water quality. The initiative was met with stern resistance by farm groups who opposed what they viewed as further restrictions on their ability to farm. Additional programs to provide for wetland protection, water quality improvement, and other environmental concerns were eventually adopted. But these programs were made voluntary to address, in part, farmers' concerns. In addition, to sell this approach to farm organizations, an agreement was reached with major environmental organizations to support the agriculture community in opposing a hostile amendment offered during debate of the Farm Bill in the House of Representatives that would have hurt farmers' income but was less directly related to environmental concerns. The unholy alliance of environmental and farm groups succeeded in defeating this popular legislative proposal.

Finally, during recent congressional debate over issues associated with the protection of old-growth forests and the northern spotted owl, most of the attention has focused on how many acres of old growth would be preserved as opposed to how much timber would remain to be harvested. In an effort to change the nature of the debate and to refocus discussions on the scientific and biological aspects of the issue, an initiative was launched by two congressional committees in the House of Representatives to bring together a group of scientists with expertise in this area to advise Congress on alternative solutions.

The panel, all of whom had been involved in a similar effort under the auspices of the Society of American Foresters, nearly ten years prior, prepared a report that drastically changed the debate. A bill introduced by the chairmen of the relevant congressional committees was based on this report. Efforts to legislate a solution to this issue, including a measure passed by the House Committee on Agriculture, are directly tied to the findings of the scientific panel. It is worth noting that the chairman and ranking minority member for one of the subcommittees that requested this science report were also members of the House Science and Technology Committee.

CAPITALIZING ON OPPORTUNITY

It is difficult to articulate what constitutes good policy and what makes a good policymaker. Certain skills and qualities may be associated with leadership in policy and legislation. But equally important are the education and experiences—both professional and personal—that affect one's sense of self and purpose.

Credibility, commitment, motivation, and moxie are key factors in the formula for leadership. Imagination, particularly as it relates to problem solving, is another key. So, too, is the ability to learn from past experiences, both good and bad, and to see beyond the crisis-du-jour to view things in a broader context.

All of these are essential elements of leadership. But unless one has the good fortune—the opportunity—to apply them, it can be difficult to demonstrate one's ability to lead.

Capitalizing on opportunity requires another important element of leadership: courage. Leaders are distinguished by their courage to make decisions and live with the consequences. I know leaders in Congress who have demonstrated that courage. Some have been recognized for their leadership and rewarded for their courage. Others have not.

I can point to specific instances in my life when opportunity arose and I was fortunate to have had the sense—perhaps the luck—to capitalize on it. Sometimes the decision to do so was difficult, but what differentiates these experiences from others was that I was willing to try my best to make a difference when it would have been easier not to.

Leaders don't decide to be leaders and then proceed to lead. Instead, they demonstrate their leadership by the decisions they make and the examples they set with their actions and accomplishments. People are faced with the dilemma of whether they should lead or follow every time a new opportunity presents itself. A leader is the one who seizes it.

REFERENCES

Burns, J. MacG. 1979. *Leadership*. New York: Harper and Row.

7 Lessons from State and Regional Resource Management

Henry H. Webster

STATE GOVERNMENTS carry out important roles in the management, protection, and effective use of a substantial range of natural resources. In some cases, governments of adjacent states work more or less closely together in carrying out these roles. Agreements between governors can often be involved, constituting, at least conceptually something approaching an informal regional level of government.

The effectiveness of state and regional government depends on a close combination of leadership and management skills, since resources and authority are often quite limited. In this chapter I examine four topics related to resource management at state and regional levels from the perspective of my personal experience. The first describes typical roles of state government as resource manager, as well as the relations among levels of government as they affect leadership and resource management. The second considers regional coalitions—first briefly, in general, and then in terms of their application to resource management. The third topic describes several innovations in state and regional resource management based on my personal experience. And the fourth cites the factors that, in my experience, contribute to leadership and allow it to occur. My experience has been directly related to state and regional governments—for fifteen years as state forester for Michigan and more recently as director of a special regional project for the Lake States Forestry Alliance. The alliance is a regional mutual-help arrangement created by the governors of Minnesota, Wisconsin, and Michigan.

My personal and professional experience began with growing up in a family that was half-American and half-Canadian in a community that is, by accident of history, in both Michigan and Ontario. I was educated first in forest resource management and then in natural resource economics. I have been a forest resource economist in the Forest Service, a forestry school director (first at the University of Wisconsin and then at Iowa State University), and the state forester for Michigan. Since 1990 I have been project director, as noted, for a major project being carried out for the Lake States Forestry Alliance in order to examine major trends and opportunities associated with forest resources in the region.

One of my strongest personal interests is history—particularly what has or has not contributed to effective national development in various parts of the world. Other interests include classical music and, of course, the Stanley Cup playoffs. Interests unrelated to the business at hand help you to maintain perspective in occasionally disorderly circumstances.

TWO MODELS OF GOVERNMENT

This chapter has three dimensions. First, I direct primary attention to resource management, not environmental protection. Second, I focus (particularly in the section on innovations) on matters related to forest resources. And third, the analysis is influenced by my experience in a part of the country where efforts to diversify regional and state economies dominated by heavy industry are a matter of great societal importance. My points concerning the genesis of leadership may apply more widely. Indeed, in many situations authority and resources are circumscribed, yet change is desperately needed. In these situations, leadership through thinking and cooperation may often be the appropriate style.

Regional coalitions are primarily positive relationships between units at the same level of government—namely states and provinces, although the federal government may also be involved on occasion. There are also critical relations between levels of government—federal, state, and local—that both limit and create leadership opportunities. Two intergovernmental links are important in resource management in the specific case of forest resources. One is the federal/state link, which is important nationwide. The other is the state/county link, which is important in parts of the country where counties own and manage sizable areas of forest land, such as the Lake States.

The federal/state link can be best examined if we understand two contrasting views of federal/state relations in an overall sense. One philosophy of how the national government should relate to states has been termed the "fabric of government" theory. It favors joint, cooperative work by multiple levels of government. This position is based on the belief that there is a distinct national interest in the economic health and vitality of all regions of the country. The federal government, therefore, is seen as an important partner that works directly with states and groups of states in this interest. This view first took form and direction in the early 1800s during the administration of Thomas Jefferson. During the next twenty-five or thirty years, numerous federal/state initiatives—for example, canals and post roads—were undertaken for the expressed purpose of bolstering the economies of what were then less developed portions of the nation. This view was also dominant during the rebuilding period following the Civil War and from the 1930s until the 1970s as the nation worked to overcome the Great Depression, fought World War II, and experienced the massive postwar economic expansion.

The other view of how the national government should relate to states has been termed the "assignment of powers" theory. It holds that each level of government has distinct and separate responsibilities. The federal government's role, in this view, should be limited to those activities that are national in scope in a sense quite separate from states and regions. Defense is the most notable example. This view was particularly prominent during the 1980s when states found themselves increasingly on their own in many respects with less federal help and support. The assignment of powers theory has alternated with the fabric of government theory over extended periods of our history.

Federal/state links specific to management of forest resources are a product of the fabric of government view (Webster, Shands, and Hacker 1990). State agencies responsible for managing forests (as well as other natural resources) receive substantial technical help and a portion of their funding from the federal government—specifically the state and private forestry branch of the Forest Service. This cooperative arrangement began early in the century with joint effort in fire control, including federal payment of part of the cost of modernizing state firefighting agencies. These joint efforts expanded progressively over the next seventy years to include a large part of the responsibilities of state forest resource agencies and, in the words of historian William G. Robbins, "virtually every arena of interest to forest owners and industrial processors" (Robbins 1985:34-121). This pattern of joint efforts suffered some reverses in the early 1980s in the face of renewed interest in the assignment of powers theory in the federal administration then in office. But joint efforts (in somewhat revised form) have since been strengthened by several initiatives, particularly the forest stewardship program. Clearly, there is a long history of joint federal/state efforts in resource management.

Relations between states and counties also follow a pattern of joint effort where counties own and manage substantial areas of forestland. Wisconsin and Minnesota are two states where they do. Joint state/county efforts are beneficial for a simple but important reason: County forest ownership and resource management works far better when backed by extensive state assistance and guidance. A striking example is in Wisconsin, where the county forest system is several times larger than the state forest system. The forest resources agency in Wisconsin's Department of Natural Resources works directly with counties, supplying technical expertise and a portion of the funding for resource management. The forest resources agency also guides adjacent counties toward reasonably similar resource management policies and related matters.

Resource management is an effective example of the fabric of government approach in terms of relationships among all three levels of government: federal, state, and local. Moreover, the fabric of government model presents an interesting theory of leadership for natural resource and environmental managers in which complexity and multiple jurisdiction and ownerships are universal conditions. This leadership model may be best applied to state and regional resource management through leadership methods that I characterize as *leadership through thinking and cooperation*. This approach is illustrated by the case studies presented later.

STATES AS RESOURCE MANAGERS AND LEADERS

State governments commonly exercise responsibility for a wide range of resources and values associated with land and water. Wildlife species, fish, and forest resources are some of the more obvious components. Water quality in a more general sense (going well beyond the effects of water on fish) is another important value included in state responsibilities. Some states also have responsibility for the quality—and placement—of development occurring on previously wild land, as in the sense of land-use planning and control. And there are emerging (and still undefined) responsibilities for protecting biological diversity. The organization of Minnesota's major resource management agency perhaps illustrates the range of resources and values involved. The Minnesota Department of Natural Resources has primary operating divisions working in the following fields: law enforcement, fisheries and wildlife, forestry, minerals, parks and recreation, trails and waterways, and waters (plus supporting units called bureaus).

Institutional arrangements for exercising state responsibility for resource management are many and varied. One involves state ownership of sizable areas. These areas typically include state forests, wildlife areas, state parks, other kinds of state-owned recreation areas, and variants of these. Such areas are then commonly managed directly by people in the appropriate unit of a state resources agency. County ownership and management of sizable land areas, sometimes with state assistance, is a variant in several states.

Direct state resource management is concentrated geographically in the Pacific Northwest (including Alaska) and in five large states adjacent to the Great Lakes. Apart from Alaska, there is approximately 30 million acres of forestland owned and managed by states and counties. Some 9 million acres of this is in Oregon and Washington. The other 21 million acres is in twenty northeastern states (broadly defined) with 17 million of these 21 million acres in Minnesota, Wisconsin, Michigan, Pennsylvania, and New York. This geographic pattern is to a modest degree a result of deliberate land acquisition. But to a greater extent it is a result of unsuccessful attempts at agricultural settlement with subsequent land abandonment via failure to pay real estate taxes—particularly during the depressed 1920s and 1930s, when abandoned land reverted to states (or in some states to counties). Obviously, direct state management of lands and waters calls for a high degree of managerial skill. But *leadership* can be a critical ingredient when major changes in the objectives and methods of management are mandated by need.

A second institutional arrangement for exercising state responsibilities for resource management involves efforts to influence management of land by private landowners. These efforts are diverse and are frequently pursued in cooperation with other organizations, both public and private. They can be grouped into two major approaches to influence private landowners. One approach is regulatory and specifies in a legal sense the land management methods that private landowners can use and how these methods are to be applied. (Forest practices acts as legislated in some states are complex examples of the regulatory approach.) The second approach involves encouragement to private landowners (as contrasted with regulation) via assistance and incentives directed toward improved land management practices and (in some cases) public access to private land for hunting and other recreational pursuits. Such assistance and incentives often involve a combination of educational and technical assistance, as well as financial incentives, made available to nonindustrial private forest owners by a coalition of public and private organizations with the state resources agency playing a central coordinating role. Leadership—the ability to lead diverse groups to consensus on objectives and practices—is essential in both approaches.

A third institutional arrangement for exercising state responsibility for resource management involves state leadership for major resource protection efforts on land under many different ownerships. Wildland fire protection and control is an important example. Obviously fire does not respect property lines. Hence strong, unified leadership is important both in preparation and in emergencies. State agencies characteristically provide this leadership—except in national forests and related categories of landownership (where close ties are nevertheless maintained). Setting sustainable harvest levels (and associated regulations) for game species of wildlife and fish is another example of state leadership spanning land and water under many ownerships.

The role of states as resource managers can be brought into sharper focus in the specific case of forest resources. The unit headed by the state forester typically has four primary responsibilities:

- *Management of the state forest system*. Management seeks to provide the best combination of outputs and values.
- *A lead role in providing assistance and incentives to nonindustrial private forest owners*. This involves focusing the efforts of a substantial number of public and private organizations that play important

parts in offering a unified package of educational and technical assistance and financial incentives.

- *Leadership for forest resource protection.* This involves wildland fire protection and control, as well as management and control of major forest diseases and insects.
- *Forest resource planning to guide the other elements.* This typically involves both charting the direction (via strategic statewide planning) and more specific land management and program planning for local areas.

REGIONAL COALITIONS

Governments of adjacent states, as noted, work together more or less closely in a variety of efforts. This makes substantial sense since state boundaries (though important in terms of administrative responsibility) often arise simply through historical accident. Conditions as diverse as major demography, principal resource conditions, and fundamental economic situations often continue across state boundaries in ways that provide an essential logic for joint efforts. The most obvious example occurs when state (or indeed national) boundaries have been drawn—as they often are—in the middle of rivers, lakes, or other bodies of water. Joint effort by adjacent states can unify borders that would otherwise divide.

Joint efforts often take the form of agreements between governors. Some of these agreements cover many subjects in a single pact or working arrangement. Governors' associations for particular regions are an example and often serve as forums for discussion of issues-in-common, as well as discussion of successful initiatives.

Organizations that analyze a wide range of regionally important issues on behalf of governors are a more specific arrangement but still cover a considerable range of topics. The Southern Growth Policies Board and the Northeast-Midwest Institute are examples. These organizations generally focus on analysis of strategic issues with the aim of helping states within their region become more uniformly prosperous and economically stable.

Finally, there are agreements that cover one specific activity. They commonly specify how adjacent state governments intend to work together in one particular field. I can offer three examples specific to resource management: a Great Lakes alliance for protection of aquatic resources; forest fire protection compacts in several parts of the country; and several forest resource management and development alliances covering (for example) southern New England, New York and northern New England, and the Lake States. In some cases, these working arrangements span the border with Canada and hence provide direct arrangements for joint efforts below the level of national governments. There are examples at each level of generality/specificity.

As an effective mechanism for integrating management of natural resource systems that cross administrative boundaries, regional coalitions present excellent opportunities for shared leadership. Such coalitions are one example of useful interaction between formal levels of government in the United States.

INNOVATIVE CASES

States and other units below the national level are frequently productive places to test innovative governmental arrangements in many fields (Fosler 1988; Osborne 1988; Osborne and Gaebler 1992). For example, arrangements for compensating workers injured on the job, for using public works to stabilize employment during depression, and for providing universal and cost effective access to health care, were pioneered respectively in Wisconsin, New York, and Saskatchewan. These programs were developed long before national interest was evident (in Wisconsin early in the century, in New York during the Great Depression, and in Saskatchewan some thirty years ago) and have now become nationwide models. These examples, wholly or partially apart from resource management, provide a historical illustration of the importance of state-like units as sources of innovation. Following are five resource management innovations drawn from my experience. I focus on how the innovation came about, including the circumstances and principal actors involved.

Case I: Developing a Target Industry Program

During a period beginning in the late 1970s and continuing until the 1990s, Michigan made a substantial effort to encourage expansion of its forest products industries. This effort began informally during the administration of Governor William G. Milliken (Republican), became a formal "target industry program for forest resources and industries" early in the administration of Governor James J. Blanchard (Democrat), and thus was informally a bipartisan effort. Several sectors were targeted in which it seemed possible to foster substantial net state economic growth.

The Michigan target industry program for the forestry sector included some twenty-five initiatives grouped under three major objectives: improve the business climate for forest products industries; give a common thrust to the activities of both public and private organizations active in forestry in the state; and assure a stable and expanding supply of timber in the state. Major effort went into providing detailed but effectively packaged information about alternative locations for new or expanded forest products plants. As well, major effort went into communicating with a wide range of firms across North America and beyond.

This program was guided by an advisory body appointed by the governor. An interagency group guided and energized ongoing efforts into common and mutually reinforcing tracks. A close working arrangement was developed between the business development unit and the forest resources unit of, respectively, the state departments of commerce and natural resources.

The target industry program was formally defined by the forestry committee of Governor Blanchard's Commission on Jobs and Economic Development. The overall commission was cochaired by a major labor union leader and the head of a major industrial firm in Michigan's dominant and troubled automotive industry. The forestry committee was chaired by the head of a Michigan-based plant of a national pulp and paper firm. Detailed work on the target industry program was done by a leading state economist (once on the faculty of a state university and later in analytic units associated with unions) and an analyst and writer (who subsequently became a policy analyst in the state Department of Management and Budget). Both knew how to ask for—and use—assistance from the forest resource unit in the state Department of Natural Resources.

These efforts to foster expansion of forest products industries were pursued against a background of severe economic difficulties for heavy industries throughout a large part of the Great Lakes basin. They also occurred at the same time that a widely endorsed statewide forest resources plan was being prepared by the forest resources unit and associated agencies and organizations. That plan helped to list the contributions of forest resources, both present and future, to economic growth and diversification. The economic imperative, the change in forest planning, and the detailed information—all supported by leadership through knowledge and cooperation—yielded results. Major expansion of forest products industries did in fact occur in Michigan, and in neighboring Wisconsin and Minnesota, where similar efforts were made.

Case II: Designing a New Basis for State Forest Systems

Michigan's state forest system covers 3.8 million acres—which is a bit more than 20 percent of all forestland in a state with more total acreage of forest than all but four of the fifty states. The state forest system is managed in aggregate for a wide range of economic, environmental, and recreational uses and values. Management was always based on a closely intermixed multiple-use approach. State forests were historically quite small. Each was managed separately by an area forester and assistants. All functioned essentially as generalists.

An important suggestion for improving public land management was made at the national level in the early to mid-1970s. The idea was to revise multiple-use management into a larger mosaic that separated uses (and users) that might otherwise conflict. Although unsuccessful at the time as a policy proposal for national forests, the idea was given early expression by the Public Land Law Review Commission and refined by Marion Clawson of Resources for the Future (Clawson 1974, 1975). Clawson analyzed which uses of forest resources were complementary, compatible, or competing when pursued vigorously in the same relatively small areas. He discovered that three were particularly likely to conflict: wilderness, highly developed recreation, and highly intensive timber growth/harvest and habitat management. He suggested separating them only where conflict seemed likely due to high rates of all uses.

We adopted Marion Clawson's idea as a guiding principle for management of Michigan's state forest system. The idea was given a name—key value management—and the categories of use were modified slightly from Clawson's: areas to be managed primarily for *natural values*; areas to be managed primarily for *developed recreation*; and areas devoted to *intensive vegetation management* for timber and wildlife. Where one use was designated as primary, management was to focus on it. Secondary uses were to be encouraged only to the point where they begin to affect the primary purpose of management.

A substantial reorganization of the state forest system prepared the way for this approach. The thirty-three small state forests were combined into six large state forests (averaging 630,000 acres in size versus 115,000 acres). This was done to focus planning at a scale more conducive to separation of conflicting use.

This reorganization also had an important (and ultimately humane) effect on personnel. Each of the six large state forests was the responsibility of a district forest manager assisted by two kinds of people (assigned from within the organization since no new positions and funding were provided). On the one hand were functional specialists responsible for directing certain activities district-wide. On the other was a modestly reduced number of area forest managers responsible for integrating activities and daily operations on subunits of the six state forests. Relaxed discussions between individual professionals and senior managers of the forest resources unit preceded new personnel assignments. Professionals were encouraged to declare their greatest interests and their own assessment of their talent. A close match proved entirely possible. Assignments were made for a limited period of time in the expectation that employees' interests and talents would evolve significantly. This pattern also helped to focus training efforts by helping personnel to strengthen their areas of greatest interest and talent.

Having a conceptual basis entirely outside the organization (that is, Marion Clawson's essential idea) helped the forest resources unit greatly in discussing the matter with administrative supervisors and gaining subsequent approval. Cooperation of all employees was fostered by open discussions and individual choice of assignment. Thus, knowledge and cooperation again contributed to success—in this instance, effecting organizational change.

Case III: Combining Organizations for Greater Efficiency

Many states originally had separate organizations for wildland fire protection and for technical aspects of forest resource management. At some point, in most states these separate organizations were combined. In some cases the process of combining was difficult and took considerable time to implement even after it was formally achieved. A difference in patterns of educational background may have contributed to the problem. Often all the principal members of the technical forestry unit were college-educated, while only a few college grads were in the fire control unit. Thus a sense that one unit was "taking over" the other (rather than two units joining together) may have bred resistance in some cases.

In other cases, including Michigan, transitions were easier and quicker. Michigan was in fact the last of fifty states to combine technical forestry and fire control units. This happened in the late 1970s as part of a DNR-wide reorganization designed to increase effectiveness by bringing related activities closer together. This was brought about relatively easily—indeed surprisingly so, given that resistance had thwarted a previous attempt in the mid-1960s.

After Michigan's units were formally combined, many technical forestry people were trained and kept current in basic fire control methods. They then constituted a built-in reserve force for high-hazard and emergency situations. Conversely, many fire control people were trained and kept current in a range of activities, particularly preparation of timber sales and maintenance and operation of recreation facilities during seasons of low fire danger. This cross-training contributed to a substantial increase in both efficiency and effectiveness.

Just how fortunate this was became apparent when a prolonged state economic and fiscal crisis took hold in the early 1980s. Despite the recognized importance of the target industry program, a personnel reduction from five hundred to three hundred people occurred in wrenching steps in the newly combined organization. Nevertheless, overall organizational outputs stayed up, fire losses stayed down, and the total amount of work done changed very little. (It may actually have increased at times.) This fortunate scenario could not have been repeated with further reductions, however. It was a case of a major one-shot efficiency gain.

Several factors may have helped this process of combining formerly separate organizations. One general factor may have been a sense of being part of an organization with a mission of enhanced importance in a state facing deep and widely acknowledged difficulties. Three more specific factors concerned people and equipment. All helped to promote a sense of joining together, not one organization taking over the other:

Shortly before the units were combined, a person of widely recognized talent in the fire control unit was appointed to a key position in the technical forestry unit as part of the overall reorganization. (He was subsequently promoted several years later.)

A seemingly trivial matter (but perhaps not) was what color the vehicles of the combined organization should be. One point of view, almost unanimously favored by forestry personnel, was that all should be the same color: green. But another view held that emergency vehicles had better be a publicly recognized emergency vehicle color: red. The solution was to make all vehicles red with some extra marking on emergency vehicles.

The process of joining together was fully completed (in a sense beyond organizational charts) when a new assistant state forester for operations and administration was appointed in 1987. He was a highly effective administrator with both understanding and pertinent vision. He began his career in the fire division and was a person with an intelligent, inquiring mind who simply did not have the opportunity to go to college. His appointment, made on merit, sealed the sense of joining. Thus, organizational synthesis was enhanced—and perhaps made possible—with good information on the characteristics of the units to be combined and the cooperation of the participants.

Case IV: Helping to Form a Forestry Alliance

The Lake States Forestry Alliance is a regional mutual-help arrangement created in April 1987 by the governors of Minnesota, Wisconsin, and Michigan. The alliance has undertaken a variety of actions: identifying the Lake States region as an important entity in forestry; encouraging continued cooperation among agencies across state lines; making joint representations to Congress on matters important to the region; and jointly analyzing trends and opportunities associated with forest resources in the region. In doing so, the alliance has subtly, perhaps unconsciously, encouraged a don't-raid-your-neighbor approach to resource development efforts among the three states. The alliance has also attempted to unify a range of interests in forest resources who might otherwise oppose each other on occasion.

While formally organized by governors, the alliance in fact emerged from activities of many people over a decade or more. The Lake States' forest resource planners, supported by their administrative leaders, first recognized that there should be joint or at least parallel efforts to understand developments and forces crossing state lines. As a result, three modest studies concerning forest product trade flows and economic impacts were carried out—jointly underwritten by the three state forest resource units and the three functional branches of the Forest Service. Each was led by a recognized authority at a major university, one each in Minnesota, Wisconsin, and Michigan. These studies, in fact, preceded the formal organization and doing them helped to form the alliance. A national coalition-builder of considerable note was then brought in to hasten this process of institution founding via two regional conferences. The support of the director of the North Central Forest Experiment Station (USDA Forest Service) was instrumental in underwriting the involvement of this national coalition-builder, thus making the alliance a "fabric-of-government" effort.

A less visible but useful factor in forming the alliance has been a willingness of the states to cover for each other when things go wrong (as they inevitably do). Covering for each other cannot create a coalition from scratch, but it can help to chink up the cracks.

Case V: Helping to Complete an International Compact

The Great Lakes forest fire compact is a direct mutual-help arrangement linking the state and provincial agencies with major responsibilities for wildland fire protection in Minnesota, Wisconsin, Michigan, and Ontario. It helps the four entities to work directly together in preparation, training, and equipment evaluation, as well as in fire emergencies. It represents a substantial simplification of working arrangements in contrast to going through the American and Canadian interagency fire centers (located respectively in Boise and Winnipeg). In a sense, it is also the fire protection area of the Lake States Forestry Alliance with a most useful addition across the international boundary.

All four state and provincial agencies participated in the process of formation from the start. There was strong agreement among them. Leaders of the fire control units took the lead with appropriate administrative encouragement. They successfully completed the first really major stage: Minnesota, Wisconsin, and Michigan were able to sign formally and Ontario functioned as a very much involved observer.

This was certainly progress, but one additional step would increase its value. As one sharp-sighted Lake States observer put it: "Ontario are the people to be allied with. They've got the Air Force." (He meant the province's Canadair CL-215 water bombers.) There was precedent but of a fairly complex kind. Quebec and New Brunswick, as well as New York and New England, have long been members of the Northeast Forest Fire Compact. But special congressional legislation had been needed in that case for states to participate in such a cross-border mutual aid arrangement. In our case, a senator representing one of the Lake States was willing to be principal sponsor if need be. The senator also directed his staff to seek a less complex solution.

A less complicated route did develop in an informal but highly effective manner. A casual conversation with a Canadian friend of some prominence suggested a way. Upon hearing the status of the matter, he responded: "I think I've already done that." He then described a new master agreement between the Canadian Forestry Service (now Forestry Canada) and the USDA Forest Service. The master agreement did indeed provide for subsidiary agreements involving units below the national level. That had long been the position of the federal government in Canada, but not so in the United States. The wording was such that doubt—and thus an opening—concerning the U.S. position were created. Other conversations confirmed the opening. A last-minute impediment took the form of a new appointee at the State Department who stalled essentially *all* new international agreements of a technical character for an extended review of protection of U.S. "intellectual property." Inspiration for hurdling this impediment came from a now-retired member of the USDA Forest Service: "This is bureaucracy at its worst. Sign the thing. Just don't officially tell us." Shortly the expanded cross-border agreement was signed by the natural resources heads in Minnesota, Wisconsin, Ontario, and Michigan.

The value of a direct cross-border forest fire compact has more than once been demonstrated to benefit the Lake States. One case involved the "Air Force." Several years ago Minnesota's fire control units were assisted on a windy, dry, dangerous spring day in the northwest zone by one of Manitoba's CL-215s. No bill was ever received. A second demonstration occurred on 8 May 1990. An exceedingly dangerous fire occurred in Michigan's lower peninsula. By the end of the afternoon, eighty-one dwellings and subsidiary buildings had been consumed. It turned out that two Ontario CL215s had been on "yellow alert" due simply to listening to the radio fire-control frequencies. Assistance certainly would have been requested had the emergency extended to a second day, which did not occur due to a drastic change in weather. Perhaps the lesson was best stated in an informal conversation by a particularly perceptive fire-control person in the Michigan agency. He thought that losses might have been reduced if the water bombers had been asked for at the beginning of the incident. This is a lesson that will guide the fire compact in the future.

In this case, *knowledge* is exemplified by the superior firefighting technology possessed by the Ontario partner; *cooperation* allowed the sharing of this technology through the promise of conventional help for Ontario from the other partners. Political *leadership* (both overt and subtle) and modest *rule breaking* were used in allowing the partnership to go forward.

LEADERSHIP LESSONS

How does leadership come about? This is a question some people appear to think has fairly simple answers. That is at least an impression given by the hundreds of books on the topic found in many libraries. Each author presumably started with an idea of how to create leader-ship that could be told (or sold) to readers. The fact that there are so many different ideas should give us pause. With so many ideas, is there any *central* notion?

Experience concerning the innovations just described, as well as observations of activities of other people and other organizations, lead me to a number of conclusions. They seem to have something to do with the genesis of leadership. But they certainly do not answer the question definitively.

First, leadership may result from *circumstances* as much as from actions. A substantial element of luck may also be involved. For example, precipitating events that make resource management strongly relevant to major social needs can do much to create opportunity for leadership. The extended decline of heavy industry has been such an event in much of the Great Lakes region. In the case of forest resources in this region, advantageous circumstances included forest growth three times harvest, lower timber prices than other major forested regions, favorable trends in technologically feasible substitutions of hardwoods for softwoods, and large imports of building and paper products into the region. Together these factors defined a sense of direction. And they did so better—and more clearly in terms the public could understand—than deliberate scheming or strategy could. Precipitating events quite beyond the control of leaders do matter.

Luck sometimes fosters leadership. A match between the needs of the time and your own background, expertise, and interests may on occasion give you something approaching moral authority of an intellectual sort. A state economy that had nearly collapsed, a personal interest in regional resource development, a long family history in a particular state (but with additional experience elsewhere)—all added up to a fortunate combination in my case. In relation to the Lake States Forestry Alliance and other regional efforts, there is a somewhat similar element of luck in my having lived and worked in four states in the region (including all three Lake States) and in having considerable Canadian family background and interests. Again, luck can help.

Actions in relation to circumstances also certainly help leadership to emerge. Actions in *harmony* with circumstances are the essential point. The following points seem to apply beyond the examples from which they are drawn:

- Relate your unit and its mission to major societal needs in a long-term sense. The depth of this relationship—and its sincerity—matter. Focusing on simple agency objectives in a short-term sense is not the same as leadership; nor is an attempt to link the mission to major social needs simply as a budgetary strategy.
- Make sustained efforts to understand links between resource matters and the rest of society and the economy. Do this in order to genuinely establish the relationship discussed in the preceding item.
- Help your colleagues to appreciate the importance of what they are doing in relation to major societal needs. Their understanding

can create an internal sense of direction and cohesion affecting both individuals and organizations.

- State goals simply even if they are, in fact, ambitions and complex. Two or three simple affirmative sentences can help greatly to create a sense of direction if they are restated periodically.
- Link up with the more perceptive among the political and staff leadership in the governor's office, legislature, and related bodies. Help them *quietly*: Remember that the governor and legislators have to run for elective office and you do not.
- Maintain an intellectual orientation, read widely, and keep in touch with university colleagues, both in and beyond your own state. Intellectual leadership often lasts better than other kinds. It gets less damaged by the collisions that sometimes occur in organizational and administrative circles. Moreover, effective leadership is frequently strengthened by help from individuals and organizations wholly outside any particular field or administrative unit. Issues, events, and situations do not respect such boundaries and neither does an effective leader.
- Take a role in resource and other matters beyond your own state. Doing so may help your state to get focused effectively and is vital to formation of regional coalitions and intellectual orientation.
- Share credit for successes widely, and help your colleagues with matters that remain *their* projects. You may be the leader of the organizational unit, but you are their helper on the project in question. There are few better ways of securing continuing support than letting others take credit for successful innovations or decisions.

These observations are far from constituting any sort of theory about leadership, but they may be helpful. A common thread in all these points is the importance of a clear, simple idea of what you are trying to accomplish, as well as considerable flexibility in pursuing that goal. This point can hardly be overemphasized, even though leadership must often take place in disorderly systems. For complex and often disorderly resources and political systems—such as forests in state and regional settings—the elements of knowledge and cooperation (as opposed to competition) often underlay activities that are reckoned to be successful.

REFERENCES

Brazer, H. E., and D. S. Laren, eds. 1982. *Michigan's Fiscal and Economic Structure*. Ann Arbor: University of Michigan Press.

Clawson, M. 1975. *Forests for Whom and for What*. Baltimore: Johns Hopkins University Press.

————, ed. 1974. *Forest Policy: Conflict, Compromise, Consensus*. Washington: Resources for the Future.

Fosler, R. S. 1988. *The New Economic Role of American States: Strategies in a Competitive World*. New York and Oxford: Oxford University Press.

Osborne, D. 1988. *Laboratories of Democracy: A New Breed of Governor Creates Models for National Growth*. Boston: Harvard Business School Press.

Osborne, D., and T. Gaebler. 1992. *Reinventing Government: How the Entrepreneurial Spirit Is Transforming the Public Sector*. Reading, MA: Addison-Wesley.

Robbins, W. G. 1985. *American Forestry: A History of National, State, and Private Cooperation*. Lincoln: University of Nebraska Press.

Webster, H. H., W. E. Shands, and J. J. Hacker. 1990. "Is There a National Interest in Regional Economic Vitality?: Forestry as a Case Study." *Renewable Resources Journal* 8 (1):8–13.

8 The Politics of Fundraising

··

W. Kent Olson

philanthropy (fĭ-lăn′thrə-pē) *n.*, . . . Love of mankind in general . . .

"I don't want this board to become a bunch of goddamn fundraisers!"
—*head of the board nominating committee of a national conservation organization*

HOW DID I BECOME a professional conservationist? It's simple: My grandfather took me camping when I was a kid. Everything else fell into place thereafter.

We'd spend weeks together each summer, mostly in the woods of Maine and New Hampshire. My mother claims I left home permanently at age six.

Gramp taught me how to get along in the woods, hike safely, sleep on the ground, angle after brook trout, appreciate the things we saw around us. A schoolteacher, he lived frugally. But he was generous with his time and knowledge, and patient with his grandson. As much as Gramp loved wildness he loved Shakespeare too, so I learned to hear "sermons in stones."

I didn't realize it then, but my professional calling grew from those times. He introduced me to the Appalachian Mountain Club (AMC), founded in 1876, one of the oldest conservation organizations. After high school, I was fortunate to land a job in the AMC Hut System, spending five formative summers in the White Mountains, amid tundra and krummholz, talus slopes, spruce forests, glacial cirques, tiny montane flora. Even today, hearing the rhythmic, two-toned whistle of the white-throated sparrow, songbird of our mountains, makes me trill inside.

My first executive conservation position, as director of the AMC Hut System, and my second, as editor and publisher of AMC books and magazines, resulted from those memorable summers. Then it was on to graduate school and a degree in natural resources management.

Eventually, I moved to The Nature Conservancy, directing the Connecticut Chapter, and also taught college courses on literature and the environment. I was doing conservation—helping get nature protected—and teaching it (and therefore learning more about it). What a combination.

The Conservancy granted me a two-year leave to assume the presidency of American Rivers, which turned into four years. Because of some superior mentors and excellent volunteer leaders at both the Conservancy and American Rivers, and with advice from inspiring leaders of similar organizations, my staff colleagues and I achieved operating surpluses every year. The general solvency enabled us to get done a decent share of the daily conservation mission. Furthermore, we had banked enough money in the Connecticut Chapter's treasury and at American Rivers to give both organizations added security for rough times. It was a visible signal to our supporters that we were serious caretakers of their benefactions.

Cumulatively I've spent about nineteen years in professional conservation, including almost ten years as the chief staff officer and most of the rest in other senior positions, now with The Conservation Fund. It's a pleasure also to serve as a volunteer trustee of The School for Field Studies.

An important lesson in my business is that generating dollars to preserve a little nature here and there—so someone we will likely never meet might hear white-throats and appreciate sermons in stones—unites people in selfless purpose. And sometimes in lifelong friendship. Just the way discovering wilderness with your grandfather makes you partners forever.

PROGRESSIVE VOLUNTEERISM

This essay examines problems that can arise in a nonprofit conservation organization when volunteer board leaders and paid staff differ about raising money. First some words about volunteers in general.

The Conservation Leadership Project of The Conservation Fund estimates that ten thousand conservation groups exist in the United States. About three hundred new ones form each year.[1] No one knows how many survive or the number of established groups that annually drop away.

In some nongovernmental environmental organizations, volunteers are the sole "staff." Many other conservation groups rely on unpaid people for board work, trail maintenance, legal services, investment counseling, envelope stuffing, testifying, budgeting, street marching, corporate outreach, organizational planning, scientific analysis, help in publishing, and other mission-driven activity.

Furthermore, an unseen legion of dollar-a-year nonprofit "employees," mostly specialists in financial management, fundraising, or direct mail marketing, is alive and well. Add the full-time staff working at half-price, and the career environmentalists earning full pay but less than the probable wage of government service or corporate trade. Finally, consider the for-profit professionals who sacrifice significant pay in order to donate time to organized conservation. Progressive "volunteerism" has many gradations.

A common element in progressive volunteer leaders is altruism: *giving the maximum within one's means to a cause one cherishes.* To a CEO, it is inconsequential whether board members contribute time, wisdom, money, or some of each. So long as the nonprofit occupies a high place on the volunteer's philanthropic list, a condition implied in serving, the magnitude of a gift is secondary to its quality. In cash terms, a small contribution from someone of slim means is as welcome as a mega-donor's check.

The thoughtful CEO strives to say well and anew the old words *thank you.* Many groups give awards honoring outstanding volunteers. Recognizing givers, whether of service or dollars, can be as satisfying as accomplishing the mission itself. Why? Because in well-managed nonprofits, a direct connection exists between every benefaction and the work it accomplishes. Conservation is philanthropy made manifest.

The job of paid staff is to convert donations into land protected, rivers cleaned, species saved, air purified, neighborhoods and workplaces made safe and healthful. Some conservation CEOs think of themselves, the staff, and the board as a unified instrument of conservation. The thoughtful CEO wants donors to know what *they* achieved through the instrument, to feel good about it, and to accept the organization's gratitude.

Every conservation executive has had the privilege of serving with progressive volunteer leaders. Many professional nonprofiteers rank their relationships with these people—as workmates, mentors, advisors, critics, confidants, benefactors, or just plain friends—as among the most important "benefits" of charitable employment.

Significantly, progressive volunteer leaders are not yes-men or yes-women. They are equable and psychologically able to put institutional needs first. They understand the positive role that organizational, personal, and financial tension can play in a nonprofit. Consequently they make excellent critics of, and foils to, paid staff, whom they challenge (sometimes hard but never unfairly), nurture, and cause to stretch professionally.

Progressive volunteer leaders promote trust as one of the foremost ingredients of successful nonprofits, especially trust between chair and staff executive, the top partners. As Peter F. Drucker has said in *Managing the Non-Profit Organization: Principles and Practices* (1990:18–19): "The leaders who work most effectively . . . never say 'I.' . . . They don't think 'I.' . . . They think 'team.' . . . They understand their job to be to make the team function."

Good board leaders encourage the CEO to operate the nonprofit in the zone of discomfort: beyond the margin of absolute safety but within the bounds of what hard work can achieve. They know that the reach of conservation—and therefore the reach of fundraising—should exceed ready grasp. Saving nature requires risks.

Sadly, though, a few volunteer leaders actually impede the necessary, stressful, and exhausting enterprise of finding money to underwrite the work. Some are honestly confused about the relationship of dollars to mission, as the following case study illustrates.

MONEY AND MISTRUST: A CASE STUDY

Excellent nonprofits thrive on two things: one, a mission-driven board and staff working as partners; and two, money.

In a financially weak organization, the board-staff alliance will be proportionately less effective than in wealthier nonprofits—balancing a budget can become more central than accomplishing the mission. When the partnership itself is out of whack, though, wealth alone will not fix it. These are commonplaces. The odd fact is that sudden riches can trigger big problems.

The following events, told from the CEO's point of view, happened in the late 1970s in an effective, prosperous environmental organization located in the midwest. The CEO had many years of executive service in nonprofits. She tells of how during her presidency the staff secured the largest contribution in the organization's history, several hundred thousand dollars. It came with a *handshake* on how it would be used. A huge, mostly unrestricted, gift for a modest-sized organization—every fundraiser's dream.

The donor requested that his proposed gift remain *confidential* until the transmittal papers were final, and he asked for anonymity. He sportingly challenged the staff solicitor: "Do you think your organization can handle a grant of this size?" Others were competing for the money. The solicitor's group, he pointed out, had little track record with big gifts. The grant had better be well used. The solicitor gave assurances.

Over the next weeks, the CEO worked confidentially with the solicitor, who worked efficiently with the donor. The two staff wanted to ensure that the gift conformed both with the benefactor's wishes and the nonprofit's five-year plan, which the board and staff had produced a couple of years earlier.

On Gift Day, a phone call from the donor's representative brought the big news. The CEO congratulated her solicitor in front of a surprised and ecstatic staff. She phoned some board members (and later wrote to all). She asked them to give kudos to the solicitor. The staff and a few board members, including the chairwoman, celebrated that evening, closing down the local pub.

At this point, says the CEO, "An alert chair would have said 'Great! Get out there and get some more!' "[2]

The CEO believed that the sheer magnitude of the grant would demonstrate that her growing institution was an increasingly worthy object of serious philanthropy. She felt that the chair, who had served well in other board positions, had helped propel the organization to the new threshold of worthiness. "I wanted our principal volunteer partner to share amply in the credit." In the CEO's view, the

grant meant more and better environmentalism, and greater financial stability. She adds, "It symbolized organizational unity and
maturity."

Within two weeks, however, the chairwoman "had begun to act
strangely. . . . She told board members that I had cut them out of
their right to decide how the gift should be used." Another board
member accused the solicitor of "hiding something." Why else was
the gift kept so quiet? Says the CEO, "People later started accusing
me of disloyalty!"

Two trusted consultants to the board, a senior board member, and
the CEO had a private dinner with the chair. All assured her that the
staff had executed a positive transaction and had properly handled the
gift.

The CEO considered the terms of the gift to be nearly perfect. "It
was restricted only in the sense that the donor had expressed certain
expectations. He trusted us to use the money accordingly." The chair
claimed not to understand why the donor didn't write out precisely
what to do with the gift.

The CEO privately told the chair, "You of all people should take my
word for what occurred in a normal charitable transaction." That is:
"Trust, not protocol or power, was the issue as I saw it." Why was the
chair making "a manifestly good thing into a bad thing"?

When the CEO cited the nonprofit maxim *The donor is always right
unless the gift contorts the mission*, the chair was "unfazed." Moreover, the
chair seemed to consider it irrelevant that the donor, solicitor, and
CEO were friends of many years. The chair continued to insist that
something was amiss and kept saying so to other board members.

Over the CEO's objections, the chair decided to bring the matter to
the full board. She made the CEO add it to the board agenda for the
next meeting. Weeks had gone by since the gift, and bad feelings
between the chair and CEO were increasing. The CEO saw that
"more time ahead would be consumed by this nonissue."

Notably, the chair had never previously questioned a grant, let alone
one with so few restrictions. The CEO believed that if word of the
chair's inexplicable actions accidentally got to the donor, he would
conclude that the organization couldn't, in fact, handle big money.
That might endanger future gifts. "It was important to contain the
whole thing," the CEO says. "I never before had to perform an end

run around any board chair and felt terrible about sneaking around to get the help of friendly board people."

She consulted with several board leaders. The night before the board meeting, the treasurer took the chairwoman aside and somehow got the gift issue removed from the agenda.

Superficially, things appeared to have settled. But over the ensuing months a rift developed between chair and CEO. For the first time in anyone's memory, board factions developed, mostly traceable to the gift episode. Coupled with later frictions, which did not heal, the rift led eventually to the CEO's resignation.

Despite the factions, the board had offered to extend the CEO's contract, thanks in part to a strongly supportive staff letter to board members. "The letter had given board moderates a foundation on which to blunt the effort to boot me summarily." The staff had opened themselves to possible board criticism or worse. Nonetheless, the CEO eventually declined the contract. Her organization was being torn apart and she realized that her continued presence would only prolong the divisiveness.

Years afterward, she still values the staff's timely support. One consultant told her it was a sign of staff respect. "He pointed out that when the staff leader is in deep trouble, the staff can take the opportunity to 'hang him out to dry if they don't like him.' Over the years, I had shielded my staff from unwarranted board attacks, and they returned the professional courtesy. I learned that loyalty begets loyalty."

Nearly a year had passed from the day of the gift to when the CEO announced her resignation. She reports: "Several more months went by as the board fought among themselves about hiring my successor. It's hard to answer your question about the actual monetary costs of all that, but they were substantial. The unpriceable stuff, like loss of spirit and union of purpose, the erosion of trust, and so forth, costs a lot too. . . . I felt sorry for our general members, the way all this was eating up their dues. It was impossible for anyone on staff to be an efficient, focused environmentalist, or even to feel that his or her work was appreciated."

As Donald Snow writes in *Inside the Environmental Movement* (1992:189), "The problematic relationship between the conservation CEO and his or her board is one of the great blind spots of the conservation movement." The root cause in this case was lack of trust between the two principals, but the precipitating event was an act of great generosity. Says the CEO: "The fuss had to do with board-staff power issues. As I was leaving, [the chair] brought up the fact that I had gone around her many months before. She didn't believe me when I said I had agonized over it. The crisis was also related to the *relative size of the anonymous grant* [emphasis added]. It was big enough that some board people wanted to poke it, maybe make some policies about it, tell the staff how to handle it, and so on. . . . Volunteers can get funny about dollars."

She quotes the chairwoman as having more than once declared, "I don't think of [our organization] as a charity." Oddly, the chair was herself a generous annual contributor and didn't hesitate to ask other board members for contributions.

The CEO says she respects those board members who tried to help, as well as the neutral ones. "Some people didn't know anything was going on until it was too late." It would have taken a "smartly delivered hip-check by a knowledgeable senior board peer to dislodge the chairwoman." The CEO doesn't think the board had reached the developmental stage at which that could have occurred. "One board person later said the whole thing probably would never have happened if so-and-so weren't the chair."

The CEO is proud of the staff's handling of the gift, the honoring of the donor's wishes, and the quality of the contribution as an empowering tool and capital base for the institution: "We got the grant efficiently. . . . Given the donor's challenge—*Can you guys handle it?*—we might have lost the money to another group. . . . Some board people tried to discourage me from taking fundraising trips during the height of the foundation funding cycle, which was about the time I had publicly announced my resignation. . . . I took the trips anyway, made some phone calls, and even received unexpected calls from concerned funders asking what was up. My simply disappearing without explanation from the funding scene would have caused some head scratching among funders."

On one set of visits, the CEO "dragged along" the person who was to become acting director: "We told the funders that a few board members and I had a dispute, which isn't uncommon in fast-growing organizations. We didn't go into details. I told the funders it was best for me to leave, that organizational policy was not in question, and that [the nonprofit] was sound and poised for a good transition to a new director. We showed continuity."

She adds: "The funders actually thanked us for coming and explaining things. Foundation officials are a smart bunch, and [the trips and phone conversations] gave them a context into which they could set their expectations about [the organization]. The year after I left was [the organization's] best year ever for foundation money raised. That's because of several previous years of hard work by board and staff and steady reinvestment by foundations—*and* because we demonstrated continuity and professionalism even while a few board members were saying things like, 'Don't go on the road to raise money.' In instances like this you follow your conscience, your own judgment. You try to keep the mission topmost."

She is proud of her quiet exit from the organization and refers to the story of Solomon being confronted by two women claiming to be the mother of the same infant. Solomon threatened to slice the baby in half. "The real mother gave up her child so the baby could live. Solomon quickly figured out who was who."

A new staff leader took over. The chair eventually left. A divided board and a shaken staff began the work of reuniting the organization. A couple of years later, the disputed grant provided a vital financial cushion against a significant budget deficit.

RIGHTEOUS DOLLARS

Star-crossed partnerships, as in the case study, characterize the governance of too many conservation nonprofits. Told from the chair's point of view, the story doubtless would have read differently. Not even the most hardbitten conservation executive would deny that criticism can sometimes justifiably be leveled at paid staff.

Even from within the conservation movement, accusations of sexism, elitism, and racism abound. And Donald Snow and G. Jon Roush's research uncovered movement-wide "deficiencies in training, communications, [and] leadership development,"[3] a failure to engage the grassroots, plus turf-mongering among organizations and poor management by CEOs. Some volunteer activists disparage full-timers as invidious compromisers attentive more to pension plans than to the environment.

Some conservation careerists certainly deserve knocks. But most paid leaders are scrupulous in financial and other dealings and are especially sensitive about the ethics of fundraising. So are most board leaders. However, the fact that fundraising sometimes takes its practitioners into gray areas is usually easier for staff to assimilate than for volunteers. Uncompensated people often regard themselves as the organization's conscience. They can hold precisely delimited ethics. As a result, they occasionally experience conflicting emotions and sometimes make naive, self-contradicting policy judgments.

One national organization's board, for example, rejected an invitation to apply for money from a politically conservative brewing company with a bad environmental record. The board discouraged the staff from seeking grants from "alcohol producers." But, interestingly, the organization decided, with board concurrence, to accept any payroll-deduction donations from *employees* of the brewery, in the event the company set up a United Way-like workplace campaign to benefit environmental organizations generally. Moreover, the conservation group holds cocktail party fundraisers, has received money from a foundation set up by a family of distillers, and counts among its largest annual contributors a spirits and tobacco heir.

An environmental organization of liberal political bent approached the same brewer directly and got $1 million. Several other conservation outfits, including grassroots groups, took grants of $5000 each. A national water protection charity received $50,000.

Whose ethics were "correct"?

A nonprofit must decide its own grant policies. Within an organization, policy should be consistent. In the greater conservation movement, many understandings of what constitutes probity can coexist. But as Peter F. Drucker (1990:112) writes: "There are always so many more moral causes than we have resources for that the non-profit institution has a duty—toward its donors, toward its customers, toward its own staff—to allocate its scarce resources for results rather than to squander them on being righteous."

When, if ever, does "dirty" money turn clean? Environmental groups energetically compete for foundation money amassed by some of the world's most famous capitalist families. Were the corporate patriarchs alive today, some environmentalists might object to the politics and means of capital accumulation. How do those same grantseekers justify plucking the fruits of that capital many years after the fact? Does there exist an "ethical discount rate"—reliant on time's passage—that assuages environmental consciences?

Does a harder look reveal what Shaw's play *Mrs. Warren's Profession* showed? His characters demonstrated that preachiness about the source of anyone's livelihood can embarrass the preacher. Can any modern citizen deny that the money he earned yesterday, or which his forbears made a century ago, may have exacted some social costs that could make reasonable people wince? John Muir noted in a different context, "When we try to pick out anything by itself, we find it hitched to everything else in the universe." So it is when charitable conservation picks up a dollar.

Nonprofits exist at the rim of the free enterprise system. If for-profits create enough wealth to generate surpluses, nonprofits can do okay. The degree to which surpluses get redistributed to charities— that is, donated—depends a lot on how the U.S. tax code encourages or discourages private philanthropy. Therefore conservationists who fecklessly condemn "the system" condemn nonprofit conservation.

Environmentalists should not exculpate business or government for poor environmental records. But we must recognize the subtle inter-dependence of a democratic polity, free markets, and private philan-thropy. A famous ecologist made the point incisively with a question. Of U.S. consumers of hamburgers made from cattle raised on slash-and-burn lands that once were tropical-belt forests, he asked: Whose hand is on the chain saw?

In conservation fundraising, no nonprofit can mature until it adopts grantseeking ethics that are at once opportunistic and principled. The terms are not self-canceling. The federal Land and Water Conservation Fund, for example, is premised on resource exploitation. Yet conserva-tionists approve of the fund because royalties from offshore oil drilling pay for nature protection. If money from government-sanctioned ex-ploitation is acceptable to conservationists, why not from private exploitation? Shouldn't corporations pay some freight for nonprofits trying to improve the environment? Several conservation fundraisers have repeated Mark Twain's quip, "Sure it's tainted money . . . t'ain't enough."

Staff fundraisers need the conscience, guidance, and ethical checks-and-balances that thoughtful volunteer leaders often bring to over-eager grantseeking by professionals. But when a board makes fund-raising policies that are prissy or inconsistent, "conscience" reveals itself as caprice disguised. The environmental mission gets over-whelmed in a tangle of collateral moral or political judgments. Money that could have supported their charity goes elsewhere. Another mis-cue at the expense of conservation. And the staff, looking venal, must rattle the tin cup yet more desperately.

LOVE VS. MONEY

In the world-wearying skirmish between lumpers and splitters, the latter consider love and money as immiscible. Thus board leaders can unanimously decide that, say, an unstaffed organization should profes-sionalize, but some of them will remain quietly ambivalent anyway. Such unreconciled tensions invariably surface, expressed most likely as anger at an executive's wrongdoings.

Often, the issue is that the executive *is* paid. The Conservation Leadership Project revealed

> some evidence of a strong anti-staff bias among the volunteers. . . . [Some] proponents of the amateur way want to keep organizations perpetually frozen in their youthful state—organized and run by volunteers, unsullied with the mercenaries who desire to become professional staff, divorced from any sense that the work . . . of conservation . . . might, for some, actually constitute a career. Said one prominent national leader we inter-viewed: "The thing I always tell people, especially leadership people, is to be careful not to become professionals." [Snow 1992:5, 130]

Board members and staff are motivated primarily by a love of nature or by moral and economic imperatives to husband the earth and its resources. Still, original motivation can evaporate. Irrational love/money dichotomies—"I'm clean, you're not"—can materialize and contribute to suppressing staff wages and, in some instances, to driv-ing professionals from nonprofit X to nonprofit Y (or out of charitable work entirely). To love one's paid work, must a professional environ-mentalist live marginally? Reconciling love/money tensions is a main task for volunteer leaders.

Progressive leaders see the moneyseeking and spiritual sides of board work as complementary. Philip D. Levin, a distinguished poet and conservation leader, typically ran interference among peer volunteers for energetic professionals with good ideas. At public events, conservationist Alexander S. Gardner, a veteran board chair, often introduced his staff this way: "To know them is to want to feed them."

"CHECK WRITERS"

The Conservation Leadership Project recommended that paid and unpaid leaders develop an enlightened view of dues-paying members, the big corps of invisible supporters behind most successful non-profits. The study sees members as human capital whose wisdom, energy, and abilities should be harnessed. It urges leaders to cease thinking of members primarily as "check writers" existing only to support a professional elite. The admonition is rational but represents an incomplete view of both membership and volunteerism.

Some conservation executives consider unsung check writers the most valued philanthropists. They contribute $20 to $5000 a year, mostly at the low end. Many check writers prefer that role. They embody charitable intent. They are volunteers of money.

These modest philanthropists prize their functional anonymity in the membership. They like being distant from policymaking and business. They may be busy with jobs and family, and perhaps with other charities in which they participate more fully, such as church. Their lives would be undiminished if they never attended another committee meeting.

Evidence of their environmental commitment includes their strong annual membership renewal rate (55 to 65 percent on average), the number of years they stay enrolled (long-time members abound in conservation groups), and the extent to which they donate beyond dues (many organizations develop "upgrade programs" to promote the annual increases, to great effect).

The director of a statewide environmental group tells of noticing his organization's decal affixed to a window of a parked car. A man was feeding the adjacent meter. The director introduced himself and thanked the man for showing the company colors. The man smiled and replied without preamble, "I'm the kind of member you like best: I pay my dues and don't bother you." He was what nonprofiteers respectfully call a "small donor," meaning a contributor of small sums, sometimes annual dues only. The director thanked him again and they parted.

These mostly unseen individuals probably make up the majority of any conservation membership. Drucker (1990:56) writes: "Fund development . . . means developing what I call a membership that *participates* through giving [emphasis added]. . . . They see support of the institution as self-fulfillment." They trust the organization's leaders and take satisfaction from afar. Check writers deserve everyone's esteem.

Today, organized conservation can claim perhaps 10 million members nationwide, or 3.9 percent of the population—an uninspiring figure, really, for 96 percent of Americans are environmental free riders! Even then, the number of alleged joiners is probably exaggerated. Legerdemain can account for big variances that are publicized little. Some, for example, are members of several organizations and are counted each time. Organizations often use multipliers to calculate "household" memberships, even if only one family member has joined. Moreover, the censusing of lapsed members differs among nonprofits—dropouts may be treated as active for extended periods.

Though nonprofit conservation is undeniably an effort lodged in the middle class, the formal movement in no way permeates that class. If environmentalism is to become a truly massive movement, it will need to multiply twentyfold or fiftyfold the number of silent, small-gift check writers. They now shoulder an unfair philanthropic burden.

Reaching nonconservationists—the unconverted, the unconvinced, and maybe, eventually, the hostile—will never occur if conservation leaders cleave to narrow definitions of "benefactor." The term must include as many faceless people as possible. We need Jane, Joe, and the kids. Our attitudes as conservation recruiters should mimic any alumni director's: Please give annually because if you like what our institution has done for you, you must periodically reinvest to confer tangible returns on future generations.

Conservation must enroll minorities, too, as paying members. Global society cannot realize a conservation ideal until present nonprofit leaders improve their own attitudes about who should buy in. We can't expect everyone to join, but many people of modest or even lower income can afford the six cents a day ($25/year) that organized conservation typically asks, no matter the color of one's collar or skin. The realignment of some nonprofit conservation programs to meet minority needs will be crucial (but is not the subject of this essay).

Conservation needs vastly more ground-level philanthropists. Environmental executives, who regularly face make-or-break financial challenges, are more likely than their board counterparts to arrive at unapologetic new convictions about fundraising.

COMPENSATORY VOLUNTEERISM

Aggressive enlightened attitudes about the seeking and giving of cash will require yet more self-abnegation in volunteer leaders—the willingness to put the nonprofit squarely ahead of personal needs. In *Managing the Non-Profit Organization* (1990:158), Peter F. Drucker says: "Over the door to the non-profit's boardroom there should be an inscription in big letters that says: *Membership on this board is not power, it is responsibility*. Some non-profit board members still feel that they are there for the same reason they used to go on hospital boards in the old days—recognition by the community—rather than because of a commitment to service."

Fortunately, most volunteers enter board service wanting to give of themselves (for example, to express love for the environment). Most finish with their interior spirit-of-giving intact or enlarged. They leave satisfied about their contribution to the mission and grateful for their affiliation with others of similar bent.

A minority of board volunteers, however, sour on charitable work while serving. They forget that charity is generosity externalized. The changed attitude can sometimes be traced to unexpressed psychological needs that compelled them to sign up in the first place. Hidden motivations lie outside the understanding of the average conservation executive, who is usually not a psychologist. But any nonprofit professional with long service knows this: People who join boards in order to make up for what is lacking at home or work, or in self-opinion, are hell to work with.

These "compensatory volunteers"—the term may have come from Vicki LaFarge, now a professor of group dynamics and organizational behavior—are sometimes blind to their own motives. But their anger is usually visible to staff, who often take the brunt of the contrariness. Compensators need the formal authority that board work grants them. They can attain a recognized station and sometimes acquire a cachet unreachable in daily affairs. They crave the formal architecture of sanctioned governance, and they operate in "rational-legal" relation to subordinates (to borrow an adjective from the sociologist Max Weber). Trusteeship can supply a pattern of order absent from one's personal life.

By contrast, mutual respect, easy courtesy, and a high quotient of trust characterize the relations among leaders who regard each other as equals. Nobody must compensate for anything. Everyone is free to discharge the mission with an all-encompassing generosity.

Peter B. Cooper, a former chair of The Nature Conservancy's Connecticut Chapter, reflecting on his organization's history, captured the idea well:

> Has there been a unifying theme or characteristic of the people who have served as Chapter Board Chairmen over these thirty years? Well, like the landscape of New England, I would say we've been a somewhat rough-hewn and idiosyncratic bunch. Yet, we have all shared a common dedication to, and belief in, the job that had to be done. Whether it was with a group of like-minded volunteers at the outset, or working instead with a highly sophisticated and professional staff organization, I think we universally tried to inspire them with the importance, the urgency, and the excitement of our common task.[4]

The opposite view—the sludge-flows-downhill school of trusteeship—teaches that staff are not partners, they are lesser hands. For compensatory volunteers it's fun to boss someone with impunity and when you want. Many are accountable only at meetings. Even then, peers don't always restrain them. A sort of diplomatic immunity is honored. In such an atmosphere, the institution's charitable intent can be lost.

If the chair doesn't control an errant volunteer, the CEO often pays the price. If the chair *is* the errant volunteer, the entire charity can suffer. In both cases, the first product to decline will likely be the one consuming most of the staff leader's time and worry—income to drive the mission.

THE NONPROFIT AS POSSESSION

In *Managing the Non-Profit Organization*, Peter Drucker (1990:157–158) describes the ideal volunteer board as the premier fundraising organ of a nonprofit organization: "If a board doesn't actively lead in fund development, it's very hard to get the funds the organization needs. Personally, I like a board that not only gets other people to give money but whose members put the organization first and foremost on their own list of donations."

In reality, though, on the bell curve of board attitudes toward fundraising, usually a small percentage of people are vigorous donors or solicitors. The center majority trusts the staff generally and therefore supports aggressive money hunts. From a CEO's viewpoint, both predispositions are welcome and valid. It's the few people at the tag end of the curve, feeling threatened or compromised by vigorous financial growth, who cause problems.

In answer to one executive's continuing entreaty for more volunteer leaders to help find money, the head of the board nominating committee of a national conservation organization declared, "I don't want this board to become a bunch of goddamn fundraisers!" This attitude is doubly misguided. It is bitterly misanthropic and therefore has no place in a philanthropy. And it is falsely dichotomous, implying that certain classes of volunteer are superior to others.

In the minds of possessive trustees, new dollar-chasing board members can signify a diminishing of the love-care-and-feeding tradition of volunteerism. Their arrival symbolizes an unwelcome change in institutional character, a dilution of "pure" conservation motives. As more fundraisers are added to the governance mix, some non-fundraising board leaders fear a decline in their own status as governors. They ask, sometimes overtly: Who owns this nonprofit anyway?

The right answer is: *No one owns it.*

Like any other nonprofit, a conservation charity is a corporate trust. It belongs not to board, staff, donors, or members. The "shareholders" are the benefactors and members, yet even they possess no redeemable certificates of ownership. Volunteer leaders and professionals are merely short-term trustees of an enduring mission and a corporate entity designed to accomplish it. The idea is to pass the trust intact—better yet, improved—to a rolling succession of new custodians.

The temporary stewardship notion is embodied in H. G. Wells' ironic admonition, "What we are given to administer, we presently come to think of as our own," a state of mind to be avoided. The best board members and senior staff "consciously work themselves out of a job," in the words of Nature Conservancy volunteer Johnnie Blum. A paid or unpaid leader is accountable to the underwriters. They, after all, entrust the leadership with dues and other gifts, and with the hope that the trust will succeed in their names.

The trust metaphor applies also to conservation's central idea: Every human generation is merely the short-term keeper of a place, whether a home, city, farm, mountain, wilderness, desert, river, biota, or planet. These, we hope, will thrive under enlightened trusteeship, one goal of a practical, well-governed, generous society.

Sometimes the most blatant transgressors of the temporary stewardship model are, ironically, ex-*staff* who are invited onto the board that once employed them. They often cannot distinguish prior professional objectives (executing the mission) from trustee responsibilities (developing policy and raising money). Their presence can smother even an open-minded CEO.

The ex-director of a large national environmental group suppresses his own return-to-the-fold urge by minimizing contact with his old employer. "Former presidents should not be seen, and they should not be heard," he says emphatically. That formula is not universally applicable, however. Some ex-staff become excellent board members.

A related class of possessory interest-holders includes the organization's founders and long-time board members. "Founder's syndrome"—the inability to part psychologically (and physically) from the institution that one helped build from scratch—can infect volunteers or staff. An example is the valued mega-donor who feels that his or her benefactions have paid for life tenure on the board. Another is the person who served from the group's inception, hasn't quit, and increasingly has become a drag on progress.

Again, notable exceptions exist. Brent Blackwelder, a founder of American Rivers, served thirteen years as chair, always selflessly. On stepping down as board leader, he graciously transferred the reins to another founder, Rafe Pomerance, a former president of Friends of the Earth. Blackwelder moved into a regular board slot, continued as an institutional progressive, friend of staff, donor, and supporter of his successor. Pomerance helped lead the organization to vigorous financial health but chose to leave after his two-year chairmanship, establishing the equally important example that fading away qualifies as honorable volunteerism too.

Both men exemplify excellent trusteeship. No simplistic wisdom about length of service explains it. In opposite but effective ways, each chairman added value to the trust, then passed it on. They loved the mission, the organization, its people. That is, they were philanthropists.

THE USES OF IDEALISM

Nonprofit conservation is charitable. It asks abundant selflessness, financial and personal, of all its toilers. When nonprofit leaders, unpaid or paid, have conflicting attitudes toward raising money, the organization suffers internally. One external result is that the natural environment is commensurately victimized at the hands of its sworn saviors.

We Americans might once have claimed as birthrights such things as safe drinking water, abundant space and wildlife, and sparkling air. They are now increasingly regarded as "gifts" that we must confer upon ourselves. Philanthropy—a love of humankind in general— formally encompasses the environment.

A sea change in attitudes toward fundraising and a dramatic rise in charitable giving cannot restore what we have already lost in biotic diversity, air quality, aquifer recharge, wetlands designations, soil cover, and so on. Nor can private contributions alone meet future environmental needs. However, an enlarged philanthropic ideal can incline America toward a powerful fusion of individual, governmental, nonprofit, and corporate energies in behalf of protecting our common natural inheritance.

The philanthropic ideal must first be forged within nonprofits themselves. Volunteer and staff leaders, working as partners, are responsible for making it happen.

NOTES

The opinions in this chapter are the author's and do not necessarily represent policies of past or present employers. Some details in the essay were altered to preserve the anonymity of individuals and organizations.

1. See, generally, Donald Snow, *Inside the Environmental Movement: Meeting the Leadership Challenge*, foreword by Patrick F. Noonan (Washington: Island Press/The Conservation Fund, 1992). The book contains the surveys, findings, and numerical data from the Conservation Leadership Project, plus interpretive essays. G. Jon Roush was senior associate on the project, which included a nationwide study (begun in 1988) of the environmental movement, its nonprofit executives, and its volunteer leaders.
2. Undocumented quotations in the text are from personal communications with the author.
3. *Conservation Leadership Project: Final Report* (Arlington, VA: The Conservation Fund, 1990), p. 4. This document consists of an executive summary and recommendations.
4. Quoted in Ogden Tanner, *The Nature Conservancy: Building a Legacy of Wild Lands in Connecticut* (Middletown, CT: The Nature Conservancy, 1990), p. 25.

REFERENCES

The Conservation Fund. 1990. *Conservation Leadership Project: Final Report.* Arlington, VA: The Conservation Fund.

Drucker, P. F. 1990. *Managing the Non-Profit Organization: Principles and Practices.* New York: HarperCollins.

Snow, D. 1992. *Inside the Environmental Movement: Meeting the Leadership Challenge.* Foreword by Patrick F. Noonan. Washington: Island Press/The Conservation Fund.

Tanner, O. 1990. *The Nature Conservancy: Building a Legacy of Wild Lands in Connecticut.* Middletown, CT: The Nature Conservancy.

III

Leadership Styles
and Experience

9 Leadership in State Agencies

Leslie Carothers

ONE DAY in the spring of 1971, I received a call from a friend who had just taken a job with the new federal Environmental Protection Agency. "You should come here," he said. "The Environmental Protection Agency will be in the seventies what the Securities and Exchange Commission was in the thirties—the best place for a lawyer to be." I took his advice and joined EPA in Washington that summer.

I had graduated from Harvard Law School in 1967 with a personal interest in environmental protection and a professional interest in economic regulation. This grew from my love of camping while in scouting and from a conviction that it was time for Americans to take back their water, air, and land from the industries and governments who were despoiling them.

After a year at the Antitrust Division of the Justice Department and another as a law clerk for a federal judge, I became a legislative assistant for a Maryland congressman whose priorities included cleaning up the Potomac River and creating the Chesapeake and Ohio National Historic Park. From there, I went to EPA.

I spent twelve years at the agency, beginning as a branch chief in Washington and ending my tenure as deputy regional administrator of the New England Region. During those years, I helped to develop the rules reducing the lead in gasoline and defended them in the lawsuits challenging EPA's decisions. In the regional office in Boston, I directed the region's enforcement programs for nearly five years before becoming deputy. As deputy regional administrator, I was the ranking civil service official and served as chief of staff for the regional administrator, a presidential appointee.

I acquired a broad knowledge of federal environmental regulatory programs—air, water, waste, pesticides, toxic substances—in addition to learning by experience how a regulatory agency works. Although I was not a political appointee and was more an insider than an outside leader, I had extensive contact with representatives of industry, state and municipal governments, and environmental advocacy groups. By the time I departed EPA, I was an expert in environmental regulation and an experienced manager of multidisciplinary staffs in both headquarters and field operations of government.

In 1982, I joined PPG Industries as senior counsel for the environment in PPG's law department. The company is a diversified manufacturer of glass, chemicals, and coatings. I chose to take a position in industry because I wanted to learn how companies went about complying with environmental rules and how the private sector got things done. I was enjoying my work with the company when I received a call from a search committee looking for someone to head the Connecticut Department of Environmental Protection.

THE CONNECTICUT DEP

Founded in 1971, the Connecticut Department of Environmental Protection or DEP is responsible for implementing all state laws and regulations for control of pollution and wastes and protection of resources such as coastal and inland wetlands. In addition, DEP manages about 200,000 acres of state park and forestland as well as the state's fish and wildlife resources. DEP also provides technical services such as mapping of state resources and educational programs for groups ranging from schoolchildren to sportsmen.

By 1987, DEP had a staff of nearly a thousand employees supplemented by another seven hundred summer employees staffing the parks. A substantial portion of the environmental regulation staff is funded by federal grants to various pollution control and pesticide programs. The federal EPA both underwrites and oversees state regulatory programs to assure that all state programs meet minimum standards of effectiveness.

Connecticut was an early leader in environmental protection. A high level of citizen interest in environmental issues has kept the state's legislature busy enacting new state initiatives. The state was one of the first to establish a groundwater program, air toxics controls, and a program of mandatory municipal waste recycling. There are many active environmental advocacy and conservation organizations in the state, including a number of regional river protection groups. In 1987, environmental and conservation issues received frequent coverage in the state's media. No state agency made the news more than DEP.

When the incumbent commissioner retired in 1987, Governor William A. O'Neill appointed a search committee to recruit nationwide for a successor. The governor decided that the expansion of DEP's staff, the length and complexity of its agenda, and the controversies increasingly attending its decisions suggested that the new commissioner should be a professional in the environmental or conservation field.

The desire to appoint a professional does not, however, alter the fact that the post of commissioner is a political appointment or that the commissioner's approach must be compatible with the governor's goals. This brief description of the DEP's responsibilities and the constituencies it regulates or serves should indicate that the department has a major impact on the state and its citizens. Its decisions are often costly and, of course, unpopular in some or even many quarters. A governor needs a person in whom he has confidence to exercise those responsibilities. The commissioner, in turn, needs the governor's support when the political seas get rough.

Connecticut's search committee consulted with representatives of all sectors interested in the department's work and asked them what kind of leader the department needed. The notes from the committee's sessions list nearly twenty attributes desired in the leader they were seeking: commitment to environmental protection and resource management, vision, integrity, charisma, strength of convictions, self-confidence, open-mindedness, fairness, consistency, credibility, common sense, decisiveness, accessibility, sensitivity, expertise, communication skills, management skills, and diplomacy. Finding no paragon displaying *all* of these attributes, the committee recommended me and the governor appointed me.

The qualities just cited are desirable for most leadership posts involving both policy direction and program administration. Some are aspects of character and temperament that are not easily acquired through formal training. But many are talents and skills that can be learned through education and experience. I would choose four skills as essential in leading an agency like DEP: demonstrating a personal commitment to environmental protection and natural resource management; setting priorities for one's tenure as a leader; decision-making skills that inspire confidence in the objectivity and openness of the process; and communication skills. The last area, communications, is a field of competence that is crucial if one is to succeed in the other three. Unless a leader and his or her staff can communicate commitment, priorities, and sound decisions, then in a real sense those things do not exist. Now let's take a look at these essential qualifications.

DEMONSTRATING COMMITMENT

People are unlikely to be good leaders unless they think what they are doing matters. This is especially important in the field of environmental protection and natural resource management where there is a strong ethical component and the benefits to the community are diffuse and realized over the long term.

It can be assumed that the people reading this book and aspiring to be leaders in environmental protection and resource protection *care* about what they are doing or they would be doing something else. But it is not enough to care. That commitment must be communicated to coworkers and constituencies by what you say and what you do about the issues. Whether you win or lose in a particular case, it is what you stood for and how well you made your case that count in establishing your credibility as a leader.

SETTING PRIORITIES

In an agency like DEP, there are dozens of issues crowding the commissioner's agenda. With an often brief tenure as a political appointee, the leader must set priorities if he or she hopes to get anything done. As an executive, the leader implements a set of laws and administration policies that broadly frame the agenda. But the leader also has an opportunity to influence those laws and policies and has substantial room to choose areas of emphasis.

Setting priorities is seldom a purely analytic process of ranking risks to public health or the environment and then choosing the big ones for attention. The leader of a government agency must respond to the demands of the situation and to the issues the public is most concerned about at a particular time. Knowing this, I did not come to Connecticut with a complete agenda devised in advance. Rather, I learned from the interview process, as well as from the advice of seasoned DEP officials, what issues were urgent. My own preferences came into play in choosing areas of personal interest and problems that would engage both the regulatory and the resource management sides of the department in working more closely together. Five key priorities emerged from this process: solid waste management, enforcement, land conservation, Long Island Sound, and agency reorganization.

Solid Waste Management

In the summer of 1987, four new municipal waste incinerators were under construction, and the General Assembly had enacted a mandatory recycling law requiring municipalities to institute recycling programs by 1991. Air pollution rules for incinerators had been proposed but not enacted, there were no rules for incinerator ash disposal or recycling, and there was only one person assigned full-time to the recycling program. Finally, there was no up-to-date solid waste management plan establishing a strategy and framework for the various forms of waste disposal being developed. What was called the solid waste "crisis" had to become a priority.

Waste incineration converting waste to energy seemed to be a good idea for a state dependent on outside energy sources and with little land to devote to land disposal of solid waste. The state's landfills were closing at a rapid rate. The issue of incineration had become highly controversial, however, due to public concern about toxic air emissions, notably dioxin, and the metals contained in incinerator ash. Environmental advocacy groups were concerned about these issues as well as the potential conflict between incineration and recycling as methods of waste management. They thought more incineration capacity would inhibit the introduction and expansion of recycling.

State legislation demanded the setting of an ambient air quality standard for dioxin—a concentration not to be exceeded in the air—as well as dioxin emission limits for the incinerator itself. Establishing numerical ambient standards for carcinogens—generally thought to lack even a theoretical threshold where no adverse effects occur—is a daunting task. Before I came to DEP, the agency had proposed an ambient standard based on an EPA risk assessment that, in its lower range, resulted in a standard below the level of detection. The EPA risk assessment was substantially more conservative in its assumptions than the assessments of other U.S. and foreign health protection agencies. By the time I arrived, DEP staff and its advisors at the State Health Department were questioning the original proposal.

They recommended to me that the standard be raised from 0.1 picogram to 1 picogram per cubic meter of air. (A picogram is one trillionth of a gram.) Although I agreed that the earlier standard was questionable, I decided that further public comment should be requested on the less stringent standard, as it represented a significant change of position on an important health protection issue.

My first six months at DEP were spent contending with the furor over the new proposal. Representatives of state and national environmental advocacy groups attacked me for departing from EPA's risk assessment. The state's leading newspaper ran articles, editorials, and even a cartoon charging leniency in the regulation of dioxin from incinerators.

The scientific underpinnings of quantitative risk assessment methodology for carcinogens are extremely complex. Our best efforts to explain the various methods of extrapolation from animal data, scaling factors, exposure and dose estimates, and why DEP chose the ones it did were less than successful. Some critics believed that we had devised an elaborate rationale for a less stringent standard just to make life easier for the state's new crop of incinerators. As a new appointee, I had not had much time to develop personal credibility.

An announcement that EPA was reconsidering its own risk assessment for dioxin—a process not yet concluded for reasons I can well appreciate—helped to restore a degree of confidence in DEP's standard. It was also helpful that there was never any basis for the charge that the proposed standard had been changed to accommodate the incinerators and helpful, too, that the governor and several respected legislative leaders supported me.

We fared better in setting standards for ash disposal. In this instance, we involved all the interested parties in discussions before proposing a standard. Ultimately DEP *tightened* the ash disposal standards originally proposed. This served as useful evidence that the agency could change its mind in both directions.

We also built up our recycling staff, issued regulations, and developed good recycling education programs. They starred Ray Cycle, a superhero in green tights, who has enlisted thousands of Connecticut schoolchildren in pressing their parents to participate in recycling programs. Though popular with most of Connecticut's environmentally concerned citizens, recycling also demands a complex program of education, collection, sorting, and marketing if it is to work. Connecticut now has a solid infrastructure for recycling and expects to achieve the planned goal of recycling at least 25 percent of the municipal waste stream.

But most important in steering the solid waste program on a steadier course was the development of the state's solid waste management plan. The plan was prepared by a task force headed by a respected senior agency official. It assembled, for the first time, all the available data on the volume and types of solid waste and defined the volumes to be managed through source reduction, recycling, incineration, and land disposal. The relative role of incineration remained a point of contention, but all parties commenting on the proposed strategy complimented the quality of the effort to lay out the facts and define a strategy.

Part of leadership is setting the course, so that people can participate and understand even if they do not always endorse the direction. The solid waste crisis would have been less of a crisis if the state had had a plan at an earlier stage. But Connecticut is now better off than many of its neighbors. In January 1992, the *New York Times* reported on the wrangles on Long Island and in New Jersey over keeping waste in the state to feed new incinerators or allowing disposers to ship it to out-of-state landfills, a cheaper but surely temporary solution. It was gratifying to read the sentence referring to Connecticut: "Connecticut, which wrote plans and long-term contracts years ago, seems to have avoided most of this problem." (See Lyall 1992:14.)

Enforcement

Giving priority to stronger enforcement of environmental laws was dictated by DEP's circumstances and by my own experience and beliefs. In 1987, the federal EPA had declined to approve the state's hazardous waste regulatory program to operate in lieu of the federal program and had threatened to withdraw authorization of Connecticut's water pollution program. EPA thought that the state was not aggressive enough in enforcing its antipollution laws. The DEP was viewed as avoiding legal proceedings and penalties in favor of a more lenient stance with regard to violators.

Few states wish to cede control of environmental enforcement to federal authorities. It makes life more difficult for the regulated community in a state, as a company or town must then deal with parallel regulatory programs and two sets of regulators. Restoring DEP's primacy in environmental enforcement was therefore a high priority for me.

I accomplished this by strengthening DEP's teamwork with its lawyers and by setting a tougher tone. I worked to solidify close working relationships with the attorney general's staff and added several attorneys to the commissioner's staff. (The DEP counsel's office had been eliminated in the seventies.) Better teamwork between the DEP technical staff and its lawyers moved cases faster and reduced the feeling among DEP's engineers that legal proceedings never got results expeditiously.

Early in my tenure, I appeared before a meeting arranged by the Connecticut Business and Industry Association and announced that I was a "hawk" on enforcement. Many of the association's members as well as many municipalities would agree that I lived up to my billing. The level of enforcement activity and monetary penalties increased markedly during my term.

The choice of enforcement as a priority did not stem from a desire to oppress companies and towns or to collect fines for the state's general fund. Vigorous and visible enforcement is essential to maintaining the credibility of any regulatory agency. It is difficult, for example, to grant permits to unpopular facilities like incinerators. What is difficult becomes nearly impossible unless the public has some reason for confidence that the facilities will be well regulated and the rules will be enforced.

Industry too has a major stake in having a credible environmental agency. The effects of the damage to EPA's credibility done by the early Reagan administration appointees are still being felt. Indeed, the public and congressional backlash against what was happening at EPA in the early eighties led Congress to enact legislation severely constraining EPA's discretion as an administrative agency. Today's laws, therefore, are far more prescriptive in the details of implementation than is desirable from the standpoint of good science or good administration.

The EPA administrator in the Bush administration, William Reilly, established a high profile on enforcement for his agency during his term. While this was doubtless done out of conviction that our laws are intended to be enforced, I suspect he was also aware that without a demonstrated commitment to enforcement, it would have been difficult for him to succeed in some of the less conventional approaches he tried, such as his highly successful efforts to secure voluntary industry commitments to reduce air toxics emissions.

The tone and style of enforcement may change. But they cannot change in ways that undermine the public's confidence in a leader's commitment to secure compliance with environmental laws.

Land Conservation

After a few months as DEP commissioner, I asked the governor to recommend a major, multiyear increase in DEP's funds for the acquisition of land for parks, forests, and habitat protection. He responded with a program to request $20 million in bond funds during each of the next five years. Some $60 million had been authorized and about $40 million spent before I left office.

When I came to Connecticut, I expected the public to be most concerned about issues such as hazardous waste dumps. Instead, I learned from my mail and my visits around the state that the biggest issue on many people's minds was the rapid pace of land development prevailing in the state in the mid-eighties. I also learned that Connecticut was the only one of the six New England states without a major program to fund land acquisition.

Adopting land conservation as a priority was also consistent with my personal interests and my goals for DEP. I have loved the New England landscape since coming to Massachusetts to college. Connecticut has maintained a pleasing blend of city and countryside for many years, an unusual situation for such a densely populated state. Moreover, the resource management and service goals of DEP's forests, parks, fish, and wildlife programs would all be advanced by expanding the state's landholdings. Practically all of the DEP's diverse constituencies enthusiastically supported a revived land acquisition program.

Administering a land acquisition program required us to develop mechanisms for ranking properties and making choices. We were slower to develop a clearer set of goals—a vision—for the program as a whole. DEP's early objective of adding 100,000 more acres to the state's holdings was drawn from a commission recommendation in the seventies. It was not a realistic target, however, given the cost of Connecticut real estate and the excruciatingly slow process of acquiring property through the state's cumbersome procedures.

By 1990, DEP was sharpening the focus of the land acquisition program. The department's Natural Resource Center had prepared new maps showing all of the state's lands under protection for conservation purposes (state, municipal, and private) together with lands owned by water companies and was working on a strategy to try to build greenways linking protected lands in certain corridors.

In the spring of 1992, Connecticut's Council on Environmental Quality, a monitoring group that reviews environmental programs and recommends improvements, issued a report focusing on the merits of greenway strategies (Connecticut Council on Environmental Quality 1992). It also recommended that the governor establish a Greenways Commission and develop goals and plans for greenways. This positive step will build on the foundation we worked to put in place in the land conservation program during my tenure.

Long Island Sound

Many states divide their environmental regulation and natural resource management responsibilities between two agencies—analogous to the federal EPA and the Department of the Interior. Connecticut does not. There is continuing concern that combining the two functions tends to submerge the resource management programs because issues of environmental regulation tend to command much more attention from the media, the public, the legislature, and, hence, the commissioner.

It is true that natural resource management programs have trouble vying for appropriate attention. One of the appealing aspects of Long Island Sound as a priority for me as commissioner was that restoring the Sound is an objective that engages practically all the professional disciplines of a unified agency—water pollution, fisheries, coastal zone management, public access to beaches and other coastal amenities, resource mapping, and many others. I saw an opportunity to capitalize on DEP's organization and multidisciplinary depth in working on the set of problems affecting Long Island Sound.

The Sound is a defining resource for Connecticut. It forms its southern boundary and contributes much to the commercial, recreational, and aesthetic riches of the state. It is also the victim of substantial pollution from the lands and rivers of Connecticut and New York and is surrounded by dense urban development at its western end. Preserving water quality and wildlife habitat, as well as public access and amenities, is a major challenge.

The issues concerning Long Island Sound are too numerous and complex to describe in detail here. It will be more useful to list some of the characteristics of the problem that are common to environmental and natural resource problems and make special demands on their leaders. The first characteristic is *scientific complexity*. For many years, a wide-ranging set of scientific studies had been conducted to identify the major problems of the Sound. Funded largely by the federal EPA, with contributions by New York and Connecticut, the study was focused in the late 1980s on diagnosing the causes of hypoxia, a condition of very low dissolved oxygen in the waters of the western Sound. Oxygen levels are a good indicator of water quality; low levels drive out or eliminate aquatic life. The study concluded that the primary culprit was excessive nitrogen loadings that were causing the growth of algae, which depleted oxygen as it decomposed. The study also attempted to discover the major sources of nitrogen and the reductions in nitrogen loadings that would be required to achieve higher dissolved oxygen.

The second characteristic is *resource restoration costs*. The findings of the Long Island Sound study involved advanced technical analyses of water quality and hydrodynamic parameters. Using computer models, they were of more than scientific interest because they pointed to the sources of nitrogen—notably municipal wastewater treatment plants—that would need additional treatment facilities. The cost estimates, though crude, predicted the need for hundreds of millions of dollars in investment in upgrading wastewater treatment plants to include a third phase of treatment to remove nitrogen.

The third characteristic is *multijurisdictional responsibilities*. The responsible political units—the federal government, two states, and numerous cities and towns—will have to make commitments of resources to address the hypoxia problem as well as others being described by the Long Island Sound study. Arguments over who owes what are inevitable when more than one unit of government is involved. They are greatly magnified when the scientific evidence is complex and the financial stakes are high. The restoration of Long Island Sound and similar resources necessarily raises questions concerning the proper roles for national, state, and local governments. Although states and municipalities must shoulder a goodly portion of the cost of abating pollution of adjacent waters, the federal government should share responsibility for protection of coastal resources when the majority of the U.S. population lives within fifty miles of its coasts.

The fourth characteristic is the *time required to show results*. It is likely to take twenty years to install the municipal treatment facilities needed to restore healthy levels of oxygen in Long Island Sound. This is a blink of the eye in the cycle of natural resources, but an eternity in the political realm.

Nevertheless, many Connecticut citizens have witnessed the dramatic improvements in the state's rivers over the past twenty years and could well respond to reminders that perseverance pays. The DEP has also pursued programs and actions with a shorter payoff to build public confidence that results can be achieved. The agency decided to press for a pilot nitrogen removal facility in Norwalk Harbor. The intent was to undertake a project with a five-year term that would demonstrate beneficial results in the harbor. DEP also stepped up the research and monitoring effort by commissioning a Long Island Sound research vessel to make visible the ongoing work to restore the Sound. Finally, we encouraged the formation of a coalition of citizen's organizations to coordinate the activities of the many groups interested in the Sound. These initiatives have all been continued by the commissioner who succeeded me.

Solving the problems of a resource like Long Island Sound draws upon the knowledge from a host of disciplines: natural science, economics, and public finance, to name a few. The information must be translated into action plans that can inspire public support and political commitment over the long term. No leader can be expected to be an expert in all or even many of these fields. Fortunately, that expertise is not necessary.

The basic talent required of any leader is to grasp enough of the specialized information to see where it points and what the strengths and uncertainties in the facts are—all with the aid of a competent staff. This kind of analytic skill and judgment is part of what legal training is supposed to develop, but it is acquired from any academic discipline, diligently pursued. And while it can certainly increase a leader's credibility and stature to be an expert in a particular field, it is more important for the leader in environmental protection and resource management to enjoy the opportunity to be a generalist dealing with many fields.

Agency Reorganization

A state agency leader must strive to take charge of the organization as well as its agenda. The DEP in 1987 suffered from a certain middle-aged spread, having added a host of new programs and divisions without any other changes to strengthen coordination among them. I consolidated most of the agency's twenty-four units under seven bureau chiefs, adding several new managers to the department in the process. This reorganization took nearly half my term to accomplish, but it improved the management of related programs and created a strong senior staff that began to work as a team—my team.

DECISION-MAKING SKILLS

The leader of an agency like DEP makes hundreds of decisions— ranging from what programs to reduce or expand to whether to allow a coastal resident to build a dock. The quality of these decisions and the manner in which they are made set the tone of the administration. They have much to do with whether you are perceived as a leader by your staff and by the public.

The first requirement of decision making is that you do it. There is never enough information or enough time, but nothing undermines the reputation of a leader faster than the perception that you avoid hard decisions. The other requirements are simple to state though hard to execute perfectly. The decision maker needs to understand the context of the decision—the statute or rules or the resource management policies at stake. You should then listen to the staff, the citizens, the business people, and the public officials who have facts and opinions to bring forward. Finally, you should explain why you decided what you did.

Good decision making is especially important in a field where many issues are both technically complex and politically sensitive. There will always be political pressures to take enforcement action against Company A or not to allow duck hunting in the waters off Town B. And there is often suspicion that scientific facts are being manipulated to support a decision taken on less meritorious grounds—a problem that plagued me in the dioxin case.

In 1987, DEP was perceived by both regulated parties and the public as inconsistent in its policies and decisions. Perhaps because I am a lawyer, I paid a good deal of attention to explaining our decisions. The commissioner hears and decides appeals from permit decisions by the staff. With the aid of my new staff attorneys, I issued a number of written decisions intended to sharpen and clarify DEP's interpretations of its rules.

These incremental improvements added up to a change that drew favorable comment from the executive director of Connecticut's Council on Environmental Quality, an advisory body that monitors DEP actions and investigates public complaints. In a report on recent trends in DEP decision making, he described the change this way:

> The old patterns are giving way to a new, more coherent, policy-based system of decision making. Reasons for the change are many, including the partial reorganization, the punctilious review of cases and relevant laws by attorneys in the commissioner's office, and a change in attitude in several DEP units. Without doubt, however, much of the credit must go to the commissioner, both for her own attention to details of the cases, and for the way she has organized the adjudicatory work. The change in "adjudicatory atmosphere" should be regarded as one of the most significant, if un-heralded, changes brought to the agency by Commissioner Carothers. [Wagener 1989:2]

The need for clarity and consistency in implementing policy was also important in the department's resource management work. The field is replete with conflicts among users of the resources. There are different interests among owners of power boats and sailboats, hikers and hunters, fly fishermen and bait fishermen, lobster pot fishermen and trawlers, to name a few. The harvesting of trees is controversial, too, depending on how and where it is done. Whether these disputes are resolved by regulation or case-by-case determinations, the agency needs to articulate a principled basis for making decisions.

I found, for example, that the staff had made a series of case-by-case decisions on whether to close certain coastal areas to waterfowl hunting. A review of past decisions revealed that common criteria for decision were, in fact, applied. It was easier to contend with new cases of pressure to close coastal areas when we stated clearly what standards we were applying.

Decision makers get into trouble when they disregard the legal or policy framework for the decision, when they ignore (or seem to ignore) pertinent facts and opinions, or when they give no reasons (or phony reasons) for their choices. Even people who are adversely affected can often accept a decision they think is wrong. What rankles is an impression that they have not been heard or that a hidden agenda has dictated the outcome. If the decision maker has done a good job, the losers in a particular case will feel that they might win the next time. And they will be right.

COMMUNICATION SKILLS

For the leader of an environmental or resource management agency, there is no avoiding the need for communication. The only question is whether it will be done well or done badly.

The communications task would be much easier, of course, if the public received a general education in environmental and resource management to form a foundation on which to build. Connecticut's citizens probably have a higher degree of general education than most, but state government has been able to make only a modest contribution to basic education in the natural resource field. DEP has a small, though valiant, environmental education staff that provides advice and materials to schoolteachers. The department also administers some excellent education programs on hunting and fishing, relying heavily on a corps of dedicated volunteers.

Much more could be done. But education programs cannot compete well for resources in the budget process. Other needs are always more urgent, if not more important. I came reluctantly to the conclusion that private resources must be sought if a stronger education program is to be mounted.

A leader of an environmental or resource management agency needs to be an educator, but he or she carries out that responsibility by communicating with various audiences on particular issues. The unusual combination of technical subject matter and a high degree of public and media interest in this field imposes great demands on the communication skills of the leader and the agency. There are plenty of technical and otherwise complex fields of endeavor for leadership. The difference is that none of them commands the same degree of interest from so many sectors of society as is claimed by environmental and conservation issues today.

Two key elements in successful communications are anticipating and preparing for issues that are difficult and contentious and explaining clearly what you are doing and why, preferably before you do it. I learned these lessons best from two cases that qualified as communication failures. One was a case where DEP authorized hunting at Connecticut's Bluff Point reserve to reduce the size of the deer herd. The other was the dioxin decision discussed earlier.

Bluff Point

Bluff Point is an 800-acre, forested reserve on the eastern coast of Connecticut. Although the property is neither a state park nor a nature preserve, the state had never authorized hunting there. Consequently, the deer herd had grown to a level estimated at seven times the deer density of the state—well above the population considered by DEP's wildlife managers to be supportable by the Bluff Point habitat. There was evidence of severe overbrowsing of the foliage in the reserve and poor health among the deer.

DEP's wildlife staff decided to allow an archery hunting season in 1990. The idea was that this mode of hunting would be less intrusive to other users of the reserve and would succeed in gradually reducing the herd. This decision was made public in the department's hunting rules for the 1990 season. It was not discussed with me or announced to the public in any other way.

As word of the program spread, controversy over hunting at Bluff

Point erupted. Connecticut has an active animal rights movement that has vigorously protested hunting and other wildlife management programs such as the proposal to control the population of mute swans in the state. Demonstrations against hunting in the Yale Forest have been an annual event. Not surprisingly, the Friends of Animals group opposed the Bluff Point hunt as an expansion of recreational hunting privileges in the state.

Many professional wildlife managers consider the positions of the animal rights movement to be emotional and unscientific. Certainly the fervor of some of the movement's partisans makes them difficult to deal with if you don't see things their way. Nevertheless, an agency with a mission to manage wildlife cannot legitimately dismiss or evade the arguments of any segment of the public. The agency must respond to the arguments as thoroughly and objectively as it can.

In fact, DEP had a very strong case for taking action to reduce the deer herd at Bluff Point. The staff's intention was not to open more areas to recreational hunting; there are ample hunting opportunities in most parts of Connecticut. The idea was to use hunting to restore a balance between the deer population and a unique natural area on a peninsula of the state.

I decided this purpose would be clearer and more efficiently served by withdrawing authorization of a normal nine-week archery season and allowing two nine-day deer hunts (using shotguns) and granting a limited number of permits to hunters. The staff also undertook to evaluate the antler beam diameter and weight of the deer taken to verify its initial judgment that the nutritional state of the Bluff Point herd was poor. When the hunt had been under way for only six days, I was informed that the number of deer taken was approaching the level DEP had estimated as needing to be culled. I therefore stopped the hunt.

Despite a good case of need for the hunt at Bluff Point and a program ultimately tailored to that need, DEP and I took a major drubbing in the media for giving in to hunting interests and disregarding public concern about what happened at Bluff Point. Some, though not all, of this controversy could have been avoided if we had laid out the facts in advance of the decision to allow hunting.

It is impossible to persuade people who oppose the killing of animals on ethical grounds that hunting is ever justified. Many people, however, can understand the need to maintain a balance between wildlife populations and the habitat that sustains them, even if they do not approve of hunting as a sport. We did not make our case to those people at a time and in a manner that might have persuaded them that DEP was doing a professional job of managing its wildlife and their habitat.

Dioxin

Although the dioxin air standard was a different case, it had a similar outcome due in part to a failure to communicate the department's position. In this case, the department was racing to meet a statutory deadline to propose a dioxin standard. The DEP proposed a range of numbers with no written explanation of the basis for its proposal and without receiving the advice of its advisory committee on hazardous air pollutants. (There was nothing for the committee to comment on before the proposal was made.) Against this background, I received, as a new commissioner, the recommendation to make the proposed standard significantly less stringent in percentage if not absolute terms. This was not a favorable position from which to start communicating about dioxin's risks.

Trying to explain the risks of carcinogens in the environment is the most difficult subject I have encountered in my professional experience. Quantitative risk assessment produces risk estimates—say, one cancer in a million people—that have a precision totally at odds with the highly uncertain assumptions underlying almost every part of the analysis. The methodology itself is nearly unintelligible to anyone other than experts. It is, however, one of the few tools we have to weigh the relative risks of carcinogens and to find the range of exposure where we can conclude that the risks are acceptably low.

Environmental agencies have often dealt with this problem by resorting to technology-based instead of risk-based numbers wherever they can. The problem is growing, however, as the country moves into the remediation of sites contaminated with industrial wastes in the past. Both industry and environmentalists commonly attack technology standards for cleanup of such sites. Industry, paying the bills, believes that technology controls (pumping and treating groundwater forever, for example) are disproportionate to the risk, while environmental groups contend that technology standards do not eliminate all risks. As the battle over quantitative risk assessments is joined, the public sits on the sidelines wondering where the truth lies.

I am not sure anyone has the communication skills to translate this debate into terms that make sense to the interested public. We need dramatic advances in scientific knowledge and greater public understanding of the limits of risk assessment methodologies to build a base for good communication about environmental risks, especially cancer risks.

The evolution of the evidence concerning destruction of the stratospheric ozone layer is a striking example of how a change in the form and clarity of evidence can ease the communication task. Scientists in the seventies were predicting accelerated ozone depletion using chemical formulas and computer simulation methodologies. While some found their predictions persuasive, the argument ended only when space age technology produced a *photograph* of the ozone hole. A picture is worth a thousand printouts. Leaders in environmental and resource management must normally communicate with much less.

MORE THAN JUST STYLE

The leadership skills discussed here—demonstrating commitment, setting priorities, decision making, and communications—are fields of competence necessary for action to advance a leader's agenda. They are independent of a leader's circumstances or personal style.

In reflecting on my own experience as a leader, I think I succeeded where I did because I was regarded as open, honest, and direct in addressing the issues facing Connecticut's agency. In the environmental and natural resource management field, the public does not want its leaders to be "political" in the negative sense that they try to please everybody or just split the difference in resolving disputes. They operate, however, in a political context where business interests fear that the leaders will cave in to pressure from environmental groups supported by the media and where environmental and citizen groups are worried that the leaders will yield to pressure to advance short-term economic interests.

The expectation of all sides is that a good leader will respect the facts and serve the common interest of protecting the natural environment for everyone, now and for the future. Attention to the facts and honesty in dealing with them are not merely matters of style. They are fundamental to a leader's credibility and success.

REFERENCES

Council on Environmental Quality. 1992. *Connecticut Environment Review*, 1991, pp. 17–29, Hartford, CT.

Lyall, S. 1992. "Suddenly, Towns Fight to Keep Their Garbage." *New York Times*, Section 4, p. 14.

Wagener, K. J. 1989. *Recent Trends in DEP Decision-Making*. Special Report to the Council on Environmental Quality. Hartford, CT.

10 National Leadership

Jeff M. Sirmon

THIS CHAPTER is about leadership in the federal government. More specifically, it describes my view of that part of government which is responsible for the management and protection of public natural resources.

A variety of agencies manage America's federal forests, parks, rivers, wilderness areas, grasslands, prairies, and the thousands of species of plants and animals that live in these special areas. As a function of their respective missions, the U.S. Fish and Wildlife Service, the Bureau of Land Management, the National Park Service, the Forest Service, the Tennessee Valley Authority, the Bureau of Reclamation, the Army Corps of Engineers, and the Department of Defense—all are responsible for some portion of our shared natural heritage.

I have chosen to focus on leadership within the Forest Service—"an institution of American life"—because it is the largest single conservation agency within the federal government and because it happens to be the one for which I have worked most of my adult life.

Those who think of the Forest Service as only, or even primarily, a timber management or firefighting agency do a serious injustice to its work force. The Forest Service is the oldest conservation agency in our government. The leadership its employees bring to their work has fostered a remarkable record of achievements that have been offered as a model for the public sector.

The Forest Service is responsible not only for protecting and managing vast tracts of public lands, but its employees also conduct forestry research, provide extension services to other public and private

165

forestry interests, and, through a recently expanded international forestry mission, are pursuing opportunities to cooperate with other nations in managing our planet's finite and life-sustaining resources. Leadership within the Forest Service has undergone a number of changes. In this chapter I will describe them and present my ideas about future managers of public natural resources. But first a few words about my own career path.

I grew up on a family farm where I learned the value of work, the results of labor, and an appreciation of the forces of nature. I was given responsibilities early and was allowed to succeed. My academic training was in civil engineering—consequently an orientation to problem solving, attention to detail, and a respect for data systems, processes, and performance.

My orientation after college was always toward management— making things happen, securing and applying resources, monitoring results. In high school, college, and church, I served as president of a number of organizations and developed the skill to make a group function.

I would say I was educated in college as an engineer, but my real skills are managerial and executive. I participated in many management and supervision training courses and experiences offered by the Forest Service in the middle and late 1960s. I was also thrust into responsible managerial positions as early as age twenty-five. It scares me now to think about the amount of responsibility the Forest Service put on young people in the mid-1960s when the service was rapidly expanding its programs.

At this point in my life, I don't consider engineering as my skill. In fact, I began a rapid shift from technical engineering to management within ten years of graduation. My career path involved eight major job moves in thirty-three years, all within the Forest Service except for a fourteen-month hitch as an officer in the U.S. Army Corps of Engineers. Each move was a test of leadership and an exposure to new constituencies both inside and outside the agency. I spent from 1958 until 1974 in engineering with assignments in Alabama, South Carolina, California, Washington, D.C., Montana, and the U.S. Army. In 1974, I was appointed deputy regional forester in the Intermountain Region headquartered in Ogden, Utah, where I was suddenly in a major line officer position over a much broader set of activities than engineering.

After that assignment, I served as regional forester in the Inter-mountain Region and the Pacific Northwest Region. From 1985 until 1991, I served as deputy chief of the Forest Service in charge of programs and legislation, which consisted of budgeting for the Forest Service, legislative affairs, policy analysis, strategic planning, and environmental coordination. From June 1991 to the present I have headed the new International Forestry Mission as deputy chief.

My career path has been somewhat different from those who now have similar positions (Table 1). Most incumbents would have had a forestry education and would have occupied the positions of district ranger and forest supervisor. I was never stationed on a ranger district nor have I held the job of supervisor. I was the first person with an engineering background to occupy the job of regional forester in the Intermountain and Pacific Northwest regions and the first deputy chief for International Forestry.

TABLE 1. Career Paths

Year	Author's Career Path	District	Forest	Region	Washington Office	Typical Career Path of Most Who Reach Top Leadership Positions
1–3	project engineer	O	X			junior forester
3–7	forest engineer	O	X			forester
7–9	engineering development officer	O		X		forester
9–12	branch chief	O			X	ranger
12–14	regional engineer		O	X		forest staff officer
14–21	deputy and regional forester		O	X		forest supervisor
21–25	regional forester			X	O	branch chief staff assistant
25–31	deputy chief for programs and legislation			O	X	regional forester or associate deputy chief
31+	deputy chief for international forestry				O/X	deputy chief

O = Typical career path of others who have reached the same level of responsibility

X = author's career path

I did not follow what was perceived to be the typical career path to top positions. In fact, there have been so many exceptions to the "typical" career path that hardly anything is typical any more. At any rate, Table 1 shows my career contrasted to those who entered the Forest Service about the same time I did.

OVERVIEW OF THE FOREST SERVICE

President Theodore Roosevelt and Gifford Pinchot supported a system of "forest reserves" that would ensure our nation a continuous flow of forest products forever. Responsible management of America's natural treasures was an idea born of their time. It was, however, an idea born not so much of necessity as of insight into what our country could become. Pinchot's vision (1987:261) fostered plans to preserve and protect our continent's forests "for the greatest good, for the greatest number in the long run." The quality of leadership that these two resource pioneers brought to their work reflected an American ethic of conservation and wise use—an ethic that has endured, in large measure, for a century.

In 2005, the Forest Service will celebrate its centennial as an agency. Comprising about one-third of the U.S. Department of Agriculture, this 34,000-person agency grew to its maturity in an age of ever-widening human settlement and burgeoning human demands. In 1906 the national forests were established by setting aside from the public domain roughly 160 million acres of land for a continuous flow of timber and favorable flows of water. Not only has the size of the national forests expanded to 191 million acres, but their purposes and use have enlarged far beyond Pinchot's dreams.

Organization

Four distinct yet converging missions dictate Forest Service activities in the 1990s. The National Forest System is concerned with the protection and management of the 156 national forests (191 million acres). The State and Private Forestry mission is concerned with forestry extension to states and nonindustrial forest landowners. The Research mission serves not only the agency's needs, but other agencies and organizations with interests in forestry by conducting research at its seventy-two laboratory locations with its seven hundred scientists. The International Forestry mission confronts natural resource issues of international scope.

The National Forest System is the most visible branch of the agency's operations and employs 95 percent of its work force. It is divided into regions, national forests, and ranger districts. The average ranger district is about 300,000 acres, and there are 641 of them in forty-one states from Maine to California and Alaska to Puerto Rico, all headed by district rangers who are usually professional foresters. The ranger executes plans and programs with a staff of three or four on small ranger districts and perhaps one hundred or more on large, resource-rich districts.

A national forest comprises several ranger districts and is managed by a forest supervisor. With a staff of interdisciplinary personnel, the forest supervisor conducts comprehensive forest-wide planning and monitors and coordinates various activities. The supervisor is recognized as a policy position and is a primary contact for interest groups and those affected by Forest Service programs. Most decisions affecting local land uses in forests are made at the forest and district level. Each forest supervisor reports to one of nine regional foresters. At this level of the organization, policies are formulated and reviewed, programs are developed for implementation, planning direction is given, and coordination is made possible among all of the region's forests and ranger districts as well as with state and local governments.

Through its State and Private Forestry branch of operations, Forest Service officers coordinate activities with individual state foresters and landowners. Through complex and ongoing cooperation, professionals of a full spectrum of resource disciplines work with a variety of jurisdictions to promote sound forestry practices under private, nonindustrial ownership and to encourage multiple use of forest resources.

The Washington office of the Forest Service, headed by the chief, is responsible for overall policy and supervises the nine regions, seven research headquarters, one state and private area office, and the International Institute of Tropical Forestry. The agency's relationship with Congress on appropriations, legislation, and review—as well as relations with superiors in the Department of Agriculture and other departments—is a critical responsibility of the chief and his staff.

The Forest Service and the Soil Conservation Service (SCS) report to the assistant secretary for natural resources and environment, who in turn reports to the secretary of agriculture. Compared with other natural resource agencies, the Forest Service is, far and away, America's leading manager of public lands and resources (Table 2).

Relationship to Others

The Forest Service operates under authorities and laws provided by key congressional committees of jurisdiction, and its business operations are guided by annual Appropriations Committee direction. In each session, Congress introduces well over two hundred bills that directly or indirectly affect forestry practices and forest management policy. Through the legislative process, Forest Service leaders are actively engaged in hearings and public policy dialogue.

Around every aspect of forest management there are well-organized for-profit and nonprofit interest groups. About fifty organizations maintain headquarters in the Washington, D.C., area actively promoting their interest as they seek to influence policy and budget decisions in Congress, with the agency, and with all other pertinent offices in the administration. Most of these organizations have field offices, as well, and members interacting with the Forest Service at the local and regional level.

TABLE 2. Relative Size of U.S. Conservation Agencies

Agency	Budget (M$)	Employees (FTEs)	land Area (M Acres)	Income (M$)
Forest Service	3,278,611	42,599	191,000	1,483,743[a]
BLM	1,111,598	11,839	272,000[b]	1,377,261[c]
National Park Service	1,442,116	18,700	80,275	99,025[d]
Fish and Wildlife	1,235,037	7,833	90,777	254,605

Note: Statistics are for fiscal year 1992.

[a]Does not include value of minerals.

[b]Additional 300,000 million acres of subsurface responsibility.

[c]Includes $1.1 million of mineral lease receipts.

[d]Includes $13,000 million of concessionaire receipts that go directly to the Treasury.

Source: Program Development and Budget Staff, USDA Forest Service, Washington, D.C.

THE EVOLUTION OF LEADERSHIP

Leaders and leadership can come in many forms and styles. While leaders act in the stream of history and institutionalize their type of leadership in their time, they must also create or strengthen systems that will survive them. No particular leadership model or style is suited for all times; rather, the effectiveness of various leadership models changes as society changes.

The Authority Figure

The dominant leadership model in the Forest Service from its beginning until the early 1960s was authoritarian. The behavior style of the federal land manager was simple: *Take charge, move out, and produce!* If appropriate laws or rules did not cover a situation, the line officer applied his own interpretation and backed up the decisions with science, experience, and related laws and regulations. In most situations his decisions were final. This model for leadership was influenced greatly by the training and experience the line officers received in fighting forest fires—very similar to the kind of training and experience received in military combat situations. There wasn't much tolerance for a lot of discussion and paper planning.

Since the earliest days, district rangers, forest supervisors, and regional foresters have occupied a very special niche in the Forest Service's management structure. The decentralized nature of this organization allowed these line officers to enjoy a unique leadership role. They were accorded a keen sense of responsibility, a high degree of flexibility, and the privilege of almost unilateral decision making.

The Forest Service had a strong line-staff style of organization. If line officers weren't around or were slow in making the right decisions (move out, produce!), staff stepped in and made them. After all, in the early years almost everyone was a forester; they went to the same schools, moved between line and staff positions in their careers, and their behavior could be predicted. The hierarchical authority-figure model was pervasive—it worked well, fit the social landscape of the new frontier, and rang true with the Manifest Destiny mindset of a very special time in our history.

In the early years, the Forest Service officer could, for all practical purposes, chart his own course. Whether he was developing projects and setting priorities at the local level or changing or initiating policies at the national level, the forest ranger was a kind of benevolent monarch. This was as true of the solitary ranger at his remote field station as it was of a forest supervisor or a multistate regional forester.

For decades the scientist-manager could describe the scientific, legal, or utilitarian needs for an action, gain some measure of support—and proceed. In many cases, and particularly at the local level, the line officer could set an agenda and proceed without challenge. This leadership role was fostered, of course, by the image of a kindly, cinnamon-brown bear in overalls. Smokey became an icon of the wise and gentle protector. We knew that everything green, natural, and true would be safe in Smokey's broad paws. In his image we saw a savior of wildlife, a guardian of human habitation—an austere, yet cuddly, caretaker of bunnies, birds, and towering stands of timber. It was a role, I daresay, that was recognized and respected everywhere.

I don't want to imply that this style of leadership didn't produce good results—far from it. Timber trespass was brought under control, our nation's losses from forest fires were drastically reduced, grazing on forestland was regulated, and deteriorating conditions on millions of acres of rangeland were reversed. Land managers took courageous positions to protect environmental qualities without the pressure of outside interest groups—they did it out of an inherent commitment to do right by the land.

In fact, agency leaders would sometimes take actions where Congress itself could not or would not. An example is the agency's campaign to control the destructive activity of miners by issuing regulations requiring the approval of operating plans for land surface operations (Wilkinson and Anderson 1985). Then came the turbulent 1960s and 1970s when the public let it be known that people wanted fair treatment in employment and demanded a voice in important policy and project decisions. The business of the federal land manager began to change rapidly and irrevocably.

More recently, environmental laws have produced altogether new policies and processes that have narrowed the line officer's flexibility. With stringent environmental assessment responsibilities, monitoring requirements, and new systems of accountability, the planning process and every other basis of decision making have changed dramatically.

The decision maker now must not only direct forest and project planning along specific courses of procedure, but must also share the decision making responsibility with the public. The social, environmental, and political complexities of the late twentieth century have dramatically altered the land manager's freedom.

Growing Pains

As social values and the awareness of our human community and natural world change, so too do the environments in which we work. For precisely this reason, Forest Service leaders began to recognize an altogether different social and political landscape. Those leaders with the most acumen began to understand, or at least to feel, the need to change or adapt their style accordingly.

After an institution like the Forest Service enjoys a long period of success, the model for successful leadership becomes a tradition. The world around us began to change faster than we could define and adjust to a new leadership model. From the relatively carefree, modestly happy, and economic robust days of the 1950s and 1960s, the public shifted—from a time of contentment and certainty that the resources in our natural world were inexhaustible to a time when even the most long-standing assumptions were open to question. The 1970s and 1980s were decades of new demands on the resources. Americans seemed suddenly to consume our natural treasures at a rate that could hardly have been predicted. It began to seem that a fundamental change in our ways of thinking would be necessary.

With the dawning of America's renewed concerns for the natural environment, Congress enacted some sweeping legislation that fundamentally changed the ways in which the Forest Service would operate. The freedom to take independent action became limited in ways that no one had foretold. For instance, the National Environmental Policy Act of 1969 made it imperative that our resource leaders give the public notice of any proposed action that might adversely affect the human environment. The National Forest Management Act of 1976 set new standards of accountability.

In recent years, the theme of conservation has begun to sound a pertinent, familiar chord. Through a wide range of interest groups, the public has begun to look—almost disparagingly in some ways, altogether angrily in others—for the kind of leadership that will ensure sustainable resources for our country and brighter prospects for our collective future. How, though, can a natural resource leader provide certainty to a future that seems to grow more uncertain with each passing day?

To a much wider constituency, managers were at once obliged to invite the public to be involved in decision making, and they were to explain the probably consequences of proposed federal actions. And, as if that were not enough, any citizen, coalition, or interest group could gain access to the courts and challenge many actions that were planned. The requirements for public involvement and effective co-operation seemed suddenly to have engaged a long-silent population, radically changed the public face of the benevolent monarch, and practically eliminated the power of line officers in the field to make unilateral decisions. Local decisions became national conflicts.

All the while, those interest groups who stood to lose their benefits because of the demands of others pressured the Forest Service to cling to the old authoritarian leadership style and protect their traditional grazing, timber, and mining interests.

New Realities

The human environment today presents a complex set of challenges to the person who would lead—challenges that seem to demand an altogether new kind of leadership. It has become increasingly difficult to retain any vestiges of the model that was so successful in the past. Those management strategies and leadership styles are simply not effective in resolving today's issues.

The land manager now faces some troubling new questions. Could it be that our leadership dilemma is only an expression of our reluctance to accept and abide in a changing world? Are we really quite ready to understand that our old tools may not be sufficient to achieve the resource goals we seek? Or are we maybe just not putting enough thought and energy into trying to understand and operate in such a completely different environment? Or is the world getting so complex that nothing comes easy and, on the whole, we aren't doing so badly after all?

The federal natural resource manager faces formidable challenges— if, that is, he or she would be a leader who resolves problems and inspires others. The challenges seem immense and the obstacles almost insurmountable: Special-interest groups proliferate; Congress and other elected officials seem unremitting and excessive in their scrutiny; national policies seem to shift in the all-too-political winds of change. Whatever happened to the swift resolution of issues?

It was not easy to change from a model that so effectively curtailed the wasteful actions of grazers, miners, loggers, and encroachers; or to lead the way for forestry research and extension in the United States. Nor has it always been clear that a new approach to leadership is needed. Yet the old style no longer seems able to deal with today's controversies, and it probably cannot oblige the new, more stringent, legal requirements.

In this writer's view, opportunities for leadership abound, and indeed a great deal of leadership is emerging in the natural resource arena today. It is occurring precisely because of the human ability to react and respond to forces in the environment. It is occurring because our instincts would have us survive. But I suspect that this leadership could occur much more efficiently if the key elements in our common, human environment were better understood. If these elements were better known, leaders would be better able to anticipate and prepare for many of the hurdles and opportunities in their path. The institution of new systems and processes, or the improvement of existing ones, would greatly increase the efficiency of our efforts.

Managing America's natural resources today calls for a much more sophisticated form of leadership—one that the agency has yet to define and embrace. New procedures and legal requirements have dramatically increased the power of organized groups, and these groups have grown in sophistication as well as size. These days, the lobbyist and the marketing specialist are quite capable of influencing land management decisions and, to a surprising degree, public policy as well. This phenomenon, coupled with the easy access to the courts and a variety of new environmental laws, allows individual citizens to stop a federal action if they believe a prescribed process isn't being followed. Of course, this begs the question: Is there, indeed, any room left for leadership and decision making?

In fact, it is exactly this situation that calls for the most mature and comprehensive approach to leadership. Sharing power does not mean that professionalism or resource management skills must be compromised. It means, rather, that leadership skills must be more finely tuned to the requirements of today's social climate. With the right leadership, the political necessity of responding to diverse clienteles can be accomplished—while incorporating the best of science and technology. As P. J. Culhane (1981:xii) observes: "The astute and fully competent federal manager can use public involvement to obtain sounder decisions and wiser actions and even enhance his own position."

The Intermediation Model

With the dawning of a new social awareness of natural resource issues, the need for a new model of leadership began to emerge. *Intermediation* is the name I give to a model that offers a means of reaching settlement among divergent groups of citizens. With this model as a guide, the leader receives complaints and suggestions from the public and fashions a solution that may be partially acceptable to all.

Although this approach seems to work well enough when disputes can be settled by technical argument (and where there is little tolerance for conflict), it does not work at all where the values in dispute are societal and strongly rooted in tradition. And it does not work well where there is little basic understanding of the pertinent issues.

Leaders using this intermediation model have been quite capable of proposing solutions to conflicts—solutions, that is, which can be found somewhere between the polar extremes, where everyone is somewhat satisfied, and no one is entirely unhappy with the decisions reached. This model has produced a brand of leadership that can quell opposition but, more often than not, can never apply quite enough of what-it-takes to resolve the issues or arrive at the *right* decision.

As there was too much residual from the authoritarian model and not enough freedom (or courage) to share more power with the interested and affected publics, a better leadership model wasn't quickly found. There still seems to be confusion between leadership and official authority, both of which carry symbolic values and traditions that enhance the possibility of leadership but surely do not guarantee it.

I have seen situations where the official with authority was able to keep issues suppressed for considerable periods and give the appearance of leadership in action when in fact there were conflicts that needed to be addressed. In fact, early in my career it was considered a failure of leadership if a forest supervisor had a decision appealed to the next organizational level. In brief, then, I view intermediation as a bridge between the earlier authoritarian model and some model for the future that is yet to be fully defined but is beginning to emerge.

The Community-of-Interest Model

Effective leadership in the field of natural resource management is not only possible; it is rapidly becoming a critical necessity. If we are, indeed, to maintain sustainable ecosystems as well as social systems, it just may be that a *community-of-interest* or partnership model will provide the means.

The leadership challenge of our age is to transform the management environment from one based on the authority figure to one based on a community-of-interest theme. Although we face a major challenge in incorporating every one of the values of a society so diverse and complex as ours, the decisions we make must take into account all values. Certainly, we must be sensitive to changing social mores and, as a result of that sensitivity, we will need to develop new approaches to the decision-making process.

The major debates facing natural resource managers today are fundamentally social. We can no longer rely on science and law alone to settle the issues. Nor can we rely on a single authority figure to comprehend the labyrinth of views and values and set a course of action that can be supported by all. I think a better model may now be emerging, and I would like to discuss some principles here and give some examples.

First, a leader articulates a vision. To Gifford Pinchot, the vision was straightforward and unmistakable. This progenitor of modern forestry was able to describe his notion of resource conservation to a very receptive president who, in turn, took historic actions that have been upheld by Congress and the public for a hundred years. Today, the more enlightened public has assigned some altogether different values to natural resources and thus has increased the competition to influence decision makers. Pinchot's vision has become blurred with a variety of visions. Values change. As a consequence, our parameters for managing the natural resources have proliferated as never before. It is no longer enough to simply establish standards for protecting resources while supporting a desired level of production of goods and services from the land. The next generation of leadership faces the challenge of having to describe a vision of sustainable resource management. And this new vision must not only allow for productivity but also the maintenance and enhancement of vital, integrated ecosystems.

The second principle describes the kind of leadership that causes work to be done. That is, the objective of leadership is to cause those within the communities of interest to engage one another and resolve the various issues that concern them. A few additional definitions that are central to this community-of-interest model may be helpful (Reich 1990):

- *Disequilibrium* is caused by change that results from new decisions, emerging issues, or anything at all that leaves the status quo *off-guard*. Leadership is needed in situations where disequilibrium must be managed.
- The *authority figure*, traditionally, was one who could calm the winds of change and restore order.
- A *leader* is one who causes work to be done.
- *Work* is the facing, defining, and solving of problems in non-routine situations. The physicist's thoughts on work seem altogether pertinent: No work occurs unless potential energy is changed. In my view, no work occurs unless progress is made toward resolving a problem.
- *Work avoidance* is refusing to face the problems before us.
- *Leadership* occurs if one causes work to be done. That is, the leader makes progress toward resolving the problem and reaching a new state of equilibrium.

Just how does the community-of-interest model differ from what is going on in the world of resource management today? The main difference is in how our leaders view the public and how the public views the natural resource leader's role. There must be more sharing of power.

Leadership must emerge from the communities of interest—communities that must discover ways of working effectively with each other. As simple as it may seem, the key to success is to keep the focus of participants on resolving issues, not on avoiding work. Effective intervention by the various communities is essential. A leader from every community must be given the opportunity to make specific viewpoints or arguments known—and be willing to receive and respect the response of those who may not hold similar views. The work to be done may require prolonged disequilibrium—quite different from a timetable established by an authority figure.

Leaders representing the various interests and values must engage each other in ways that lead to agreement and result in a new state of equilibrium. A solution that is imposed by a third party—or does not satisfy the community of interest—isn't a solution at all. To the participants in such a dialogue, a forced solution represents only a distraction from the real work to be done—a postponement, as it were, of the time when the issues must be addressed.

The federal resource manager is more than a convener of the community of interests. He or she must also be an effective *intervenor* and actively participate in dialogue and interchange with the communities. The effective federal leader will also be an educator, a provider of data, a developer of viable alternatives, an interpreter of law and regulation, and a representative of those not able to participate in dialogue and intercommunity transactions. As if this were not enough, the effective natural resource leader must also serve as protector of nonhuman interests and future interests, as well. In short, the resource manager must ensure that the productive capacity of the land is neither exceeded nor abused.

This model of leadership can be effective at all organizational levels—from the ranger district to the forest service chief and his or her staff in Washington. At every decision level there are interested parties who are ready, willing, and able to engage in shared power and the spirit of decisive participation. In a community-of-interest forum, good decisions and effective leadership can be accomplished democratically. And, with the proper finesse, the federal land manager will not be seen as a person failing to exercise the proper authority.

There are risks in using this new model, since the leader does not control the schedule for making decisions. Prolonged periods of uncertainty may result, along with all the attendant criticisms and exasperations they might bring. Or there may be "assassination attempts" by those who don't like the direction a decision is headed. Here are two recent examples of the community-of-interest model in action.

Silver A comprehensive recovery plan would be necessary to restore 96,000 acres of forest that burned in the summer of 1987 on the Siskiyou National Forest in Oregon. Known as the Silver Fire, the affected area comprised exceptionally rugged terrain, and the involved lands and resources had long been the subject of contentious debate. Proposals to develop a system of forest roads that would afford access to the affected acreage had brought protest demonstrations, lawsuits, and special relief legislation over several years preceding the fire.

The forest supervisor convened interested and affected parties and challenged them to come forward with a recovery plan on which they could agree. In this setting the communities of interest (including the Forest Service) designed alternative strategies for rehabilitation of public resources using information and computers furnished by the forest supervisor.

By formulating a full range of alternative management strategies, this true *congress* of divergent interest groups was laying the groundwork for the decision maker in a way that had never been tried before. Facilitators were on hand to explain the particulars of sound resource management, to describe the applicable laws, and to help the participants define feasible management options. The proposals that resulted outlined, by varying degrees, how much timber might be salvaged, how much environmental protection would be given to which resources, different ways to protect wildlife and fisheries, which measures would be used to prevent soil erosion, and what combination of economic and social considerations should be given weight in the approved strategy.

The community of interests used state-of-the-art computer technology and a database that was constructed by the Forest Service to create various alternatives and displays, and each interest group was encouraged to defend and challenge its plan. This approach resulted in a knowledgeable public and, eventually, a solution that all parties, including the Forest Service, could support. Not only was the result a successful rehabilitation effort, but the contributing groups and individuals even monitored the effects of the aspects of recovery for which they were responsible. There were no appeals or lawsuits—a rare accomplishment in these days of protracted legal challenges.

The Gorge For over 100 miles east of Portland, Oregon, the Columbia River flows through some of the most spectacular landforms on the continent. Cited by a variety of advocates as a likely candidate for national park status or other federal regulation, this popular area became the target of national organizations who wanted to impose some kind of federal protection of its scenic beauty. Over 40,000 people live along the Columbia River Gorge, however, and about 61 percent of the acreage there is privately owned. There was no local support for any kind of outside control or protection.

The outcome seemed clear in 1983: Inevitably, some kind of control would be imposed on development in the gorge and, probably, one form of government or other would be making some very sweeping decisions. Who would do it? How long would it take? And would the locals have any influence on shaping the controls?

A Forest Service person was assigned the task of working with the communities of interest, both within and outside the gorge, to see if community leaders could agree on some principles—*if* controls were imposed on development.

It took three years to get the communities of interest to the point where they were willing to put forward ideas they were willing to live with or talk about. With the Forest Service as the catalyst, networks were formed, information was packaged and distributed, forums for debate and issue analysis were arranged, and dialogue between leaders was facilitated.

In 1987 legislation was introduced in Congress to make this site a national scenic area. And within six months—in a single session of Congress and despite a very conservative administration on such measures—a bill was passed by legislators and signed by the president. It called for further state legislation that would set up a bistate commission and complex zoning guidelines, all accomplished within a short time.

The comprehensive work by the communities of interest prior to the introduction of legislation and the subsequent debates further laid the groundwork for successful implementation of the complex legislation. The same communities-of-interest model would be used to design the detailed planning, zoning, and administration of the area.

Processes, Networks, and Beyond These are two examples in which leadership occurred over a short period of time—one to three years. Many changes sought by leaders take much more time and public debate. Demands and rewards for leaders in the public natural resource arena don't mesh well with issues that take a long time to resolve. Since most leaders don't stay engaged in an issue from beginning to end, leadership is shared within the agency on a single issue.

Leadership today is to a large degree processes and networks. The issues are too technical or multifaceted for a single leader to resolve. Further, resolving the problems requires the skills and participation of a much wider audience than the leader's own organization—especially true for the managers of public natural resources.

Sometimes the political and public pressure on both sides of an issue is so strong and entrenched that an agency leader cannot resolve it—even Congress itself cannot come to grips with such issues and continues to deal with them incrementally. Examples are below-cost timber sales, clearcuttings, user fees, old growth, and private forest-land regulation. Frequent changes in public policy perpetuate the hope of all parties that their side will prevail if only they can prevent resolution until their stars are aligned. Just enough victories result from this strategy that no one is motivated to reach resolution without a crisis.

The leadership style that seems to work in this situation at the national level (Washington, D.C.) is one that creates an extensive network with all interested parties—plus a leader who knows what he or she wants, understands the ever-shifting political winds, and is able to communicate with key players on the Hill, within the administration, and with leaders in interest groups. The leader has a sixth sense for daylight (an opportunity that typically doesn't stay open long) and knows how to run for daylight with fire cover from friends. Making progress on long-standing issues in Washington takes extraordinary patience and persistence. No is never a final no in Washington. Yes is hardly ever an unequivocal yes either.

Networking is essential to government leadership and to the leader's success and survival. No single person can tower over the business and complexity of today's work and project the clarity and direction that will compel many to follow. They need networks made up of advocacy groups, editorial boards, association leaders, political leaders, intellectuals, and others.

NEW TERRITORY AHEAD

To be a leader, one must have followers. Today the followers within the Forest Service are quite different from what leaders found in the early years. As described by Herbert Kaufman in *The Forest Ranger*, the old managers were of like mind, shared similar values, came from similar backgrounds, and went to the same few forestry schools. They were fiercely loyal to the organization.

Today, there are over a hundred disciplines in the Forest Service. Employees come from dramatically different backgrounds and represent a wide range of values and have much less loyalty to the organization or its leaders. Effective leadership must deal with this new population if it is to be viewed as capable of solving their problems or achieving their goals. Today's leader must perceive the needs and moods of employees throughout the ranks of the four levels of administration to gain their trust.

"Our . . . governmental processes, functioning at their best, are designed not to impose arbitrary solutions but to preside over the peaceable competition of conflicting interests, and to reconcile those interests within the framework of our shared purposes," says John W. Gardner in *On Leadership* (1990:102). It isn't that the Forest Service has been imposing onerous and arbitrary solutions on the public. Rather, the emergence of new values and demands has made it imperative that we seek collaborative ways to resolve conflicts. Gardner calls for pulling together "networks of responsibility." My term, "communities of interest," is a similar concept. The Forest Service leader not only convenes and maintains the various interests, but also leads them to a resolution and takes the product of that resolution and moves forward with action programs.

Leadership in government will become more difficult as competition between resource use and conservation becomes more intense. The stern authoritarian style will not be successful in resolving issues or projecting a vision toward which our publics are willing to commit.

Nor can leadership succeed by hanging onto the old model while experimenting with new techniques and maintaining the hope that the world will return to the good old days. The tendency to blame other forces—these new laws, Congress, the press—for failure to resolve today's issues simply compounds the problems and distracts from the need to prepare for tomorrow's world. More energy has to be put into dealing with change and planning for the future than is put into strategies for defending today's actions and yesterday's deeds. Our everyday world is clearly in transition.

In the part of the government I'm in, leadership must be reexamined in the context of this world in transition. It should be redefined—with the realization that power has to be shared. We operate in a very enlightened society. We are truly a community of interest. The current environment cannot be transformed to the one in Pinchot's time. There are too many diverse aspects of our society, and indeed the science of forestry no longer permits the old leadership models to work.

The time is ripe to forge some new dimensions in our thinking about leadership in government. Never before have we had such a high level of public interest and understanding of our natural resources. Nor have we had such a mix of talent and enthusiasm within the ranks of the Forest Service to respond to scientific and managerial challenges. These two elements make for an overwhelming resource ready to be called upon.

The Forest Service can chart new territory by endorsing a *community-of-interest* leadership philosophy and assigning priority to fleshing out the concepts so they can be taught and rewarded. The agency is receptive to community leadership. The next steps shouldn't be too difficult. Let's hope our children will look back and agree with the words of the Chinese philosopher Lao-Tzu: "When the best leader's work is done, the people will say 'we did it ourselves.' "

REFERENCES

Culhane, P. J. 1981. *Public Land Politics*. Baltimore: Johns Hopkins University Press.

Frome, M. 1984. *The Forest Service*. 2nd ed. Boulder, CO: Westview Press.

Gardner, J. W. 1990. *On Leadership*. New York: Free Press.

Kaufman, H. 1960. *The Forest Ranger*. Baltimore: Johns Hopkins University Press.

Owen, H. 1990. *Leadership Is*. Potomac, MD: Abbott Publishing.

Pinchot, G. 1987. *Breaking New Ground*. Washington, DC: Island Press.

Reich, R. B. (ed.) 1990. *The Power of Public Ideas*. Cambridge, MA: Harvard University Press.

Sample, V. A. 1991. *Land Stewardship in the Next Era of Conservation*. Milford, PA: Grey Towers Press.

Wilkinson, C. F., and H. M. Anderson. 1985. *Oregon Law Review* 64 (1–2):246–260.

Wondolleck, J. 1991. "Natural Resource Management in the 1990's and Beyond: Problems and Opportunities." Unpublished paper prepared for the Pinchot Institute for Conservation Studies.

11 International Leadership

Ralph C. Schmidt

IN 1969 I WENT TO COLOMBIA as a Peace Corps volunteer with the National Agrarian Reform Agency to work with subsistence farmers in a tropical moist forest area. This sparked a lifetime interest in tropical forests and the people who live in and around them. I studied at Yale F&ES and spent eight years in Puerto Rico, first at the Institute of Tropical Forestry and later as head of the Commonwealth Forest Service. I worked at FAO for four years on management of natural forests, and I am now UNDP senior program advisor on forests and biodiversity. I have worked on tropical forest issues in more than thirty countries in Latin America, Africa, and Asia.

WHERE HAVE ALL THE LEADERS GONE?

Leadership is often hard to define, but you know it when you see it. Or in the case of international forestry in developing countries, you know it isn't there when you don't see it. In this chapter I want to review a number of important events and programs designed to address our critical international forestry problems. Specifically I want to trace the history of the Tropical Forestry Action Plans, the Forest Convention, and the Bush administration's Forests for the Future initiative to illustrate the complex world of international leadership. I will not, for the most part, focus on the personalities involved and their impact on events. Although they definitely are significant throughout the events described in this chapter, I don't believe personal qualities are the determining factor. Several figures from North and South possess the

185

normal qualifications for leadership, yet no leader has yet emerged. I believe, and will show by example, this is because the institutional structural environment simply does not permit it.

Leadership in the intergovernmental arena requires a worldview, not a nationalistic or regional perspective. This means that leadership in one's own region on the hard issues may be indispensable for intergovernmental leadership. Agriculture subsidies in Europe make it very difficult for the Third World farmer to compete, for example, perpetuating the poverty that leads to population explosion and ecosystem degradation. An EEC leader who could sell the slogan "Save the Rain Forest, Eliminate Crop Subsidies at Home" would be in a position to lead in international forums. However, a leader has not yet arisen who can persuade his or her own followers to forgo immediate nationalistic needs in order to benefit a collective world vision.

Apart from the hard task of promoting a worldview, to say nothing of insufficient institutional structures, leadership in international forestry is especially difficult for a number of important reasons. Most often issues involve many organizations and countries with often conflicting objectives and interests. Currently huge deficiencies exist both in human resources and basic information about people and resources. The balance between political sovereignty and donor assistance is always fragile. And related to all attempts to protect forests are fundamental social issues of poverty, education, health care, and landownership. Finally, the scope, urgency, and geographic scale of natural resource problems pose special challenges to international leaders. The implications of these factors for international leadership will be illustrated throughout this chapter.

WORLD LEADERS ON FORESTRY ISSUES

Tropical forest destruction, with a chunk the size of Nebraska disappearing permanently every year, has for the first time ever gotten world political leaders involved in forestry issues. The tropical forest is the scene of the greatest destruction of the earth's biodiversity. The impact is *present*, not projected, and is even more irreversible than the ozone destruction and rapid climate change that seem imminent.

Thus it was not entirely surprising, but still unprecedented, when a summit meeting of the seven major industrial powers—the G-7 in

Houston in the summer of 1990—called for an international forest convention and urged revamping the Tropical Forest Action Plan (TFAP). Prior to this summit, François Mitterrand had organized a high-profile international meeting on forests and Margaret Thatcher and Helmut Kohl had called for at least a doubling of their countries' international assistance for forestry. More than two years after the summit, we have no forest convention and the renewal of the TFAP has hardly taken the direction the industrialized world leaders had hoped. An analysis of what happened will provide a way to examine the role of leadership, or its absence, in international forestry matters.

THE EARLY TFAP

The TFAP was one of the most exciting things ever to get started on the international forestry front. It was an attempt at leadership generated by a few figures within the many organizations dealing with international forestry. In the early 1980s the Food and Agriculture Organization (FAO) of the United Nations published country-by-country reports showing that 11 million hectares of forest in developing countries were being converted to other uses every year. At that time (1983) about $300 to $400 million of international assistance was dedicated to forestry (meaning conservation, community forestry, sustainable management, reforestation, and land-use planning, not just silviculture and harvesting). This is less than the budget of New York City's fire department and not very much when spread among more than a hundred countries and three billion people. Each organization and donor country had their own program and ran it their own way. The list may be tedious but shows the complexity of the situation: the World Bank, the Africa, Asia, and Interamerican Development Bank, US AID, Canada, Sweden, France, Great Britain, Germany, Japan, Finland, the Netherlands, Belgium, Switzerland, Norway, Denmark, Spain, and the UN Development Program (UNDP) and FAO are the major actors. Not all of these players operated in all countries, but many, often a dozen, might be at work in any one developing country.

The resulting chaos was inevitable. Analysts in some of these organizations—plus very significant nongovernment organizations (NGOs) such as the World Resources Institute (WRI) in Washington and the International Institute for Environment and Development

(IIED) in London—began to think there might be a better way. The idea was to create a framework under which all the donors would operate: the TFAP. Within this general framework each participating developing country would develop its own program, "The National Forest Action Plan." Developing countries would declare their interest; donors would consult to field one team with general participation; a common plan would be drawn up with the countries that everyone could fund together. The objective was to promote international cooperation for development and conservation of tropical forests.

Significantly, most of this thinking and design was done by foresters. Of course higher-ups made the big money decisions, but in the early 1980s international foresters were left to run their own shops without interference or interest from their superiors. In those days there were lots of conferences and discussion about leadership or followership within the profession. This situation has now completely changed in an environment where heads of state and major international organizations are directly interested in forest programs.

What went wrong with the TFAP? The situation up to 1990 is well documented in WRI's review, *Taking Stock*, written by Robert Winterbottom. He found that an elegant plan drawn up by foreign consultants providing fundable projects for interested organizations did not have much impact on resource degradation and destruction or on the way business was conducted and life was lived in developing countries. Country plans might contain fifty well-presented and much-needed projects. The problem was that those same countries did not have even ten people who could manage these multimillion-dollar projects. Moreover, ambitious plans were drawn up when the information base was not adequate to define the true situation. Thus the developing countries entered into the plan with the prospect of more donor assistance but without truly owning or being committed to the national plans. Back to the drawing board.

THE NATURE OF FAO

There was another key complication in the implementation of the TFAP. The lead agency for world forestry within the UN system is FAO. Never mind that UNDP funds most of FAO's field projects or that the 1.5 percent of World Bank loans devoted to forestry is almost twenty times greater than FAO's annual forestry budget of about $12 million. As lead agency for world forestry, FAO's intergovernmental committees, where governments' representatives direct its work, were telling it in late 1983 to start a major new program for tropical forestry. At about the same time WRI, World Bank, and UNDP were authoring *Tropical Forests: A Call for Action.* Those involved still differ on who started first and who led whom.

The result was an agreement in 1985 that all would join forces to support one program and that FAO would take the lead in implementing TFAP. Any alternative was really unthinkable for FAO as the lead organization for forestry. FAO has fifty experienced foresters from around the world at its headquarters and hundreds in the field. There are things it can do better than any other organization. There are things it is not the best at doing because of its structure, however, things that are essential for effective TFAP implementation.

FAO's presence in forest field projects in a developing country depends on the government telling donors that it wants FAO involved in the project's execution. This means that operatives can hardly criticize the government or use their persuasive powers for change. After all, when deforestation is rampant and poverty pervasive, change is what TFAP must be about. This arrangement also means that international, and possibly national, NGOs that might get involved in project execution are direct competitors for funds. This provides two compelling reasons for FAO to keep NGOs at arm's length within the TFAP. Yet in virtually all developing countries, NGOs are by far the most effective organizations in working with people at the village level for positive change.

There is no question that if we could figure out how to go about it, seriously confronting the deforestation crisis in developing countries would take considerably more financial resources than are now deployed. The developing countries are especially convinced on this point. But FAO is in a position of soliciting, not providing, funding to developing countries. This means that any resource mobilization activity is suspect due to the element of self-interest. If a donor has $50 million to invest in a developing country and approaches other donors suggesting that they invest together concentrating on different subprograms, this is more likely to be well received than an organization asking donors for $50 million that it wants to spend for them.

FAO has another structural problem in dealing with forests that we will return to later: It is largely governed by the agricultural ministers of the world. Thus its budget for forests represents only 4 percent of its resources, even though its largest donors have consistently called for a greater share for forestry. Entrusting world forest leadership, as embodied in the TFAP, to FAO becomes less promising when forestry places so low in total FAO funding.

Yet blaming the TFAP's shortcomings on FAO alone is an oversimplification. Most of the long list of organizations involved in international forestry in developing countries have continued to do their own thing, and this includes their activities within the framework of TFAP. Some of the shortcomings of FAO taking the lead in tropical forestry were probably predictable, but everyone was making the same mistakes—such as overreliance on expatriate expertise—and a lot was learned in the first five years about how to tackle these problems. Since top decision makers had never before taken the forest situation seriously, the learning curve was particularly steep during these years. It will probably stay that way for some time to come.

THE INDEPENDENT REVIEW

By 1990 NGOs were directing strident criticism at the TFAP, considerable political pressure was brought to bear in the donor countries, and it was clear to all involved that TFAP was in trouble. FAO was advised by its donors, by UNDP (a chief provider of field project funding), and by the World Bank (the largest source of funding for international forestry) that a high-level independent review should be undertaken. To its credit FAO accepted this task and appointed three distinguished independent leaders who published their conclusion in June 1990 (very interesting reading for those wishing to delve further).

There were several recommendations on how things should be done in the developing countries that might fall into the category of easier said than done but which have come to be generally accepted. These focused on more leadership by developing countries and a less donor-driven process. There also was a call for a steering committee of interested parties (bilateral donors, developing countries, NGOs, the World Bank, UNDP) that would not be within the formal structure of FAO. And there was a call for a forest convention just a month before the Houston Summit statement mentioned earlier.

How did the independent steering committee's recommendation go over with FAO? Perhaps the reader can guess. But a little information on UN governing bodies is necessary if we are to understand the reaction and the context for any leadership to be exerted within the intergovernmental system.

UN GOVERNING BODIES

The committees and governing councils of FAO and all UN organizations are made up of representatives of the member states. In theory the organizations have no power of their own, only that which emanates from these meetings. This arrangement produces several characteristics:

- The meetings are inherently time-consuming and inefficient because so many countries have the right to speak and there is no superior control. Leadership requires great patience and tact.
- Many of the representatives, especially those from developing countries, spend their tours of duty at the headquarters of their assigned organizations. The Ambassadorial Syndrome then kicks in—that is, one tends to identify more with the organization than with one's own national interests. This is especially so when the organization's interest is clearer and more urgent than national interest. Leadership may depend on extensive personal contacts.
- The organization can muster experienced and skilled professionals for the secretariats of these meetings. Although they are directed by member states, these secretariats can have a great influence over the proceedings and conclusions of the meetings. Leadership requires thorough knowledge and perhaps financial influence over the organization involved.
- Alliances between blocs of countries tend to form according to strategic global interests. During the cold war this was East-West; now it is North-South. The developing countries are highly loyal to these alliances and may act against their better interests on particular issues in order to maintain strategic alliances. Leadership requires a profound understanding of strategic interests and their impact on specific issues (which is often the exact opposite of what one might expect).

When the independent review of TFAP was released, a number of complex reactions were set off around the world. First the heads of state of the seven most economically powerful countries of the world stated in a brief communiqué that they wanted a forest convention and a revamped TFAP. About this time someone influential convinced the president of the World Bank that its record on forests needed improvement. At $200 million per year, forest-related loans comprised only 1 percent of the portfolio. (World Bank governance is completely different from the UN: Voting rights are proportionate to contributed funds, not one country one vote.)

One can only speculate on the bank's internal considerations. In any case, this was an international program on forests in need of a substantial overhaul. The bank needed to improve and increase its lending program in forestry. Forestry was rising to the top of the international agenda, and the organization exercising leadership might greatly increase its stature and funding in the near future. The temptation to be the white knight riding to the rescue must have been overwhelming. It is known that the World Bank urged the top leadership of FAO to consider real changes in the TFAP. One obvious change, perhaps not stated directly, was a steering committee where the World Bank and others would wield significant influence.

UNDP—FAO's direct partner in field programs on forestry—perhaps viewed the situation similarly, but through a slightly different lens. UNDP had not been criticized as severely as the World Bank for "bankrolling environmental disasters," but perhaps it saw the writing on the wall. Located right next to the Secretariat of the UN itself, the Brundtland World Commission on Environment and Development was greatly influencing UNDP's thinking. Environment and development were linked, but UNDP had traditionally concentrated on development, and the UN Environment Program was set up for international monitoring and reporting, not field projects. UNDP needed to begin serious work on environmental programs as quickly as possible. A more substantial role in TFAP was one obvious way to do this.

The position of the World Resources Institute was an especially interesting case. In a way WRI had spurred the original action in forestry and had first blown the whistle when serious problems with some of the national processes had become apparent. WRI's continuing involvement with what was seen as a failed program of UN vested interests was leading to bad press within the environmental NGO community. WRI was being accused of that most dreadful of all sins: selling out. Despite its desire for influence and positive change, WRI announced after the March 1991 meeting on TFAP that it would no longer be a cosponsor. This was clearly meant to distance WRI from the program.

The bilateral donor governments, especially in the United States, Canada, the Netherlands, Great Britain, and Germany, were in trouble with politically powerful environmental groups for supporting TFAP. They were being accused of contributing to rather than slowing down deforestation and needed a substantial change in the program to take home. The developing countries, as usual, were sandbagged. For five years they had been urged to join in the TFAP process and promised more donor support if they did. Suddenly it appeared that the donors, and their NGOs, were abandoning the program.

These cross-currents began to make real waves at the meeting of the FAO Committee on Forestry in September 1990. This normally placid and diplomatic meeting was fraught with charges and countercharges on FAO's handling of the TFAP and the review. Finally, it was decided to ask FAO to form a group with the World Bank, UNDP, and WRI in order to set new objectives and governance mechanisms for TFAP. This led to a meeting two months later where these four agreed to write a paper together to be discussed at a meeting of six developing countries, six donors, six NGOs, and six agencies. Tremendous importance was attached to this meeting, and all four organizations were represented at a top management level.

THE CONSULTATIVE GROUP ON TROPICAL FORESTS

After considerable jockeying on drafts and invitees, the meeting was held in March 1991, new objectives were drafted with much greater emphasis on protection of forests and empowering indigenous people, and an independent informal Consultative Group was recommended. World Bank, FAO, and UNDP then met to put together a concrete proposal for the Consultant Group that was accepted by all three. Almost one year after the review of TFAP had been published, and after eight months of constant negotiations, FAO announced that this informal group must be approved by its council.

What was FAO's concern here? It can only be assumed that the main concern was a loss of control and leadership over the TFAP that might result in a loss of prestige and perhaps funding for field programs. In truth, a seriously polarized North-South debate on forests had been brewing. Based on a charitable or a cynical view of FAO's leadership, one can say that the organization wished to solicit and respect the views of developing countries—or that it saw an opportunity to deflect the intrusive initiative of the World Bank and UNDP by taking advantage of the developing countries' views on forests.

THE EARTH SUMMIT

The UN Conference on Environment and Development (Earth Summit) made the front page of the *New York Times* ten days in a row when it was held in Rio in June 1992. The first meeting to prepare for the conference was held in Nairobi in August 1990. These meetings were similar to the intergovernmental gatherings that have been described; all countries can talk on all issues. The significant event for forestry at the first "Prepcom" was that FAO arrived with a proposal to lead and service the negotiations for a forest convention. (As mentioned earlier, the G-7 heads of state had called for this two months before.) Again one may conclude that FAO was eager to serve its member states in this capacity—or that it was eager to maintain a lead role in all forest matters and perhaps even deflect a bit of attention from all the criticism about the TFAP.

But the Prepcom held real surprises for many on forest issues. There was strong opposition to a forest convention from developing countries headed and catalyzed by Malaysia. FAO quickly withdrew its offer to lead negotiations on a forest convention. It is quite possible that some who favored a convention in principle breathed a sigh of relief.

THE FOREST CONVENTION

The cause of the opposition to the forest convention remains somewhat speculative. Malaysia's outstanding leadership in opposing the convention has been a principal element. They exerted this leadership through tried and true methods. They did their homework, often through the night, on the endless drafts and proposals, studying each one carefully and formulating well-defended positions. They systematically canvassed and consulted with their colleagues from developing countries, convincing them and leading them so that theirs was always a consolidated Southern position. They were fearless and tireless in the debates and impervious to peer pressure to take the path of least resistance now and then.

These were the tactics of their leadership—to be sure a leadership opposing and not promoting change. Malaysia's reasoning against the forest convention may have run something like this. They perceive that there is international economic competition that is close to warfare; they believe, as well, that the rich countries wish to exploit and dominate the poor countries by rigging the system in their favor. (With present hard currency net annual transfers of $50 billion from poor countries to rich ones, it is not hard to see why they might reach this conclusion.) Moreover, most of the global toxic waste, as well as water and atmospheric pollution, including greenhouse gases, has been produced by the industrial nations. Now there is worry about the global environment, and the rich countries want to focus attention on the one area where poor countries would have to take action to conserve the world environment: tropical forests. Thereby the rich nations avoid taking action to regulate their own economies and instead suppress economic activity in developing countries and hence maintain their dominance.

Malaysia has the most qualified national cadre of tropical foresters anywhere, and its export earnings from forest products are $3 billion per year. We have seen that $1.3 billion was the total, for all countries, of international assistance for forestry in 1991. So it is not hard to see where Malaysia's bread is buttered. No assistance program could possibly approach the sums currently generated by forest exploitation.

There was another twist to the forest-related negotiations during the two-year process of the Earth Summit. Tropical forests emerged as the one thing developing countries had that industrialized countries were deeply concerned about. Thus forest agreements, or leadership for them, could not stand on their own merits. They were held as a negotiating chip by developing countries for progress on issues like trade, debt, and international economic relations. Furthermore, the correct perception that industrialized countries were deeply concerned about tropical forests revived serious apprehensions in the South concerning possible efforts by rich countries to undermine the sovereignty of developing countries over their resources. These fears revive very understandable sensitivities regarding colonial domination.

The convention issue was not completely stonewalled by the South. Negotiations proceeded through all the subsequent meetings, finally resulting in "A Non-Legally-Binding Authoritative Statement of Principles for a Global Consensus on the Management, Conservation, and Sustainable Development of All Types of Forests." The title speaks for itself. Many believe that a forest convention is in the future, though few predict when. A forest convention makes sense when you consider the importance of the issue for rich countries, their willingness to invest, and the importance of cooperative assistance to the developing countries.

DEFLECTION OF THE REVAMPED TFAP

The general point here is that forest convention discussions were occurring simultaneously, but in different forums, with the process of attempted reform of TFAP. Some of the figures involved were the same; many were not. Under normal circumstances, recommendations on how to manage TFAP put forward by FAO, World Bank, and UNDP would have been accepted without much questioning from governments. But the high-profile, pivotal position of forests in the overall Earth Summit negotiations meant that governments—again lead by Malaysia though Brazil, Indonesia, and India also were critical—did question the proposed reforms. The key concern was whether World Bank, UNDP, and the donors were trying to assume much greater control over international forest policy and whether conservation NGOs (mostly Northern) would be placed on an equal footing to criticize governments.

In June 1991 the FAO Council refused to accept an independent group on tropical forests; all donor countries spoke in favor and several developing countries spoke against. Subgroups were set up to discuss the situation, and these meetings continued until September 1992, when most of the donor countries, simply to end the saga, accepted the developing countries' position that the group be set within FAO. Thus it appears that the reform of TFAP's governance has led to no significant changes.

FORESTS FOR THE FUTURE

Another important and related story concerns President Bush's Earth Summit proposal: Forests for the Future. From the public information on this initiative, several conclusions may be drawn.

Having dehorned the Climate Convention and having refused to sign the Biodiversity Convention, the United States clearly needed something positive to say. The forests initiative was it. That forests were the one area where the president would promise to find new money and urge other donors to do so also speaks for the universal support the issue can generate in the country. One is reminded of Bill Clinton mentioning tropical rain forests in the New Hampshire primary debate.

Two contrasting views may have validity regarding the sincerity and usefulness of the proposal generally. When the president's announcement was made, American voters were not aware that two years of negotiations on a convention as well as a new framework for international cooperation for tropical forests had essentially failed. Thus the initiative was not responding to, but was in fact running counter to, the thrust of the conference. It had no chance of uniting the international community on the issue in any real way.

Conversely, the offer of additional assistance through bilateral channels would be accepted by many developing countries, and one could certainly argue that the multilateral—that is, the UN—system had failed so completely for so long that the only option was to get on with the job directly. One might say that the initiative is positive in its increase of funding but negative in that it seems to neglect the remaining problem of reaching international consensus on forest stewardship. After all, the TFAP came about because the bilateral system of operating parallel programs in developing countries was not sufficiently articulated and unified.

THE FIGHT AHEAD

Perhaps this chapter seems to have concentrated unduly on the TFAP and the Consultative Group to manage it. The real work in forestry goes on in the field and, increasingly, with the local communities involved. Ironically, developing countries, donors, governments, and NGOs alike are agreed upon this. But a thousand points of light of good local projects can't really hold back the enormous surge in degradation and impoverishment of natural resources. Perhaps nothing will until people have access to decent health care, education, and sustainable livelihoods. In any case, comprehensive national programs to sustain natural resources are indispensable, and these must be continuously put together and recast based on broad consultation and participation with all of the interested actors.

There appears to be no alternative to a TFAP kind of process in developing countries if the negative trends of deforestation and forest degradation are to be addressed—whether the action is carried out under the TFAP label or not. An independent, informal, but high-level group to monitor the success of the programs from all viewpoints is absolutely key to providing universal and impartial leadership to this critical process. At this point in time, however, this arrangement is not acceptable to FAO and its leaders.

FAO is the lead intergovernmental agency for forestry, and recent experience suggest that there is a crisis of leadership. Can useful conclusions be drawn from this? Ralph Roberts, Stan Pringle, and George Nagle, three distinguished international foresters, albeit all from North America, published a paper on leadership in world forestry in September 1991. They point out that FAO has had excellent staff, but the contributions to leadership they are capable of have not been realized because of fundamental structural problems in the organization.

The most serious of these problems is the historic conflict of interest in the governing bodies, which are controlled by agriculture ministers and functionaries who are rightly concerned with agricultural issues. Forest-sector priorities have little prominence and forestry budgets are hard to secure. The forestry share of the FAO budget peaked in 1956 with 9.1 percent of the total. By 1984 it had declined to 4 percent. The 1992–1993 budget proposes 4.5 percent. This despite continuous calls from donors for greater funding for forestry programs. The FAO's regular $12 million per year forestry budget would indicate that the world doesn't give much of a damn about forestry leadership. Many of the other facts laid out in this chapter belie that conclusion.

Roberts and colleagues call for a thorough feasibility study for a World Forest Organization. This could be a UN organization or an international organization with an innovative governance mechanism such as the Consultative Group for International Agricultural Research (CGIAR) of the World Conservation Union (IUCN). Only six countries in the world have more than 100 million hectares of forest, and they happen to be split evenly North and South: Brazil, Canada, Indonesia, Russia, the United States, and Zaire. Together they account for two-thirds of the world's forests. One wonders what would happen if these six united in a head-of-state initiative to invite other countries to join in establishing a World Forest Organization.

One thing is certain: If such a move were taken, a majority of governments represented in the intergovernmental organizations concerned with forestry (FAO, ITTO, UNEP, IUCN, UNIDO, UNESCO, WFP, UNDP, the banks) would have to get their act together to clarify and align the fuzzy and conflictive mandates of different organizations. Then and only then will world forestry leadership emerge. And we know we only have a few years at most if the vast forest areas present throughout human history are to remain.

REFERENCES

FAO. 1991. *TFAP Operational Principles*. Executive Summary. Rome: FAO.

International Task Force Staff. 1985. *Tropical Forests: A Call for Action*. Washington, DC: World Resources Institute.

Multi-Donor Trust Fund Project. 1992. *Report of the Joint Evaluation Mission and FAO's Comments*. Project in support of the Tropical Forest Action Plan.

Roberts, R. W. et al. 1991. *World Forestry Leadership*. Discussion paper. Toronto: Canadian International Development Agency.

Tropical Forestry Action Plan. 1990. *Report of the Independent Review*. Kuala Lumpur: TFAP.

Winterbottom, R. 1990. *Taking Stock: The Tropical Forestry Action Plan After Five Years*. Washington, DC: World Resources Institute.

12 Local Voluntary Organizations

■■

James J. Espy, Jr.

EARLY IN MY SENIOR YEAR OF COLLEGE I recognized that a career in the environmental field was suited to my interests, temperament, and specific geographic addiction. I enjoyed the outdoors, wanted to work in a small organization, and, most important, wished to stay right where I was upon completing college—in Maine. Contrary to the popular wisdom that one should follow a career wherever it may lead (especially at age twenty-two), I had no intention of leaving Maine even if that meant certain doors would be closed to me.

Within six months of finishing school, I was headed to work in Washington, D.C., for one of the largest environmental consulting firms in the country. So much for well-laid career plans! It would be six years before I returned to Maine and began a full-time position with a small, nonprofit conservation organization.

The career path I have followed is probably like that of many others in the environmental field—circuitous (at times tortuous) but, like a maze, logical when viewed from above. Having spent considerable time during my childhood hunting, fishing, and canoeing, I developed a keen interest in the natural world. The environmental professionals I met and studied under in college helped me envision the type of position I someday hoped to hold. A near-infatuation with the landscape and culture of Maine provided a focus for my growing environmental commitment.

Before leaving Maine, I spent the summer working as an intern with the Maine Bureau of Parks and Recreation under the auspices of the Massachusetts Audubon Society's Environmental Intern Program (now known as the Environmental Careers Organization, Inc.). I was

200

responsible for conducting an economic impact study of three state parks.

The following year in Washington, D.C., I spent as a gofer for several senior environmental planners and project leaders. Fortunately, my superiors had tired of monitoring events on Capitol Hill and handed me the task of attending committee hearings on environmental and energy legislation: a crash course in civics. I then moved to corporate headquarters in Concord, Massachusetts, and received a new title, associate planner. Here again I assisted senior planners—this time preparing environmental assessments and impact statements for proposed industrial facilities. The work was interesting but I knew that I had not yet found my niche.

Working as a consultant helped me recognize that I would need more education to expand my horizons within the environmental field. I also realized through the experience that I was not cut out for a career in science or research. I became hooked on the idea of working in a managerial or policy role with a nonprofit group and began searching for graduate programs that would prepare me for such a position. Yale University offered a joint master's program through its School of Organization and Management and School of Forestry and Environmental Studies. I was accepted none too soon, it turned out, as the recession of the early 1980s was taking a toll on environmental consultants, myself included.

During the two summers in graduate school, I was able to arrange internships with Maine Coast Heritage Trust (MCHT) and the Natural Resources Council of Maine (NRCM). Working first in land conservation and then in environmental advocacy, I experienced the wide spectrum of "environmentalism" in Maine. MCHT worked behind the scenes helping landowners to conserve important land resources. NRCM, on the other hand, was out front advocating an environmental agenda in the policymaking arena on a wide variety of issues. Through these two wonderful apprenticeships, I learned a great deal about my personal strengths, weaknesses, interests, and styles of professional interaction. I learned that the tangible rewards of protecting land inspired me more than any other endeavor ever had. Although I admired those who could sit in the advocacy hot seat, I learned that the nonconfrontational and less controversial nature of land protection better suited my disposition. I preferred quiet negotiating to public wrangling.

Upon graduation, luck had it that the associate director position at MCHT was available and I was chosen for the job. Three years later, I was promoted to my current post as president—the chief staff position for the organization.

MAINE COAST HERITAGE TRUST

Maine Coast Heritage Trust is a private, nonprofit corporation dedicated to protecting land of scenic, ecological, and cultural significance throughout the state of Maine. Since its formation in 1970, MCHT has assisted landowners, local land conservation groups, and government agencies at the federal, state, and municipal levels to conserve roughly 50,000 acres of land.

The mission of MCHT is far-reaching: "to protect land that is essential to the character of Maine, its coastline and islands in particular." MCHT involves itself in a broad range of land protection projects: Farmland, working harbors, wildlife habitat, recreational lands, scenic waterways, old-growth forests, and sensitive ecological areas are all resources MCHT seeks to conserve.

MCHT has two primary programs—Land Protection Services and Land Trust Assistance. Through its Land Protection Services program, MCHT offers assistance to landowners who are interested in voluntarily conserving properties they own. To accomplish its goals, MCHT relies heavily on gifts of conservation easements from landowners. MCHT staff work directly with property owners to provide guidance in evaluating various conservation options, developing conservation plans for their properties, sorting out the legal and tax implications associated with land protection, and drafting conservation easements. Apart from facilitating gifts of land and conservation easements, MCHT occasionally purchases threatened properties and helps government agencies to acquire new public lands.

The Land Trust Assistance program of MCHT was formally established in 1987 to provide technical assistance and training to local land trust organizations throughout Maine. There are currently seventy-three independent local land trusts in Maine, each incorporated as a tax-exempt corporation (501(c)3). Most are all-volunteer groups operating with minimal budgets. MCHT offers professional help to existing and prospective land trusts and often works in partnership with them to protect important land in their regions.

MCHT has a staff of eleven operating from two offices. It is governed by a nineteen-member board of directors and a fifteen-member advisory council. MCHT has been blessed with an exceptionally able and active board of directors. Many of its directors have served the organization since its formation twenty-one years ago. Most directors and council members function as fundraisers as well as policymakers.

The Trust is funded almost entirely through private contributions and foundation grants; individual donations comprise nearly three-fourths of annual operating revenues. The operating budget for MCHT in 1991 was approximately $550,000.

As president of MCHT, I am one leader among many both inside and outside the organization. The presidency is the most visible and recognizable leadership post, but the trust is led at various levels by numerous persons. In terms of hierarchy, the board of directors, headed by the chairman, truly leads the organization. MCHT's board is the only body empowered to make decisions concerning the Trust's direction.

Of course, staff actually run the organization day to day. It is they who observe conditions in the field, synthesize information, recommend courses of action to the board, and implement the board's decisions. Staff must present a full and articulate account of the salient facts affecting a decision if the board is to perform its duties properly. The board's ability to make wise decisions hinges on the quality of information it receives from staff. In this respect, the staff leads the board.

THE LEADERSHIP EXPERIENCE

Much has been written about the qualities of leadership. What makes a good leader? Are leaders born or made? Can leaders change their style and develop their skills? Do they share certain universal traits?

In discussing this topic, I offer two caveats: One, my experience is limited to my work at MCHT; two, I am not sure how those I serve would grade my leadership abilities. The problem camper is often the last to know that he is the problem. And this is especially true of people in leadership positions. Few wish to serve as sacrificial messenger.

It seems to me that leaders are created and shaped by the internal and external environment of their organization. I can cite six primary factors that influence my leadership position at MCHT: job title, vision, inspiration, management, knowledge, and humility.

Job Title

One of the reasons I feel quite strongly that leaders are created, not born, is my own experience ascending from the number two position at MCHT to chief of staff. The board's simple act—promoting me from associate director to president with its associated duties, responsibilities, and powers—irrevocably changed my relationship with staff, directors, and the outside world. I was anointed "leader," transformed from worker bee to head of the hive. I began to view my role within the organization much differently. My allegiance became stronger. I was now required to cross the line separating board and staff and to serve both masters. Within the organization, I was viewed as the intermediary among staff members, between board and staff, and between MCHT and the world beyond. I was both the "enabler" and the "disabler"—empowering or disempowering staff as they sought guidance on a multitude of tasks. Juggling became my vocation.

To the outside world, my new job title meant that I now was chief spokesperson for MCHT. My statements might have been overridden as associate director, but my proclamations as president were generally viewed as final by outside parties. The job title also suggested to many on the outside that I was somehow the most knowledgeable staff member on the full range of services MCHT offered. Countless times, staff and board have agreed that I should be the one to speak with someone or sign an important letter, confirming my suspicion that leadership is as much image as reality.

The new job title also gave me access to persons of far greater power and leadership. Nonprofit organizations are especially well positioned to attract the attention of community and business leaders. While MCHT is a relatively small organization with a modest budget, its mission appeals to many community and state leaders. To some extent this is a function of Maine's small population and the accessibility of its leaders and media, but it is also a function of the public constituency we serve. Recognition of my status as a leader by other community leaders and the media continues to reinforce my legitimacy as a leader both inside and outside the organization.

Vision

Vision is commonly cited as a key ingredient of successful leadership. I agree. But in my experience, vision has not been the sole purview of the titular leader.

To see beyond the horizon, one must have some advance information and possess reasonable powers of deduction. To obtain advance information, the leader must confer with those who have sailed closer to the horizon—those who may already have a clear vision of what the future holds. In my experience, field staff are generally the first in the organization to become aware of new opportunities and threats. By serving clients day to day, they see patterns emerging.

Advance information also comes from people working in other nonprofits that are a bit further along in terms of organizational growth. Experts in certain fields related to land protection (tax regulation, environmental law, real estate) can also provide valuable information about what may lie ahead.

Throughout MCHT's history, the board of directors has recognized important trends and equipped the organization to address future challenges. MCHT is blessed with an unusually visionary group of directors who foresaw the need for a land conservation organization such as MCHT fifteen years before the 1980s development boom.

To provide vision for an organization, its titular leader must perform three important functions. First, the leader must continually communicate with a wide variety of people on a wide array of topics. To do this effectively, the leader must foster a working relationship with many people. He or she must take advantage of opportunities to circulate within the community whenever possible. Second, the leader must synthesize disparate bits of information and identify patterns or trends—an ability, I sense, that improves with experience and a widening circle of acquaintances. Third, the leader must articulate a plan for achieving future goals and be willing to adjust the plan in response to comment by staff and directors. This collaborative process permits clearer vision and a sense of "ownership" by staff and board.

Inspiration

I have always admired those rare individuals who can somehow project strength, confidence, and competence without even speaking.

Likewise, I have admired those whose passion and contagious enthusiasm can ignite the energies of others.

Unfortunately, I possess neither of these qualities and hence must rely on other means for inspiring those I lead. There are two traits, I suppose, that allow me to quietly inspire staff, board, and clients. First, I am firmly committed to the mission of MCHT. I eagerly espouse land conservation's social benefits to receptive listeners and willingly defend its virtues before hostile critics. All staff and directors of MCHT share this commitment, of course, but I view articulating our mission as one of my most important duties.

Second, I try to abide by my firm belief that actions speak louder than words. The greatest inspiration to everyone associated with MCHT is the completion of a land transaction. Likewise, it has been our *work*, rather than our pitch, that has attracted supporters and donors to MCHT over the years. As leader I can inspire to the extent that I enable land protection. I enable land protection to the extent that I allow flexibility and creativity. My willingness, and that of the organization, to try new conservation techniques, take calculated risks, and remain entrepreneurial is fundamental to MCHT's success.

Management

I have often heard people complain that so-and-so is an inspirational leader but cannot manage or that so-and-so is a great manager but offers no vision or leadership. From observations of MCHT and other groups, I have concluded that leadership (in its broadest sense) and management do require different skills. Someone who is inspirational and visionary may not always be organized and task-oriented. Nevertheless, successful leaders must not only provide competent management but tend to the less tangible duties of leadership if they and the organization are to prosper.

Administrative management has been one of the greatest challenges in my position. I constantly struggle with my tendency to operate on policy decisions immediately, while leaving administrative decisions lingering in the waiting room. At best, this crisis management style is inefficient. At worst, it frustrates or even alienates other staff members.

I am lucky to work with a staff of highly competent and organized people. My managerial weaknesses are generally balanced by their strengths. I have been able to delegate administrative tasks to various staff members with the knowledge that those tasks will be completed with skill and finesse.

Of course, delegation can be carried only so far. As the staff and budget have grown in size, I have found that I need to concentrate more time and effort on administrative matters.

"People management" is one role I feel I must personally perform as president. To foster communication within MCHT, I maintain an open-door policy and am generally accessible to discuss issues as needs arise. While this policy is somewhat frustrating in that it seldom allows me large blocks of uninterrupted time, the benefits of regular and spontaneous communication with staff far outweigh the frustrations. I cannot imagine anything more demoralizing for staff than having a supervisor who doesn't offer guidance on a regular basis.

Knowledge

It may seem self-evident, but I have found that knowing the business is an essential ingredient of leadership. The leader of a small nonprofit group must know as much about the organization's product or service as any member of the staff or board. This is not to say that the leader has to be *the* authority on every technical matter. In fact, MCHT comprises staff who by training or experience have developed expertise in specific areas. But to lead MCHT, I must be able to shepherd a land conservation transaction from start to finish, stay current on the myriad of real estate tax laws, and keep up with new conservation techniques. Thus, I continue to carry a "client load," pared down to accommodate my other responsibilities. Only by working in the field can I continue to speak articulately about MCHT's mission, assist staff and board in evaluating land projects, and make decisions affecting the future of the organization.

Humility

As location is the key to investing in real estate, listening is the key to investing in leadership. Listen to others. Accept constructive criticism. Embrace sensible new ideas. And, above all else, try to understand and recognize your own limitations. I find all of this easier to say than do, of course, but I clearly recognize that I am only one member of the MCHT team.

As president of MCHT, I am first an associate, second a boss. During my tenure with the trust, the people joining the staff have been highly motivated—not by leadership but by their personal commitment to land protection. These are people who are drawn to MCHT not by money (heaven knows they could make more elsewhere), and not by a desire for career promotion (Maine is a small state with few environmental jobs), but by the organization's mission and purpose. To perform their duties, these people require direction, not directives.

Likewise the directors of MCHT, the landowners we assist, and the local land trust leaders we advise seek guidance, not dictation. Although a chain of command exists, decisions are almost always consensual. My job is to build that consensus. The free exchange of ideas among all who serve MCHT is the reason for the organization's prosperity.

PREPARING FOR LEADERSHIP

Most of the leaders I know among nonprofit conservation organizations never actually sought skills to prepare them for leadership. Instead, they sought skills that would allow them to pursue an interest. They are generally people who began contributing to an environmental issue or cause and later got tapped for leadership. Those who lead state or regional environmental groups come from a wide spectrum of fields and a broad range of professional and academic experiences. There is no formula.

That said, there do appear to be some similar traits among the leaders of small nonprofits:

- They are deeply committed to the mission of their organization.
- They are able to articulate the purpose and public benefits of that mission. They may not always be the most entertaining or inspirational public speakers, but their message is clear.
- They like to work with people.
- They are skilled in delivering the organization's services.
- Their style tends to be entrepreneurial—they look for opportunities and are willing to take calculated risks.
- They tend to operate as consensus builders rather than unilateral decision makers.

- They are energetic and creative.
- They are people of integrity and character.
- They were blessed with a certain degree of luck, having been in the right place at the right time.

Many of the conspicuous skills of leadership—management, public speaking, consensus building—can be learned through study. But most of the inconspicuous traits of leadership—vision, creativity, character—develop with experience, both on and off the job.

WHAT IT TAKES

Leaders of state and local nonprofit groups must have many of the same skills that all effective leaders require. With the power of position comes the responsibility to articulate mission, supply vision, instill enthusiasm, offer direction, provide management, and remain knowledgeable about products and services.

There may be further leadership characteristics peculiar to small, volunteer-governed, professionally staffed organizations. In my experience, most decisions must be reached through consensus. Nonprofit work is, almost by definition, a labor of love. Directors and staff must genuinely feel that they "own" the organization to continue contributing to it. Autocratic leadership is not likely to be tolerated.

At MCHT, group involvement extends beyond decision making to include vision, inspiration, and management. The leader's primary internal function is to facilitate communication, creativity, and the personal growth of staff and board. The ability to listen is tantamount.

To the public, the leader is chief advocate and spokesperson for the organization. He or she must project the virtues of the group and absorb any criticism hurled in its direction. Since the organization and its chief are often seen as one and the same, the leader must be thoroughly knowledgeable about organizational policies and services. The credibility of the group hinges on the credibility of its titular leader.

Leaders of small nonprofit organizations are created, not born. While some skills can be learned in academic study, many are acquired through experience. The perpetual financial struggling of most nonprofits does have an unexpected benefit: All staff are asked to assume an unusual amount of responsibility. The opportunities for on-the-job training are plentiful.

REFERENCES

Knauft, E.B., A. Berger, and S. T. Gray. 1991. *Profiles of Excellence: Achieving Success in the Non-Profit Sector*. San Francisco: Jossey-Bass.
Snow, D. 1992. *Inside the Environmental Movement: Meeting the Leadership Challenge*. Washington: The Conservation Fund/Island Press.

13 Corporate Leadership

William Y. Brown

BIRDWATCHING as a youth got me interested in conservation. We lived in the country near Oakton, Virginia, and I could see what was happening to the forests where I spent time. I often hiked to Bowman's Lake, where I would see many bird species and often spend an afternoon without seeing a single person. I went back a few years ago. Now called "Lake Audubon," it is surrounded by condominiums.

Once in college, I majored in biology and planned to teach high school. But after a brief, frustrating teaching experience in the fall of 1969, I applied for admission to a Ph.D. program, I studied seabirds in Hawaii, and I became a professional naturalist. But I was not a professional scientist at heart. What I foresaw for myself in that profession was mostly attention to detail, patience, and competition for meager fruits of knowledge and recognition. After Hawaii, I taught biology for a year at Mount Holyoke College and got my seabird work published. Then I went to law school at Harvard. I wanted to get involved in conservation.

My first job after law school was as executive secretary of the Endangered Species Scientific Authority. ESSA had been established by an executive order of the president to serve as the U.S. Scientific Authority under the Convention on International Trade in Endangered Species of Wild Fauna and Flora (CITES). The United States had signed the treaty and now had to implement it. ESSA was an interagency group. A new International Convention Advisory Commission followed ESSA with a similar function, and I was made its director.

I stayed at the commission until James Watt took over at the Interior Department in 1981. Although chaired by CEQ, the commission was funded by Interior. Watt considered me and my group holdovers from the preservationist Carter administration and proposed to zero-budget the commission. I decided that my time in government had passed, at least for the moment, and went to the Environmental Defense Fund.

I was at EDF from 1981 through 1984. Most of my work was on wildlife and nature conservation—emphasizing endangered species and wetlands protection. I worked as a scientist and a lawyer. For most of 1984 I was the acting director of EDF, commuting between Washington and New York every week. I learned much about finance and a bit about fundraising. I did not have much time for issues that year—it was almost all management. By the time 1984 ended, I was ready for something different. It turned out to be Waste Management, Inc.

I have been with WMI for over seven years, and I continue to like my job, which is to help shape the company's environmental vision and help keep it on a sound course. My enthusiasm stems in part from the importance of the services that we offer in dealing with environmental problems as well as their scale and diversity. WMI now has 65,000 employees and 900 operating divisions around the world. The company deals not just with trash and industrial wastes, but also air and water pollution, and with pollution prevention as well as control.

I like the novelty of much that the company does and the constant growth and change. I am challenged by the constant controversy that surrounds the things we work on and the wild range in public perceptions of the company. WMI is not perfect by any means, but many good people work for it and are trying to do right by environmental protection. The controversy keeps me on my toes.

I like the diversity of my own responsibilities, which range from public policy and cooperation with environmental groups to internal education and compliance issues. I give speeches and often deal with the press. I sit on several nonprofit boards and manage our environmental philanthropy.

If there is a lesson to be learned from my experience to date, it may be that a person can do a number of things in his life and still have a job. But I also think that these different experiences help me to see things in my job more quickly and clearly.

CORPORATE PRINCIPLES

Diverse companies now give more priority to environmental issues than ever before. Many executives accept the validity of environmental problems and want to address them. Furthermore, the environment's *political* stock has risen. Polls put popular support for environmental protection at a historic high. Indeed, the environment has become an issue on which elections can stand or fall.

This is a good time for companies to reflect on their businesses and the environment and to develop new environmental principles for their activities. Several areas for such examination are reviewed here, followed by a look at the principles that might advance the quality of environmental advocacy.

Compliance

An effective program for compliance with environmental laws is the *sine qua non* of corporate environmental leadership. The features cited here are incorporated into WMI's compliance programs and should be generally appropriate for larger companies operating under detailed environmental regulation:

- Assignment of facility or division environmental compliance responsibility to general managers of these units and provision for compliance monitoring through environmental management programs reporting independently of these managers.
- Specification, assignment, and scheduling of employees' environmental compliance tasks at facilities and divisions.
- Training and testing of employees to assure adequate understanding of environmental responsibilities.
- Compensation systems that reward superior compliance and penalize poor performance.
- Procedures for disciplining employees who violate legal environmental requirements.
- Systems designed to assure that compliance issues are noted and resolved promptly on an ongoing basis.
- Periodic audits of facility or division compliance status by the major business units of a corporation in which facilities are lo-

cated. These audits should give priority to operations that pose the most environmental risk and are subject to more complex regulation. Audits should include mechanisms to correct any problems.

- Mechanisms for regular review of facility or division compliance by top management of larger business units.
- Periodic review of overall larger unit compliance by top parent company management, combined with an appropriate parent company audit program and involvement of an independent firm in assessing the soundness of compliance management systems.

Pollution Prevention

Leadership requires more than carrying out laws that others have promulgated. Leaders must find out which voluntary activities contribute to environmental improvement, and they should codify long-standing commitments in policy. Pollution prevention is a key field for initiative. At least three areas warrant particular attention: commercial goods and services; design and operation of internal facilities; and environmental initiatives.

Commercial Goods and Services Companies in the environmental sector can give priority to offering goods and services advancing pollution prevention. WMI has done this by establishing consulting groups to advise waste generators on source reduction and recycling opportunities and by rapidly expanding its own commercial recycling services. One of the most promising new endeavors, undertaken by WMI's Rust International group, is concentration on source reduction and recycling opportunities in engineering and construction services. The service was inaugurated in October 1991 through a $500 million project with Hoechst-Celanese to design pollution prevention and control measures for eight plants in the Southeast. The project is expected to reduce overall chemical air emissions by 70 percent.

Facility Design and Operation A second key area is assuring that a company's own facilities are designed, built, and operated in an environmentally sound manner. In a country like the United States or in EEC nations, regulatory compliance gives a strong measure of assurance that this standard is met. However, the same cannot be said of the developing world. To implement a pollution prevention policy, companies operating in the developing world must have baseline environmental criteria or, at least, a management approach that assures an adequate level of environmental professionalism whether or not required by law. This does not necessarily mean applying all the legal requirements and typical practices of more developed nations. Some of these regulations and practices may have minor significance for the environment and may be too expensive for developing countries to afford.

Environmental Initiatives A third leadership area in pollution prevention concerns the opportunities for administrative environmental initiatives. Corporations vary widely in the nature of their activities, but all have offices that are major consumers of office supplies and energy for lighting, heating, and cooling. All generate waste. In addition, office administrators manage procurement activities that reach into every corner of a business. Every institution has significant opportunities to prevent pollution through purchase and use of products and through "good housekeeping" in office management practices.

Many businesses, government agencies, environmental groups, and others are currently buying paper with recycled content. The concept of "buy recycled" is reasonably familiar to the public in the case of paper and enjoys broad support as a necessary adjunct to collection programs for recyclables.

Less understood, but no less important for environmental quality, are efforts to buy items other than paper with recycled content as well as items that advance source reduction (to choose acceptable alternative products with less packaging, for example, or to use pigments and additives free of heavy metals). Purchasing for energy conservation— such as well-insulated windows, energy-efficient lights, and efficient heating and cooling plants for buildings—is another important category of what can be collectively called "purchasing for environmental quality."

Institutions purchase *services* as well as goods—offering further opportunities. Cleaning and landscaping contracts, for instance, might be modified to specify low-toxicity cleaners and pesticides.

The details of an environmental purchasing program will differ from institution to institution just as demand for goods and services differs. Furthermore, any effort to buy environmentally superior products will be qualified in some way by their cost and their capacity to serve the basic function for which they are purchased. Nevertheless, companies can demonstrate leadership in pollution prevention by instituting an environmental purchasing program. Such programs should include a mission statement and general guidelines for instituting internal efforts to identify and buy environmentally superior items when quality and cost allow. Implementation also requires a serious mandate from the top to spur the effort and provide environmental expertise in procurement activities.

The way in which products are used and offices managed is also significant. Do employees copy on both sides of the page wherever possible? Do they turn out the lights when they leave a room? Do employees or cleaning staff adjust blinds to keep out direct sun and reduce cooling loads? Is the office recycling all the items it can? Are grounds watered at night to conserve water? Does the company help employees to carpool? Examining such housekeeping practices is a logical complement to instituting an environmental purchasing approach.

Nature Conservation

Nature conservation is a natural complement to pollution prevention in corporate environmental leadership. Many companies have improved their properties for wildlife, and this should be commended. But the time has come to get more systematic about corporate nature conservation programs.

Waste Management has endorsed a "no–net–loss" policy for wetlands and other key reservoirs of biological diversity on its properties, such as prairie grasslands and forests. The company has made grants to the World Wildlife Fund in support of the group's report on this subject as well as a conference held in December 1991 to review it. The WWF report specifies guidelines that companies might use for conservation of biological diversity on their lands. WMI also retained a consulting firm to assist the company in preparing pilot conservation plans for three of our properties and setting guidelines for conservation of biodiversity. More recently, a WMI subsidiary—SEC-Donohue—has established a detailed program to assist in implementing the policy.

The WWF report and the WMI draft guidelines were used extensively by the president's Commission on Environmental Quality in its biodiversity project. Commission members include the CEOs of WWF and WMI. The commission organized company demonstration projects identifying management practices for biodiversity conservation on private lands. Practices identified include such concepts as:

- Look at the big picture to promote regional and global diversity.
- Promote native species and communities.
- Endeavor to provide larger areas of unbroken space.
- Protect sensitive environments such as wetlands.
- Recognize and protect unique species and communities.
- Avoid unnecessary harm in development activities.
- Compensate for unavoidable damage to priority ecosystems.

Besides such stewardship principles themselves, the commission is recommending implementation steps including inventory, conservation planning, plan implementation, and monitoring of results. The work done by the president's commission should serve as a benchmark for leadership in voluntary conservation efforts on corporate lands.

Public Policy

It is often the perception that companies are intrinsically at loggerheads with the public environmental interest. For corporate environmental leaders, this should not be the case. Company management can help to counter negative perceptions by making a public commitment to supporting environmentally sound public policy and by explaining how the commitment is being met.

WMI has made such a commitment, and we are explaining our position on major issues in the company's public environmental reports. Most of our positions are clearly positive for the environment, but few require discussion, such as the company's opposition to bans on interstate waste shipments. Company management is confident that this position is the right one from the perspective of environmental protection, however, and our articulation of reasons has been useful from everyone's perspective.

Training and Recruitment

Environmentalism is a new concept for many corporate employees. Yet employees must understand and work toward environmental goals if they are to be achieved. Hence training and recruitment are essential.

Training ranges from the specific information required for compliance-related operational tasks to sensitizing managers to trends in national and international environmental policy. For compliance tasks involving hazardous wastes, WMI has developed "standard division practices" or SDPs. The SDPs are intended to take the guesswork out of compliance for hands-on work subject to regulatory specifications, which themselves may be less clear.

Training on more sophisticated matters is no less important. General managers of facilities and divisions, for example, are critically important to environmental excellence in companies, including WMI, and these managers must genuinely appreciate the big picture or excellence will not be achieved. Training of this kind requires input from the whole range of players who define the parameters of environmental concern: policymakers, local officials, environmental organizations, the press, academics, and technical experts of various kinds. Ways to accomplish such training include company-sponsored workshops, training modules used on-site, and exchanges with academic institutions. Whatever the specifics, environmental training programs should be developed and then implemented energetically by a corporate environmental leader.

Training should be complemented by efforts to recruit professionals with environmental experience and skills important to corporate environmental performance. Such recruitment is particularly important in the case of managers. It is especially difficult to provide, on the job, the sophisticated training and experience needed to make managers at home with the broad environmental parameters that affect the success of their business. The difficulty is alleviated to the extent that otherwise qualified people can be recruited from schools and organizations providing this kind of environmental experience. Corporate environmental leaders should have recruitment programs that connect with such institutions and consider qualified applicants.

Executive Attention

Environmental principles addressing *process* complement commitments in other areas. Executive attention and communication are key areas of leadership. Every large company needs an executive group close to the CEO to keep the firm attentive to environmental issues. In WMI, the Executive Environmental Committee serves this purpose.

Its membership includes top management from operating groups and top environmental management. The committee develops internal reports and recommendations and is responsible for preparing the public annual environmental reports on progress in implementing the company's environmental policy. A number of other companies have similar committees, but some do not. Corporate environmental leaders also must fully integrate environmental considerations into planning. Those implementing programs of "total quality management" should make environmental excellence a fundamental element of the TQM system.

Communication and Disclosure

Companies have generally earned their reputations as bad communicators on environmental issues. Corporate statements are often defensive and empty. It's time to change this. More candor is in everyone's interest.

A key initial step for improvement is a commitment to issue an honest public annual report on activities affecting the environment. Ideally, the report should document progress in implementation of a sound overall corporate environmental policy. Such reporting has both internal and external benefits. For the company, the effort establishes a mechanism for useful self-examination and education. For the public, the report is a way to reduce the public's distrust of companies and their perceived secrecy. When problems occur, people are often tolerant so long as they believe that company management is candid in disclosing them and forthright in correcting them. Many companies will have much positive to say in such reports. WMI prepared the first report of this kind for 1990 and issued the 1991 report in the spring of 1992. WMI's environmental policy commits the company to these annual environmental reports, and living up to the commitment has been a useful and positive experience for the company.

PRINCIPLES FOR ADVOCACY

This is a time of great challenge and opportunity for nonprofit organizations as well as for companies. Media attention has never been so intense. It is a time of heady power and a time to make a difference. It also is a good time for some introspection. Nonprofit environmental organizations are well advised to follow the advice that they themselves are now giving to corporations. They should evaluate their own principles for doing business.

The first part of this chapter addresses principles for corporate environmentalism. Here I want to support general principles for advocacy by nonprofit environmental organizations. There is room for improvement in all quarters. The following principles are offered as a reminder to the organizations that play a seminal role in the development and adoption of society's policies for environmental protection.

Be Truthful

Neither government, corporations, nor environmental organizations have been especially fastidious about telling the whole truth. Yet environmental problems are *real*, and no falsehood or distortion of the facts is required to justify actions on them. In the end, dishonesty and intentional or negligent inaccuracy are their own worst enemies. Credibility takes time to earn but can be lost in a moment. Environmental organizations are fortunate in that many enjoy high public trust— more trust than is afforded government or private industry. Such trust and power should not be wasted through inaccuracy.

Practice What You Preach

Environmental organizations should pursue a vision that is challenging—even revolutionary if appropriate. But members and staff of environmental groups should give themselves a reality check on what they advocate. Don't pursue a vision you are not prepared to live with. Don't seek to stop oil production unless you have studied the alternatives realistically and are prepared to embrace them. Don't oppose all landfills and incinerators unless you have found a way to recycle all of your own discards (and good luck!). Don't object to plastics manufacture in a document typed on a PC encased in plastic and stuffed with plastics. Do what you ask others to do.

Address Real Problems

Environmental issues are hard to rank. Yet environmental organizations should rise to the challenge and focus their attention on what will really make a difference to human health and the environment. The alternative is to become a tool of money or the media. No bright line exists. Environmental groups must raise money to do their job. Restricted foundation or corporate support may be available for legitimate work that fits a group's overall objectives and should be done, even though the project funded would not be undertaken if the same funds were given for general support. Dull direct mail doesn't work—but a direct mail piece or the verbal presentation of a canvasser may add a little drama without spinning a yarn. Furthermore, environmental organizations need to work effectively with the media—to get the message out to the public and policymakers.

Somewhere, however, there is a line that should not be crossed: where going for the money is your first impulse; where your objective is a name in print or an image on television. Most environmentalists, so long as they are paying attention, know when they are at the line. They should pay attention.

Embrace Experience

Ignorance is no virtue, and diverse professional experience is an indispensable element of education. Yet environmental organizations do not always put much stock in experience. Perhaps it is considered at odds with enthusiasm for social change. But this is clearly not always true. Moreover, dismissing experience fosters an unsophisticated arrogance that is not particularly effective. Environmental organizations should include some staff with industry and government experience. Sound advocacy and public education cannot be based on perceptions that have evolved from narrow experience.

Confront as a Last Resort

Sometimes confrontation is necessary—in litigation, in a legislative showdown, in peaceful demonstrations. But confrontation should be preceded by an effort to reach cooperative solutions. Not just because fighting should be avoided if possible (although nothing is wrong with good manners), but because fighting can be counterproductive. Confrontation usually offends the one on the receiving end and creates a resistance to compromise that may last for years. Few issues are resolved with a clean victory for one side or the other. Why not try for the compromise sooner rather than later? The environment may deteriorate while the war rages on. Any organization inclined to fight first and talk later should ask itself whether solving environmental needs is its priority or whether ego gratification, media attention, and fundraising are heading the list.

THE FUTURE?

Significant change in corporate environmental practice calls for a heroic marriage of vision and consensus. Government regulators have provided little direction or support in addressing environmental priorities. Scientists advising EPA have long been frustrated with the agency's (and Congress's) failure to base program priorities on risk. Recently, the EPA has put more emphasis on pollution prevention and risk reduction. Even so, too little, in my view, continues to be spent on some of the greatest risks: global warming, ozone depletion, indoor air pollution, and loss of biodiversity.

The challenge for EPA and other agencies faced with budget restrictions is in finding *anything* that warrants less attention than now received. When it comes to government programs, it seems easier to ignore even the most significant of forgotten needs than to wean the smallest of concerns already fattened at the public trough.

Companies, however, may be able to move forward where government has not. Many environmental initiatives—pollution prevention and energy conservation—can reduce next year's costs. As never before, customers, shareholders, and employees are expecting environmental excellence from the companies in which they have a stake, whether or not the government requires it or even seems to care. I think they are going to get their way.

14 Academic Leadership

··

James E. Crowfoot

FROM 1983 TO 1990, I was dean of the School of Natural Resources at the University of Michigan, which was renamed in 1992 the School of Natural Resources and Environment. Before that I was a professor in this school. My Ph.D. in organizational psychology with an M.A. in social psychology provided me the background and expertise to teach and do research on processes of organizational and social change. Earlier education and degrees in physics and theology helped prepare me to focus on complex social problems involving science and value questions. I was initially appointed in 1972 as an assistant professor to teach and do research on processes of social change in response to environmental and natural resource problems.

THE ACADEMIC CONTEXT

Academic natural resource units, until relatively recently, have been led most often by people with graduate degrees and careers focused on biological aspects of natural resource management (specialties within forestry or fisheries, for example). More recently, some deans of these units have come from more diverse backgrounds including landscape architecture, natural resource economics, and social science of outdoor recreation. Related academic units focusing on environmental studies or environmental science have leaders from backgrounds as diverse as history, geology, political science or policy, and chemistry.

In describing and analyzing leadership here, I will draw directly on my own experience while generalizing to other academic units focusing on natural resources, environmental science and policy, and environmental studies. Some environmental and natural resource units are specific departments within colleges of agriculture or colleges of arts and sciences while others cut across a number of departments within a college or a number of colleges. Occasionally these units are relatively free-standing research institutes or centers within large universities and as such exist outside of any college.

In my situation, the School of Natural Resources was one of seventeen colleges at the University of Michigan. Each of these colleges has a high degree of autonomy including its own bylaws, its own faculty and other personnel, and its own budget and administration. The deans of these colleges report to the academic vice-president and provost of the university, who is the number two person in the hierarchy of administrative authority. The provost is the chief academic and budget officer of the university and exercises authority over the colleges in both these areas. Deans are appointed by the regents (another term for trustees) after a search process involving recommendations to the provost, who selects the short list considered by the regents. My appointment followed this process and my role included reporting to the provost. Within the school I had responsibility and authority within the policies of the university and the bylaws of the school for:

- Overall leadership
- Financial budgeting and expenditures, appointing faculty and staff personnel, and managing the physical plant and properties
- Administering the teaching and research programs within the policies of the university and school
- Representation to other university units and to external organizations and constituencies
- Fundraising

In most of the university's schools and colleges, including the School of Natural Resources, the deans share executive authority with a faculty executive committee. This committee is nominated by the faculty and, at the recommendation of the provost, appointed by the regents. Final responsibility for the school's operation rests with the dean, and by tradition it is a role that includes substantial organizational power.

In other universities where environmental or natural resource units are separate colleges or separate centers or institutes outside of college structures, the dean has similar responsibilities for leadership, administration, and external representation. Differences exist among universities in the relative autonomy of the environmental and natural resource units in relation to fiscal matters, personnel, and academic programs. There are differences, too, in the relative power of the dean's role and the specific areas where the dean shares authority with the faculty. My role as dean required certain leadership skills:

- Organizational vision
- Strategic planning
- Resource acquisition and allocation
- Business and academic program administration
- Selection, evaluation, and development of faculty and staff members
- Exercise of power
- Individual and group motivation
- Communication (including selling)
- Self-reflection and criticism

THE SCHOOL AND ITS ORGANIZATION

The School of Natural Resources in 1983, when I became dean, had forty faculty and about four hundred students. The faculty was organized in five program areas: forestry; wildlife and fisheries; landscape architecture; natural resource policy and economics; and environment and behavior. Instructional programs operated at the undergraduate, master's, and doctorate levels. Faculty members pursued their own research programs. The school's mission, while not explicitly formulated, was to prepare students for professional natural resource roles in management, policymaking, and planning and design as well as research in these areas.

This school had been founded in 1928 as the School of Forestry and Conservation. In 1950, it was renamed the School of Natural Resources to reflect its broadened concern for all renewable natural resources and its concerns for both the biophysical aspects as well as the political and social aspects of natural resource management. The university originally became involved in this subject in the 1880s as deforestation and the management of the nation's forests became major issues. Instruction was organized into a separate department in the arts and science college as a result of the regents' desire to respond to Michigan's forestry problems.

Throughout the United States there were parallel developments of academic natural resource programs in many universities, particularly land grant universities with their special attention to agriculture and related topics. For different universities the dates and other circumstances of the founding and evolution of instruction and research on this topic varied in response to regional natural resource concerns and the interests of their academic leaders and trustees. Generally, natural resources were seen as a commodity amenable to efficient and wise use by means of applying scientific investigation to understanding how best to manage the resource to gain the desired commodity outcomes. Biological and physical sciences predominated in these academic units; economics and policy matters did not come into the curriculum until later.

Typical of developments elsewhere, from its founding the enrollment of the School of Natural Resources at the University of Michigan increased but also was subject to major fluctuations caused by the Depression, World War II, and subsequent changes in public attitudes toward natural resources and the environment. These events also affected employment opportunities for graduates. Generally, the natural resources colleges—or, often, departments within colleges of agriculture in land grant universities—were small in comparison to other colleges and departments. Their size reflected the low priority of natural resource and environmental concerns among the academic priorities of universities, among the intellectual priorities of the academic disciplines, and among public policy and overall business priorities of the country.

In the early 1970s, as public concern for environmental problems grew rapidly, so did student interest. This led to expanded enrollments, faculty, and curriculum. It also began a shift away from a commodity view of selected resources to a broader ecosystem focus along with a concern for preservation and other new issues like the urban environment and the human health consequences of environmental problems. In this period at the University of Michigan, enrollment in the School of Natural Resources grew from below three hundred to over nine hundred, and new areas in the social sciences (environmental education, communication, advocacy) were added to the curriculum. This rapid enrollment growth—along with demand by students in other colleges for environmental courses and the consequent faculty and curriculum changes—resulted in an overextended faculty, a lack of curriculum coordination, and great pressure for more courses in this area.

Toward the end of the 1970s and in the early 1980s, public concern for environmental matters waned along with the interest of political leaders. The renewed emphasis on economic growth included a perception that environmental and natural resource concerns were alarmist responses that contributed to bothersome or even destructive consequences for economic growth. In the politics of these years, this perception led to a major loss of emphasis on the environment and natural resources and encouraged forces advocating weaker environmental policies and fewer regulations. In higher education at the end of the 1970s, there was growing awareness of the approaching end of the period of continuous growth in enrollments and research funding that had begun at the end of World War II. There was also a negative reaction to curriculum additions of the 1960s and 1970s that resulted in attempts to trim back or eliminate these courses and areas of curriculum. Moreover, in some states and some universities there were financial crises prefiguring the now widespread financial problems of higher education in the 1990s.

The University of Michigan was deeply affected by the state's financial crisis of the late 1970s and early 1980s, a crisis rooted in the decline of the U.S. auto industry. All of the university's schools and colleges faced budget reductions, but these were differential reductions reflecting judgments by the president and provost about the relative importance, costs, and revenues from different units. These decisions were controversial and the actual criteria (quality versus prestige) and decision-making style (autocratic versus collegial) were much debated. At the University of Michigan, the School of Natural Resources was, along with the Schools of Art and Education, targeted for major reduction or even elimination. Parallel events were occurring at other natural resource colleges, as well, particularly those that were part of non-land-grant universities. I became dean a year after this university-wide program of major reductions had been initiated—and at a time when a tentative decision had been made to continue the school but with a major budget reduction in the range of 20 to 30 percent to be phased over a five-year period.

Appreciation for these changes in academic natural resource units is essential to understanding their leadership. The history of my own school—and related academic units throughout the United States— indicates how even the academic aspects of natural resources and the environment intertwine with economic and political conditions globally, nationally, and locally. This profile also describes how politics (spelled with both a large P for public decisions and a small p for organizational decisions) determines to what extent, if at all, teaching and research in natural resources and the environment will be funded in universities.

Political and organizational leadership decisions, along with changing public attitudes and priorities, are involved here. These actions and attitudes affect the interests and choices of students as well as the attitudes of higher education's college and university trustees, administrators, and faculty members. Taken together, these are major shaping conditions of academic environmental and natural resource units that also shape their leadership needs. Other major forces shaping these academic units, as well as their leadership needs, include:

- Pressures for productivity and reliance on bureaucratic assumptions and means regarding it—especially hierarchical authority, explicit and specialized roles focused on science-based expertise, rewards and incentives tightly coupled to specialized role performance, standardization of policies to accomplish organizational goals, and separation of behavior in work organizations from other social roles
- A tradition of faculty governance in which the faculty through democratic processes determines academic goals, curricula, and faculty qualifications for hiring and promotion
- A history of northern European white male faculty membership and leadership despite growing numbers of female students (often approaching 50 percent) and early signs of an increasing proportion of persons of color

- Growing recognition of extensive and major environmental challenges resulting from unprecedented human population growth, economic growth (and in some places high levels of affluence), and damage to the biosphere and ecosystems—which, in turn, is related to all areas of knowledge and aspects of human behavior
- Growing economic inequities between the North and South globally and within the United States as well as related impacts on the natural environment and efforts to address environmental problems

As well as needs that are specific to an academic unit and university, general leadership needs result from these forces:

- A vision of the societal, local, and global changes necessary to meet the environmental challenges and their implications for universities and academic units focusing on natural resources and the environment
- A commitment to innovative and high-quality research and teaching and other activities directly addressing these changing conditions
- An ability to advocate the interests of an environmental or natural resource academic unit that tends to be small
- A vision of the organizational mission, structures, and culture needed for a future-oriented academic natural resource unit and the skills to develop such a unit
- The ability to involve and motivate faculty, students, staff, alumni, and other collaborators to achieve high performance as well as major changes in the program, organization, and external environment
- A commitment to higher education along with goals for change that involve the natural resource and environmental unit in major university policy debates and changes in the university's mission, program, and structure
- The skills to gain support and resources from government, private corporations, nonprofit organizations, and individual citizens with major interests in the natural environment

At the time I became dean, the School of Natural Resources had specific leadership needs as well:

- An ability to gain the cooperation and commitment of all groups involved in the school in order to cope with a major budget reduction, plan for the school's future, and successfully implement these plans
- Skill in reallocating resources—including downsizing the organization along with attendant program and administrative changes
- An ability to work both cooperatively and where necessary competitively with university powerholders and groups that could affect the school's future
- Commitment and skill in developing increased revenues for the school, especially from new sources

LEADERSHIP PRACTICE IN ORGANIZATION

My view of leadership has been shaped by the organizational situation I have described as well as my prior socialization as a middle-class white male in the United States. My view is changing, however, due to my perception of deepening environmental and social problems, both global and local, my aging and experiencing a later stage of the human life cycle, and my growing awareness of diversity. My view is changing, too, due to my personal efforts to heal past hurts and to transform old coping patterns that no longer satisfy me and in fact impede my effectiveness in working with others.

In the past I viewed leadership as basically having the power and expertise to influence people to get things done. I saw leadership as plentiful and based primarily on specialized expertise and lengthy professional experience that merited having power. In my earlier thinking, leaders (mostly white, male, and upper middle class) were quite autonomous individuals who demonstrated their competence through competition. Leaders determined the right answers and, by being dominant, influenced their followers to do what they directed. My emphasis was on individual, conscious, rational thinking in response to the leader's perception of a situation.

Now I am coming to see the crisis proportions of the human race's damage to the biosphere as well as to human communities and relationships. These multiple problems of destructive and violent behavior are causing great suffering and threaten the future viability of the natural environment including human social life and, ultimately, life itself. These problems are intertwined, rapidly changing, and involve great uncertainty. I am coming to recognize that I myself am enmeshed in these problems and that they involve socialized patterns of exploitation which are internalized in the values, norms, and practices of institutions and individuals. These patterns include unconscious behavior.

Leadership is ways of being; it is actions that enable life. I conceptualize such leadership as a circle of distinct but interrelated values and behavior. In this section I describe six aspects of this circle: being compassionate; knowing what is and what could be; acting interdependently; sharing power; honoring and conserving resources; and promoting change.

Being Compassionate

Leadership is deeply respectful and accepting of self, others, and groups as well as the environment. Each of these elements is so important that it requires continual appreciation and constant learning. Being compassionate means always struggling to honor and, as much as possible, understand what is "different," "strange," or even "threatening and abhorrent." Full understanding, while sought, is never realized. Compassion continually reexperiences the goodness, intelligence, and meaning in the other and the need to attend to the other with respect.

Compassion for self means caring for esteemed aspects of oneself, unattractive parts of oneself, as well as dimly perceived parts of oneself. Such compassion is never perfect and must be developed in ever deeper ways while it is accepted for what it is: partial and in process. Without compassion for different aspects of oneself, a leader will project these inner realities onto other people and situations and deny important aspects of her or his own values and behavior. Such projections not only distort one's perception but also bring with them hurtful judgments of others and blind spots with regard to aspects of the leader's person.

In being compassionate to others, the leader learns their needs, wants, and ideas. Such compassion also invites collaboration with others through which the leader seeks honest responses to his or her principles, ideas, and initiatives. Compassion tends to be generative and expansive and contributes to shared leadership as it is reciprocated and shared in other ways.

I have seen behavior in the School of Natural Resources that I would call compassionate, but it is rarely considered desirable or even necessary for leadership. Rather, leadership is expected to be pragmatic and focus on utilitarian considerations in the interest of achieving organizational goals in an efficient fashion. Furthermore, formal authority roles in academic organizations are deeply intertwined with European male culture, including hierarchical authority, "hard" work to accomplish specific tasks, competition, and "hard" science. In this culture, compassion is not a word often heard. Indeed, in this culture the word connotes softness, tolerance for what is lesser whether in terms of productivity, intelligence, or quality, and a host of other characteristics that are frowned upon or harshly rejected.

Leadership in the traditional academic culture presumes hierarchies of power and decision making, unemotional and rational responses, detachment and objectivity in thought and judgments, unilateral commitment to specific and circumscribed goals, and treating subordinates as means to achieving these goals. These values, which place the highest priority on rationality and instrumentalism, stifle compassion.

Natural resource and environmental organizations in academia are occasionally, though cautiously and often indirectly, exercising compassion toward the natural environment. Few of these organizations explicitly connect behavior toward the environment with behavior toward other human beings. In other words, these organizations have yet to discover that compassion toward both the natural environment and people is mutually reinforcing—and necessary to protect the biosphere and life.

Knowing What Is and What Could Be

Leadership is discovering what is and what could be. This most basic information about the present and the future is not a given; it must be discovered. Such discovery is not a one-time project but an ongoing process of learning that includes gradual, incremental phases as well as surprises and startling insights that radically change individual and collective views. At its best, this element of discovery is a creative process involving oneself and others in diverse ways of knowing, evaluating, and synthesizing information. It involves rationality and intuition, conscious and semiconscious processes, individual and group activities, quantitative and qualitative data (including stories, pictures, and music), and people with diverse backgrounds and views. We all tend to see what we want to see—both consciously and unconsciously—and tend to be deeply embedded in things as they are. To discover something different requires seeking out and appreciating the views of others—particularly others who differ from oneself and hold views that diverge from one's own. We often avoid discovering "what could be," including the potential futures of the organization we are leading (and its possible ending). It frequently is threatening to seek such information and give it careful consideration. Compassion greatly enhances one's ability to learn from conflicting views and from people who are different.

In my own experience I found it challenging and difficult to seek out conflicting views about the school's present functioning and effectiveness as well as what its future mission and performance should be. My own initial views were based on what I considered to be good information, but they were still my views and thus subject to inevitable bias and distortion. I found it essential to find conflicting views, learn from them, and change my own initial views in order to understand the school's current state.

It took effort to engage people who were different from me; after all, I had more familiarity, comfort, and contacts with people like me. Sometimes I had inaccurate information and biases toward other groups. I learned it was impossible to understand the school's true performance and potential without learning from the views of people different from me—different in disciplinary training, professional experience, organizational position, race, gender, socioeconomic background, age, and nationality.

The discovery dimension of academic leadership is called upon again and again because leadership involves problem solving, whether the focus is curriculum, budget allocations, faculty and staff evaluations, or the many other issues that are essential to the functioning of an academic organization. Motivating diverse individuals and groups to support the mission and goals of the academic organization is greatly enhanced by discovering—and including—the views of the people you want to motivate. To communicate effectively outside the organization and advocate collaboratively on its behalf, the leader must know a great deal about "what is" and "what could be" and continue to learn more.

Formal authority roles provide both helpful support and serious barriers to realizing the discovery aspect of leadership. Spending time outside the organization—as well as controlling the dollars and power to conduct information searches and engage consultants—can help discovery if they are used in ways that expose conflicting views and result in their creative synthesis.

Often people in authority are cut off from others—and the information they have—due to norms and fear and approval seeking. Isolation and selective communication to the leader of only "good news" become serious barriers to discovery. Moreover, the status and income of many leaders separate them from key groups and individuals and hence valuable information, creativity, and other resources.

Acting Interdependently

Typically leadership acts unilaterally on behalf of individuals, groups, and organizations viewed as separate entities. Compassionate leadership—which discovers what is and what could be—is in a position to act interdependently. Such action requires recognizing, creating, and valuing interdependencies and promoting cooperation among all these individuals and social units.

Complexity and interconnection are key characteristics of our biophysical environment and, moreover, increasingly characterize our human sociocultural systems. Leadership is urgently needed that discovers and fosters these interdependencies. Such relationships are needed to achieve creative problem solving and realistic actions. Acting interdependently can increase an organization's effectiveness and efficiency and minimize adverse impacts due to its failure to anticipate negative consequences—including destructive conflicts.

Acting interdependently requires boundary spanning. Group and organizational boundaries must be crossed; communication must be established and maintained. Such communication needs to reflect differences and should include conflicts as well as areas of agreement. To do this inevitably requires leaders to be educators and mediators helping members of interdependent social units to know and respect what each perceives, thinks, and expects.

In helping to create interdisciplinary academic programs focusing on the conservation of biological diversity, I found it essential to foster the inclusion of the perspectives, methods, and information from biological ecology, landscape ecology, and human ecology as well as related natural and social sciences along with the humanities. There were many pressures to allow one perspective to dominate in determining the organizational home for a new program, its requirements, and its personnel. As new programs were developed, it was essential that the representatives of the different areas of expertise voluntarily decided not to simplify and exclude but rather to acknowledge interdependence and act to further it. Getting to this point required dialogue, mutual education, and discovery of commonalities and differences.

Sharing Power

Leadership that shares power—personally and organizationally—is very different from leadership that amasses power and seeks to defend hierarchies of authority. Apart from supporting compassion, discovery, and interdependent action, sharing power includes diverse groups and individuals and helps to gain high levels of participation and commitment from them.

For people to genuinely participate in organizational affairs, including decision making, requires that they have power. Without it they are either excluded or present in name only. Without the power to participate, they cannot offer their true ideas and concerns; they can only comply with directives and prevailing values and norms that sometimes are not their own.

In sharing power, leadership seeks the freely chosen yes, no, or maybe of others and responds to it. This process enhances mutual trust and commitment. Thus accountability between leaders and members is enhanced.

Leadership without power sharing relies on control and domination, whether or not the leader is conscious of it. Sometimes followers affirm such domination as leadership. When this occurs, it is because it's the only kind of leader/member relationship they know or because it's the safe thing to do. Often leaders reinforce such a distorted understanding of leadership and interpret compliance as freely given assent.

When such responses of compliance exist, they include distorted perceptions and expectations of leadership in which leaders are seen as all-knowing but resented, all-powerful but resisted, and others are seen as in some ways deficient, inadequate, and dependent subjects (but deserving better). Such views impede understandings of interdependence, feelings of mutual responsibility, and the exercise of compassion.

The control patterns that prevail in the absence of power sharing are characterized by certain feelings: numbness, suspicion, anger, and isolation. Awareness of power dynamics and their consequences is lacking. Some level of denial is present, as well. This can include the dominant leader's denial of such realities as self-serving exploitation, grandiosity, and viewing the subordinate as inferior. Denial can also be present in the follower. This can include ignorance of one's own worth, acceptance of mistreatment, reluctance to develop one's skills, and belief in the negative image of subordinates communicated by leaders and others. The absence of power sharing brings with it threats, coercion, and unfair distribution of rewards and punishment. Such treatment of others is harmful to them and in turn hurts the organization as members are less willing to contribute.

Power sharing is required to accomplish the participation necessary for interdisciplinary environmental problem solving. Such problem solving should include the many social groups experiencing the problem and is necessary for effective implementation of solutions. There is a rapidly growing recognition, for example, that public natural resource planning requires extensive participation by diverse social groups. There is even the beginning of acknowledgment that this participation should include resource sharing to mitigate power inequalities and consensus building as a means of tapping the ideas of all participants, developing agreements, and getting others committed to the plan and its implementation.

In academic organizations, including environmental and natural resource units, there is a tradition of democratic faculty decision making in academic matters. Power sharing is the foundation of this tradition, but the sharing rarely extends to students or staff. Even in the case of faculty, power sharing rarely extends beyond academic matters.

Present financial difficulties in higher education, along with other cultural changes, are causing increasing reliance on hierarchical authority and growing disregard for even the tradition of faculty governance. These changes are being made in the name of increasing the pace of organizational change and improving productivity, thus emulating private business. Reduced commitment by faculty, staff, and students is one of the consequences of such changes, even though these impacts are rarely acknowledged. Some universities are starting programs that focus on group-oriented problem solving. These programs are intended to invite—and use—the ideas of individual employees in new ways that inevitably involve some power sharing. Leadership will determine whether these programs, including their power sharing, become institutionalized or disappear as a passing management fad.

Honoring and Conserving Resources

As leadership inevitably works to protect and enhance life, it is involved with employees, consumers, neighbors, technology, facilities, information, money, the natural environment, and other elements. Typically, leadership treats these elements as means to an end and, in so doing, sacrifices them to the higher good of the goals being pursued. True leadership, in my view, honors and conserves these elements while using them as resources in accomplishing goals.

Each organizational resource is also an element with its own integrity and hence merits recognition and respect. Those who use them should not be wasteful and should honor the element by respecting its limits so as not to damage or destroy it. This requires an ethical relationship with all of the resources (including oneself). Ethics is a primary matter, not an optional concern.

Compassion is a foundation for relating to resources ethically. Acting interdependently and sharing power can help conserve resources by incorporating multiple values and providing checks and balances to prevent domination and exploitation. Given our society's affluence, materialism, and patterns of exploiting the natural environment and people, honoring and conserving resources demands that leadership continue to deepen new values, attitudes, and practices of conservation and preservation.

In criticizing the common treatment of organizational resources as means to achieving organizational goals, I recognize that these practices are accepted and legal. Here, as in many other matters, leadership must depart from traditional practices—especially when these practices are destructive of life.

In academia's environmental and natural resource organizations, as in other academic organizations, numerous goals and practices run contrary to this aspect of leadership. Rarely do organizational goals include—much less place high priority on—honoring and conserving the natural environment and advancing employee wellness in ways that recognize today's high levels of stress and other conditions that harm employee health. Annual targets for research and tuition revenues often fail to include holistic analyses of trade-offs and impacts on organizational resources and outputs. Core values—such as academic quality and institutional rank relative to peers—are seldom explicitly examined in terms of their implications for the treatment and use of all organizational resources. Never in my experience has honoring and conserving organizational resources been an explicit organizational value. Rarely are academic administrators encouraged to honor and conserve themselves by limiting the hours they work or to enhance their wellness by playing, pursuing outside hobbies, or spending plenty of time with their families.

Promoting Change

Change is a fundamental condition of life and a major challenge to individuals and groups. Leadership involves understanding change and discovering future options including attendant dangers and risks. Leadership promotes change by helping others to recognize and understand it and by working with others, not only to adapt to change but also to shape it.

In our time the rate and scope of fundamental change have been increasing. Ready examples include atmospheric processes, human population dynamics, and global cultural patterns—to say nothing of soil erosion and disappearing plant and animal species and the growing scarcity of fresh water. These changes and others are multifaceted and include cyclic and discontinuous patterns of events.

Change represents both welcome opportunities for improving conditions as well as the threat that conditions may get worse. Change cannot be controlled completely; sometimes it cannot be controlled at all. In facilitating change, leaders themselves must accept these realities and work with others to face both the positive potentials and these difficulties. Leaders need to recognize that because they benefit from the status quo they often act to maintain it while attempting to control change. When leaders act this way they obstruct real opportunities and confuse others' understanding of change.

Promoting change involves working with people, groups, and organizations to plan for, decide on, and implement new goals, new ways of operating, and new programs to achieve certain ends. The complexity of change and people's strong reactions to matters involving change make this element of leadership exceptionally demanding. Leadership sets an example of coping with change and helps create processes including conditions for safety and creativity within which others can grapple with the threats and opportunities of change. Each of the other elements of leadership—particularly discovery, sharing power, and acting interdependently—contributes strongly to an effective process for promoting change.

All academic units, particularly environmental and natural resource organizations, face major changes. Yet these units and their leaders are more oriented to the past and to stability than to promoting change. While it is quite clear to most academic leaders that undergraduate liberal arts and many professional curricula currently do not lead to basic environmental literacy for graduates, for example, there are very few examples of major change initiatives addressing this serious deficiency. Even in academia, where major attention is being given to the future and crucial changes, there is generally insufficient commitment and cooperation to really facilitate change. In 1988, for example, the School of Natural Resources prepared a second major strategic plan in response to a central administration directive. Although it was extensive and future-oriented, this plan was virtually ignored by the central administration—which thereby communicated its support for the status quo. The plan itself relied too heavily on the central administration rather than embracing interdependent action with a variety of other actors. In the face of these conditions, leadership in the central administration and the school failed to promote change because they did not place a high enough priority on the effective strategic planning to ensure that all involved parties could commit to it.

LEADERSHIP IN MY ORGANIZATION

It is difficult to characterize how leadership is perceived by others in my organization. Part of this difficulty can be traced to the wide diversity of views coming from three different academic cultures:

biological scientists, social scientists, and planners/designers. Each of these cultures, along with the interests of its organizational units and the people within them, leads to differing expectations of organizational leaders. The difficulty of characterizing this diversity is exacerbated by the fact that my information is impressionistic rather than systematic. Furthermore, having been the dean, I carry biases and blind spots. Nonetheless, I will try to provide at least a cursory picture of the faculty members' perceptions of leadership. Remember the source of this information, however, and its attendant limitations.

Central to the thinking of most faculty is the survival, financial well-being, and academic reputation of the School of Natural Resources. They expect leadership to give highest priority to these issues and to achieve positive results. The continued employment of faculty depends on the organization, on faculty members' satisfaction and pride in their work, and on the school's reputation and achievements. Leadership is expected to be highly committed and responsible for the unit's survival, to have adequate finances, to operate a high-quality instructional and research program, and to be well regarded by the university's regents (trustees) and executive officers (president, provost, and vice-president for academic affairs, as well as other vice-presidents) and by the faculty and administrators of peer units.

Faculty want leadership to be responsible for these matters so that they themselves can concentrate on their research and teaching. The organization's requirements for faculty involvement in, say, strategic planning, curriculum development, and marketing of instructional and research capabilities compete for time and other resources faculty need in order to pursue their teaching and research. They want leadership to understand and respect these needs.

To ensure the organization's well-being, leadership is expected to develop a vision of the organization's future and to mobilize support to implement this vision. The vision is both the property of the leadership and the membership (faculty, staff, students, alumni) and is developed through mutual influence. But initiative in creating, maintaining, and modifying this vision is the responsibility of the leadership. Faculty expect leadership to attract resources from outside the organization and to gain resources equitably from different program groups and people within the school.

Leadership is expected to demonstrate outstanding academic performance as a basis for wise judgments and legitimacy in dealing with peer administrators and faculty. This academic performance is also supposed to provide a model for faculty performance and a basis for leadership's evaluation of faculty program groups and individual faculty members. In this way leadership plays a major role in developing and maintaining standards of performance and ensuring that they are applied to groups and individuals. Another aspect of maintaining standards is to say yes or no appropriately and provide regular informal and formal feedback indicating what is expected and what is not acceptable. This guidance is important, whether or not it is always popular, and faculty expect leadership to provide it.

Leadership is expected to respect faculty governance over the academic program, curriculum, and individual courses. It is also expected to respect academic freedom in relation to faculty decision making within the individual's area of specialization and within matters relating such specializations to wider academic and social policy matters. Underlying these specific expectations is a general expectation that leadership will seek the input of faculty on organizational decisions that will ultimately affect them. Staff have different expectations, but they too want to be consulted on decisions that will affect them personally or in their work. Staff want leadership to recognize that the staff have high value to the academic organization and merit respect whether they are professionals or support staff.

Leadership is expected to have administrative expertise and to ensure effective and efficient management of the organization. Faculty see such work as onerous but necessary and expect leadership to participate in leading it and delegating it. Furthermore, leadership is expected to ensure that such work is done in ways that are directly helpful to faculty and indirectly supportive of the faculty through advancing the well-being of the overall organization.

Leadership is also expected to articulate the strengths and accomplishments of the unit and to view its future with optimism. Leaders are expected to be the spokespersons of the unit and to do this articulately and persuasively whether verbally, in writing, or by demeanor. Such communication is to be directed to different groups including faculty, staff, students, alumni, and central administration, as well as external funders, accreditation organizations, and other external organizations interacting with the academic unit (legislative bodies, public agencies, private for-profit and not-for-profit corporations). Yes, leadership is expected to do cheerleading for the organization and to promote its value, contributions, and aspirations.

Leadership is expected to play a key role in promoting a positive work environment. Faculty, staff, and students want a supportive and task-oriented environment that welcomes initiative and recognizes contributions. Leadership is expected to recognize problems that detract from such an environment and initiate action to improve it. Leadership is expected to model attitudes and behavior that will create and maintain such an environment.

Beyond being pleasant, leaders are expected to demonstrate fairness, respect, and concern for others. This expectation also means that leaders must listen and respond favorably to the people and groups with whom they may conflict. Fairness involves not only interpersonal actions but clear and well-understood processes that are scrupulously followed. Leadership is expected to make exceptions for people experiencing difficulties not of their own making. Moreover, in the face of work-force diversity and other differences, leadership is expected to follow the maxim "equal treatment is not the same treatment." Leadership is expected to be courteous and considerate, of course, and to make every possible effort to listen to concerns and do whatever is consistent with policy and colleagueship to assist faculty, staff, and students.

Some of the differences in faculty expectations focus on the degree to which leadership:

- Seeks input and consensus before making decisions
- Is concerned with task and content as opposed to process
- Seeks individual accountability to the organization's mission and goals as opposed to encouraging individual autonomy
- Imparts information about the academic unit as well as organizational matters that affect the unit
- Is part of the faculty as opposed to being part of the administration
- Acts as an apologist for university policies as opposed to a thoughtful critic and proposer of new policies
- Is influenced by the organization's history and present goals and policies as opposed to future opportunities and new policies and programs

These differences in expectations for leadership can influence the choice of formally appointed leaders and informally chosen leaders. Such differences can also affect the level of conflict and dissatisfaction within the organization. And, finally, these differences in expectations can affect the behavior of the leadership.

The expectations described here determine who is accepted and respected as a leader and how such a leader can proceed in exercising and maintaining leadership. Expectations of faculty, staff, and students cannot be ignored in defining and achieving organizational leadership. Yet these expectations can also give leaders considerable latitude in what they do and how they do it.

Leadership is desired—and if effective, it is trusted. Faculty, students, and staff *want* leadership. Often, however, they expect more than leadership can possibly provide. And despite frequent criticism, rarely is effective leadership challenged or ignored. When this happens, it is almost always the result of leadership violating what is expected and furthermore failing to explain its action and listen to criticism.

PREPARING FOR LEADERSHIP

One can prepare for leadership in many different ways. Here I suggest some basic requirements for leadership in academic natural resource and environmental organizations. Moreover, I offer my perspective on matters that have affected my own preparation for leadership. Although one can intentionally prepare for leadership, certain key aspects of preparation are neither planned nor intentional.

Knowledge and Experience

Leadership of academic environmental and natural resource organizations requires preparing oneself to do research and teaching focused on environmental and natural resource problems. This preparation involves both undergraduate and graduate study as well as work experience focused on the environment. To qualify for an entry-level, tenure-track, academic position requires a doctoral degree and a record of strong performance in academic study and related professional and volunteer work.

In addition, preparation for leadership in these organizations requires an outstanding record of performance as a faculty member, which is generally reflected in promotions to the level of professor. This record generally includes leadership activities inside and outside the university. Such activities include administrative responsibilities in natural resource and environmental organizations, innovative and widely recognized research and related public policy participation, and other responsibilities demonstrating contributions beyond those expected of the typical faculty member.

Often preparation for leadership includes experiences and responsibilities that have nothing to do with academics or natural resource and environmental issues. Such preparation occurs throughout K–12 education and college and includes participating in innumerable scholastic and community activities, particularly those that challenge the person and assist her or him in developing social confidence, gaining organizational experience, and leading activities.

All these experiences provide one with specialized knowledge and skill to do research and to teach on environmental and natural resource topics, as well as knowledge and skill in getting important tasks accomplished by motivating and organizing people.

Personal Values and Characteristics

In my experience, certain personal values and other characteristics have helped me prepare for leadership. Willingness to work hard and achieve high-quality results has been central to my continual learning in preparation for leadership. Being able to perceive power—and selectively challenge it without alienating powerholders—has consistently led me to question the status quo and advocate needed changes. Willingness to listen to others and make requests of them while at the same time being perceived as fair has allowed me to develop relationships and trust in the midst of conflict and differences. My interest in several areas has allowed me to see things differently and, as a result, to continually seek to develop new programs and courses that have attracted the attention and respect of others.

I recognize that racism and sexism are pervasive in our society and that they affect one's preparation for leadership. Because of these patterns of discrimination, many of my experiences as a white male have been different from those of people of color and white women. Change is occurring, true, and it must continue if we are to eliminate restricted access to educational and employment opportunities. A major goal of achieving work-force diversity and multicultural organizations is to recognize, develop, and reward leadership by white women and persons of color. Different leaders have different personal values and characteristics, and I strongly support development and acceptance of this diversity.

EXAMPLES OF SUCCESSFUL LEADERSHIP

From my experience observing leaders, I have found a wide variety of characteristics that, in different configurations and in response to different situations, result in successful leadership. The characteristics and examples listed here are based on my personal experience as a leader and thus reflect my personal style and the situations I have faced.

Individual Characteristics

For me the most important individual characteristic for achieving successful leadership is this: knowing your limitations, failures, and weaknesses as well as your potential, successes, and strengths and then using this information in working with others to achieve common goals. Self-knowledge leads to doing that which one is capable of and seeking assistance from others in areas of weakness—and all the while learning. It also leads to more accurate perceptions and better understanding of other people, which in turn affects a leader's goals, strategies, and behavior.

Limits must be respected. No one is perfect. Everyone fails. Each of these realities is seemingly obvious, but people often ignore them, especially people with power. Leadership requires self-knowledge that recognizes limitations and failures along with the importance of taking risks in order to learn and develop. Over the course of my deanship, I learned more about my own strengths and weaknesses. To do this I sought evaluative feedback. While I would have benefited from earlier and fuller learning in this area, in my experience there were no systematic organizational processes for the annual evaluation of deans based on the observations of faculty, staff, students, and others in a position to assess a dean's performance.

Two other key characteristics have contributed to my leadership: high commitment to the organization's mission along with respect and concern for individuals—faculty, students, and staff who make up the School of Natural Resources. I was not always able to balance these two concerns. When this happened, my commitment to the organization's mission and productivity was sometimes stronger than my consideration for its members. While this may have resulted in short-term productivity, it sometimes led to overcommitted and overloaded personnel, lower morale, and other conditions that detract from long-term productivity.

Other characteristics, as well, contributed to successful leadership:

- Involving faculty, staff, and students in decision making
- Recruiting and hiring personel who are highly qualified and motivated
- Sharing information widely and minimizing organizational secrets
- Minimizing surprises by telling people what would happen *before* action was taken
- Being fair in allocating resources
- Establishing goals and timelines
- Developing new collaborative programs involving multiple units and new sources of revenue
- Maintaining an organizational culture focused on pride in mission, quality of teaching and research, outstanding accomplishments, and progress toward long-range goals
- Being responsive to university-wide priorities and superiors' expectations
- Advocating vigorously on behalf of the organization

Specific Situations

Based on my experience, I will offer a few examples of what I perceive as leadership in three important situations: program; process and function; and values and norms. While each example could be described at great length, my primary objective is to communicate a variety of examples of leadership.

The core of any academic organization is the program. Through these activities the organization creates its primary outputs of education and research—its basic reason for being. Examples of leadership in programmatic matters include:

- Eliminating a long-established, autonomous instructional field studies program and replacing it with a comparable but jointly operated and less costly program
- Initiating exploration of a new program on population/environment dynamics and finding possible leadership and funding
- Articulating a view of interdisciplinary problem solving to catalyze faculty discussion and decision making about the focus of instructional and research programs

In order to operate, an organization requires processes of communication and decision making along with administrative functions. Examples of leadership in this aspect of organizations include:

- Designing and negotiating acceptance for a new organizational decision-making process to determine financial cutbacks and personnel reductions
- Developing a new administrative function of enrollment management in order to become more competitive
- Changing the basic orientation of administration and support staff from routine, inwardly focused functioning to becoming proactive and competitive in relation to external peers

Personnel is a central aspect of work organizations, but it is particularly critical to academic organizations given the nature of teaching and research. Examples of leadership focusing on personnel include:

- Initiating conversations with potential early retirees and achieving retirements that meet both organizational and individual needs
- Creating a new faculty position, gaining faculty support for it, and recruiting an outstanding person to fill it
- Instituting new evaluation processes based directly on organizational goals calling for greater productivity, including higher quality

- Engaging the services of an outside consultant and mediator to help settle conflicts involving valued employees

Values and norms are central in defining an organization and its culture, and leadership plays a critical role in articulating and defending these values. Examples of this behavior include:

- Actively supporting new organizational values of work-force diversity by providing funds for new personnel and activities, being personally involved in combatting sexism and racism, and speaking persuasively for these values
- Intervening in day-to-day organizational functioning in order to prevent violation of policies, stop dishonest practices, and end unfair treatment
- Employing a consultant to work with administrative leadership to understand individual differences and improve means of problem solving
- Advocating high standards for teaching and research

These brief descriptions are selected examples of leadership I have observed in an academic natural resource organization. Anyone wishing to learn about leadership should look for such examples and develop their own casebook describing such situations in which they perceive true leadership in action. Such a casebook will contain a rich reservoir of leadership ideas as well as material for refining and further developing one's understanding of leadership.

FUTURE NEEDS

The future, I think, will force academic environmental and natural resource organizations to change more rapidly than they have in the past twenty years. Four developments will have major impacts for their leadership: deepening environmental problems, the changing dynamics of the U.S. economy, the changing racial and gender composition of the U.S. work force (as well as changes in the roles of people of color and white women), and the growing costs of violence. These changes will require new leadership styles and new skills.

As environmental problems continue to grow worse, more and more academic specializations and units will be dealing with these problems and more societal organizations will be wanting assistance from academia. Leaders of academic environment units will need skills in developing temporary coalitions and new networks. These skills will be needed to create extensive university-wide collaborative programs and to develop new consortia of private and public-sector organizations that can work with academia to reduce specific environmental problems. To do this, academic environmental leadership will need skills in joining generalists and specialists in highly effective task teams that address pressing environmental problems in ways that are not only scientifically sophisticated but practical in terms of cost-effective and widely supported implementation. These leaders will also need more sophisticated organizational change skills and styles that evoke in organizational members strong, sustained commitment to fundamental organizational change. These new change skills will be needed because of the extensive and rapid changes in the environmental disciplines and professions, changes that will undoubtedly affect the demand for services and intensity of competition. Organizational change skills will also have to include more effective ways to terminate programs and deal with consequent losses while at the same time creating new and different programs.

The changing dynamics of the U.S. economy will provide many challenges for leadership in academic environmental and natural resource organizations. New fundraising skills will be needed along with financial ingenuity in changing the patterns of support for these academic programs. At the same time, these leaders will have to be able to work out methods of reducing costs and otherwise operating programs in ways that are congruent with environmental values and economic justice. Economic changes also will bring increased conflict over inequities. These conflicts will be present in the operation of the academic organizations as well as in most efforts to reduce environmental problems. Leadership will be challenged to develop new ethics addressing inequity and to model their implementation. The globalization of the economy will call for leadership to operate in partnership arrangements throughout the world with peer organizations, potential students and other customers, and transnational networks of non-governmental organizations, businesses, and governments. New language and cross-cultural communication skills will be demanded along with styles that are not nationalistic and function in diverse cultural settings.

The changing demographics of the U.S. work force will bring more persons of color and white women into these academic organizations. Continued development of movements for social and economic justice will lead to more white women and people of color in higher levels of organizations and thus in leadership roles. Leaders will be needed who are skilled in developing and administering multicultural organizations. New skills will be needed to combat racism and sexism and discrimination based on income and status. Leaders must be able to apply these skills in academic organizations and in the communities where employees live. Particularly for white males, this will require giving up traditional privileges and developing new commitments to sharing resources. These changes will be attended by a variety of conflicts that will necessitate new skills in functioning in conflict situations—situations where personal involvement in disputes is more highly charged than has typically been the case in organizations. As the composition of the work force changes, these conflicts will include very different styles of conflict and dispute settlement. Leaders will have to be familiar with this greater diversity of styles.

As the world experiences explosive population growth along with growing inequities and exceeds critical thresholds in natural systems, the intensity of social conflicts will increase. Coupled to these conflicts are the availability of very destructive military and police technologies along with individual and group histories of socialization into violence. These conditions will lead to high probabilities of interpersonal and collective violence. In its extreme form, this violence has the power to eliminate life on the planet and even short of this point has devastating potentials that are almost beyond comprehension. No organization or individual, including environmental academic organizations, will be insulated from escalating social conflict and the threat of catastrophic destruction.

Because academic environmental organizations focus on vital and scarce resources that will increasingly become objects of conflict and because these resources will increasingly be affected by violence, academic environmental leaders will have to place major emphasis on what to do about violence. This task will require them to explore the sources of violence and the means of containing it whether in the workplace, in the community, or among ethnic groups or nations. Leadership will need to acquire new ethics, new commitments, new styles, and new behavior in relation to nonviolence and be able to model these changes personally.

Given all these dramatic social changes, future leadership will have to be much different from what I have experienced in my generation or read about in modern history. My own understanding of leadership—as ways of being and action that enable life—has been stimulated by my experience in academic environmental organizations and my growing awareness of social and global changes. In the preceding pages I have described six aspects of leadership that, I believe, begin to respond to the early manifestations of major future changes. But these six dimensions—being compassionate, knowing what is and what could be, acting interdependently, sharing power, honoring and conserving resources, and promoting change—represent only the initial stage of thinking about the major leadership changes needed in the future.

Is such change possible? I don't know. But I am hopeful when I think about changes during my own lifetime, including changes I myself have made and am experiencing. It is clear that humankind has immense capabilities for change, among them formidable knowledge and information. But it is also clear that using this knowledge *effectively* in the face of emerging problems will require acknowledging what we do not know and having unprecedented commitment and creativity—including a deep desire to learn, to share, and to change. I hope you will find ways to contribute to this future leadership.

ACKNOWLEDGMENTS

I am indebted to the late Professor Stewart Marquis for his critical review of the first draft of this chapter. His inspiration helped me pursue my thinking and writing on this topic. I appreciate also the suggestions for revisions from Joyce Berry, John Gordon, and Barbara Dean.

15 Foundation Leadership

....

Jon M. Jensen

THIS IS A PERSONAL ACCOUNT. It is not based on any extensive research, nor is it meant to summarize the sum total of wisdom regarding leadership in foundation work and grantmaking. These comments are not intended to be critical of the grantmaking and grantseeking community and the many fine individuals that work in it. It is simply a summary of observations and understandings I have acquired along the way.

This chapter consists of three general but overlapping areas. The first describes my career path and certain experiences that I believe have shaped the development of my interests and skills. The second is a brief glimpse into what life is like working for a private foundation. The third is my own opinion of what skills I believe are essential to good grantmaking. I offer these thoughts as part personal history lesson and part philosophy born of that experience. The most striking examples, of course, are my mistakes.

OVER A DECADE OF GRANTMAKING

If you ask people in the environmental movement how they began their career in this field, the most frequent response would be "by accident." While my high school work in biology and undergraduate work in psychobiology at Albright College touched upon conservation issues (such as the conservation of bat populations in West Virginia), I didn't really engage in environmental work until the latter part of my graduate education. While completing my master's thesis

252

in animal behavior at Bucknell University in 1979 I took a part-time position as coordinator of an experimental environmental studies program. This program sought to draw on faculty from nine different departments (from philosophy to engineering.) It was a challenging position for a number of reasons. First, I had to bring together a highly diverse faculty—a group not used to working together on a common educational program. Second, I had to structure their diverse perspectives into a coherent framework for the students to follow.

The degree to which I contributed to the successes (and failures) of the course, was, I believe, due to my energy, patience, and willingness to "walk and talk"—that is, to spend a lot of time in each faculty member's office (often in as many campus buildings as there were participating faculty members) and serve as a communications link for what each faculty person was thinking and doing for the course. This job involved a good measure of diplomacy skills (such as when we discovered that the team of faculty for one course had assigned enough readings for *two* courses, and I had to go back and tell them they were overloading the students). It was also fascinating, since each faculty visit was a window on that discipline's special perspective on environmental studies. It sensitized me to the fact that even if people don't see the same thing in quite the same light, they aren't necessarily wrong.

A Small Conservation Nonprofit

I finished my master's in animal behavior from Bucknell University with the firm conviction that neither teaching nor research was in store for me. I decided instead that my future was in administration—but in higher education, not the environment. In 1980 it was only "by accident" that I obtained my first full-time career position as executive director of the Wildlife Preservation Trust International. WPTI is a small conservation nonprofit organization that raises funds for endangered species and then awards these funds as small grants for captive breeding programs and related research, fieldwork, education, and reintroduction. Given that our office consisted of myself and two secretaries, the title "executive director" was a bit expansive in the impression it gave. (I likened it to being "vice admiral" of a rowboat.) But it was right on the mark in terms of the range of tasks that the job required. Within this one position I was responsible for board relations and meetings, program planning and development, fundraising, membership services and communications, financial management, and office management and personnel.

Add to this the management of an international program and the travel it entailed, and you have a day-to-day workstyle that demanded flexibility and an ability to move quickly from one task to the next. This experience was invaluable to me. Not only did it give me an opportunity to hone my skills in a variety of areas, but it required that I learn to prioritize and plan so that a diverse set of organizational activities moved forward in concert. Moreover, it increased my tolerance of frustration in that I had to learn to work on a variety of tasks without necessarily seeing any one of them come to completion that day.

The WPTI experience also gave me a chance to see how the various elements of an organization's activities interconnect (or fail to). Many organizations regard program activities, communications, and fundraising as separate elements, for example, either in terms of how they approach them or staff them. Insufficient thought is given to how their program goals relate to their communication strategies and how communication, in turn, enhances their fundraising ability. These understandings are critical to providing sound leadership to nonprofit conservation organizations.

A Large Private Foundation

In 1985, I accepted a position as the first full-time senior program associate for the Conservation Program of Pew Charitable Trusts, a private foundation based in Philadelphia. While the Pew Trusts was a large foundation (awarding over $138 million in 1985), the Conservation Program was relatively modest ($2.6 million was awarded in 1985, only 2 percent of the total).

This position provided an almost unlimited horizon of institutions and projects, as well as the interesting people who undertook them. Because Pew's Conservation Program at the time I joined it was very broad, a wide range of institutions approached the foundation for support. There were three major challenges in dealing fairly with this avalanche of requests: to find the appropriate niche for the foundation's program, to balance this with the philosophy of the founder and the board (which at that time was still relatively conservative), and to integrate it with my assessment of what was needed most and what the conservation program could do best at that point in time.

Most foundations limit the scope of their grantmaking along a number of parameters, including geographic limitations (local, regional, state, national, international), topical limitations (toxics, energy, biodiversity), and sectoral limitations (grassroots activism, policy, research). The focus I developed ran somewhat counter to these typical (and quite valid) approaches to restricting grantmaking programs. Instead, I instituted a focus on supporting programs to develop the "infrastructure" of the conservation movement via training and education—investing in human resources on the assumption that, as issues and approaches change, well-trained leaders would be able to shift with those changes. This program, for the most part, cut across geographic, topical, and sectoral boundaries. One grant, for example, supported the development of the Land Counselor Program by the Trust for Public Lands that trained staff of local land trusts in the management and technical aspects of operating a land trust.

Another emphasis of the Conservation Program was on applied research and technical transfer—supporting the application of sophisticated techniques developed in other sectors (such as computer technology) to the conservation movement. One of the most fascinating aspects of the conservation movement is that, because of its relative youth as a field of endeavor (compared to education, health, or culture, for example), there are many techniques and approaches from other arenas that have yet to be tested. In the mid-1980s, for instance, conservation organizations began to develop debt-for-nature swaps— a conservation-supporting variant of deals that had been a practice in the business world for many years.

I realized early in this position that my intrinsic knowledge of conservation issues would be, under any circumstance, limited relative to the broad scope of the program. To set myself up as an "expert" and act solely on my own counsel would have been risky at best, given the large sums of money that the program was awarding. Instead, I placed primary emphasis on listening to the array of the movement's leaders that I met and exploiting (in the best sense of the word) my role as a "bottleneck" for the many ideas that passed through my office. I tried to understand the themes, trends, and collective problems that cut across institutional boundaries and attempted to provide funds to address these core issues on a broader scale. In effect, this was a sort of "leadership from behind."

A New Association

While working at the Pew Trusts, I had the good fortune to meet a number of people in other foundations who, like me, were dedicated to environmental grantmaking. Until the mid-1980s this scattered group of people had not met for any extended time or communicated in any systematic fashion. As a means of supporting the voluntary efforts of my colleagues in other foundations who were setting up retreats and meetings for this budding group I established a small secretariat for what became the Environmental Grantmakers Association (or EGA, for short). This secretariat also published a newsletter to increase communication among this fledgling group in regard to grantmaking and other environmental activities. I also started a directory for members.

As the first voluntary host of the secretariat I was involved in setting up EGA's bylaws and, with the aid of others, setting out EGA's three-part mission: promoting communication and cooperation among environmental grantmakers, encouraging other grantmakers to make environmental grants, and explaining environmental grantmaking activities and interests to the grantseeking community.

EGA started as an informal set of people with a common interest. Today EGA numbers over a hundred and fifty member foundations and supports a full-time staff person, a variety of publications, and an annual three-day conference and weekend retreat. Indeed, the evolution of EGA has been a remarkable example of the power of volunteerism. Most of what occurred happened because people stepped forward at a key point and committed time, energy, and enthusiasm beyond what was expected of them.

An International Fellowship Program

In the process of reviewing an enormous number of proposals, I came to a fundamental conclusion about the progress of the environmental movement: At the core of every successful project, program, or institution there are a few key figures who make it work. Individual initiative is the key to progress in the conservation movement. It was with this goal in mind that I helped develop and now administrate the Pew Scholars Program in Conservation and the Environment, a relatively new program that provides significant support ($150,000) to early to mid-career "conservation scholars." Recipients are rooted in scholarly work ranging from the humanities to the physical sciences and the professions, yet they must be committed to active environmental problem solving and advocacy for change.

This program has allowed me to focus on leadership development in the biodiversity community. It has, even in its early stages, led to insights on the barriers to success that these hybrid scholar/advocates face. It has afforded an early view of the dynamic energy that can be generated when you bring people of such diverse backgrounds together to focus on a single problem. Most interesting, however, has been the opportunity to create a new program and to develop the whole review and award process from start to finish.

In looking back over my career history, I realize that I have been a grantmaker for about twelve years—first as a "small grants" person for a highly focused nonprofit, then as a generalist for a broad grants program for a private foundation, then as administrator of a prominent international fellowship program. While each of these settings was very different, they provided insights that are common to all grantmaking.

The Other Side of the Table

All these career experiences were spent on the staff side of the board-room table. One of the most personally fulfilling and educational aspects of my career has been born of time spent on the "other side of the table"—that is, as a voluntary member of the governing board of a nonprofit organization.

I serve on the board of directors of three national nonprofit organizations: as treasurer of American Rivers (dedicated to river conservation), as a trustee of the Institute for Conservation Leadership (providing technical and management training to grassroots environmental groups), and as chair of EGA. Every good board member has to be more than just a warm body at the table. They have to be constantly asking themselves this question: What talents, connections, or resources do I have that can assist this group in its mission? Unfortunately, this question is not raised enough.

Board participation allows one to step back from the day-to-day crises that characterize most nonprofits and the ensuing tunnel vision that can afflict even the best-intentioned staffer. It allows one to look at the broader issues of the organization's role and question some of the givens that become ingrained in the institution. This is important to the nonprofit you serve on a voluntary basis, but it is also instructional in terms of what you take back to your own job. For example, in 1990–1991 I participated in a long-range planning process for American Rivers. The goal was to develop a new five-year plan for the organization—one that would extend its mission to the broad range of river conservation issues and establish American Rivers as the nation's principal river-saving organization. This exhausting process took over a year and a half of the board, staff, consultants, and advisors' time. It was a process of stripping away all of the prior assumptions about what was important and what the organization could do, "blue-skying" every idea of what tasks the organization could possibly undertake, and then sorting all of these potential goals and activities into a framework of priorities that could be achieved in the five-year time frame.

The planning process helped me understand the enormous range of issues involved in river conservation, among them the science of river quality and biodiversity maintenance, as well as economic, social, and legal issues. There is also a wide range of ways that the organization can address these problems, ranging from high-level policy development (such as promoting the federal Wild and Scenic Rivers Act) to local grassroots education on the need to protect rivers. The success of the planning process would not have been possible without extensive staff work. But it was strengthened, too, by the diverse perspectives of the board.

It probably comes as no surprise to a foundation staff person that a primary reason for being asked to serve on the board of a nonprofit is for their fundraising knowledge. So long as no conflict of interest exists, this is appropriate. What sometimes surprises the nonprofit is that—because of their contact with so many other nonprofit organizations and their knowledge of management structures—foundation staff can offer assistance on many other fronts.

As a foundation staffer, working on a nonprofit board lets you see how a nonprofit really operates, the pressure it faces, and the amount of time that goes into activities that are generally invisible in grant proposals—that is, administration and fundraising. You can see the vagaries of cash flow and how that instability affects the organization's ability to execute the plans it has made. It is a dose of reality you need.

LIFE IN A FOUNDATION

One consistent characteristic of foundation work is that you are always in demand—whether on the phone, in person, or via the mailbox. Foundation work sometimes feels like being under a waterfall, as you are constantly inundated with requests for conversations, meetings, and consideration of yet another request for support. Much of your energy can go to simply keeping your head above water. Although there is nothing inherently wrong with this, the load can often be so extreme that it's hard to keep up with the demands. Colleagues have often said to me (in reference to one foundation contact or another), "So-and-so never returns my calls." Even under the best of circumstances and the best of intentions, foundation people can be hard to reach.

Life Under Water

One subtlety of foundation work is the understanding that most foundations are primarily in the business of *making* grants, as opposed to following up on grants and evaluating how they worked. This is not as simple as it sounds. Most of a foundation's energy goes into the review and decision making surrounding the awarding of funds. Following up on the progress and impact of funded projects takes on lower priority in the day-to-day activities of the staff person. Few foundations have a significant *evaluation* component—and when they do, it is usually focused more on financial auditing than program assessment.

For example, I once asked a colleague in another foundation what grants were on the agenda that had just been voted on by his board a few weeks ago. I received, in reply, a blank stare that signaled his inability to remember any of the grants he had made at that meeting. He was already so focused on the next set of grants, he had forgotten those he had just finished.

The pressure to keep moving forward is so great that looking back becomes a luxury. As might be expected, grantees may feel neglected because they receive few if any follow-up calls from the foundation and get little or no comment in response to the lengthy and carefully crafted progress reports they submit.

The Potato Chip Syndrome

One of the truly stimulating aspects of foundation work is the unceasing flow of ideas that come into your office in the form of grant requests. Each one usually represents a new issue, a new idea, or a new approach to problem solving. A major frustration of foundation work is the fact that your involvement with these new exciting projects is usually brief. Your contact is usually limited to the time you can spend in reviewing and framing the request for a board decision. After the grant is made, you must move on to the next request. A subtle workstyle influence of this brief contact with grants is what I call the "potato chip syndrome." In this instance, the constant pressure to review, make a decision, and move on to the next grant request can shorten your attention span. People with this syndrome find that they are always seeking the next idea, moving on to the next item with impatience, and have less tolerance for in-depth work with one grant or project. Like opening up a bag of potato chips, you find you can't eat just one.

The most effective way to combat the syndrome is to engage yourself with at least one long-term project—maybe a proactive grant that you have personal interest in, or perhaps writing, or some type of research or involvement in a particular grant. Voluntary work for a nonprofit organization can help as well.

Serving Multiple Constituencies

At its worst, foundation work can be a very isolating existence. Staff can be isolated from the community—and the issues they need to serve—by inclination, time, and distance pressures. (The "in" box can be a tyrant preempting that interesting conference or site visit.) Contact with other grantmakers may be limited. The board of directors may be remotely involved or poorly informed on decisions to be made. The traditional private foundation has an independent endowment that supports its grantmaking, but the independence this provides is at once both a strength and a weakness. This independence can reduce accountability to many of the constituencies that a foundation staffer should be responsive to:

- The affected population (people near a toxic waste dump, for instance, or an endangered species)
- The grantees (or potential grantees) who are undertaking to resolve the problem
- Staff and board of the foundation (who exercise decision-making authority or provide technical assistance)
- Peers and colleagues in other foundations (whose opinion of your professional ability counts)
- The U.S. government (via the IRS and entities that monitor foundation activities)

A foundation staff person with an appropriate perspective must be able to balance the need to be responsive to each of these constituencies. That is, you should understand what each constituency needs from you and understand your responsibility to each constituency. Moreover, the foundation staff person needs the important ability to resolve conflict—for these constituencies are not always in agreement, and your role is often to mitigate the differences.

Often I found myself serving as a translator and advocate in working with the accounting staff of the foundation—people whose role is to make sure that the funds are spent appropriately and as planned. Accounting and grants management is an important aspect of the organization. Accountants serve as the watchdog for the foundation's board by monitoring the expenditures on grants and by certifying that they are staying within the legal bounds of their grantmaking charter. More often than not, accounting staff have little working experience in the real world the grantees live in. Many times I found myself explaining to the accounting staff things like: "The principal investigator had to postpone the field study until June because there was guerrilla activity in the area and they couldn't get to the study site."

The Pile of Money

Some of the more cynical comments that I received when I began working for a foundation included snide comments that I would "never eat another bad lunch" or "ever tell a bad joke." While these comments were perhaps too cynical, they illustrate some of the built-in uncertainties of foundation staff as they stand in front of the "pile of money." They never know whether people's interest in them is based on their own knowledge and abilities, or because they are simply a conduit to something the grantseekers want. Some grantseekers, in their anxious desire to get a favorable response, may curry favor. After the foundation staff encounter this tendency a few times, they may become suspicious of all encounters.

Foundation staff cope with this dilemma in various ways. Some simply believe that all the praise for their wisdom and perspicacity is absolutely true. Others become suspicious and defensive. Most fall somewhere in between these two reactions; they learn to sort out false praise from genuine comments. Still, even in the best of circumstances there is always a nagging uncertainty as to one's intrinsic value. What can sustain a person in this situation is a sense of one's own ability and self-worth, based in part on the candid feedback of a few good friends.

KEY LEADERSHIP QUALITIES

Like the environmental movement itself, grantmakers represent a wide range of backgrounds and abilities. This diversity is a strength of the grantmaking community. While I do not believe there is any "right" background for working for a foundation, I think at least three types of career background are important to being a good grantmaker.

The first is *nonprofit experience*. It is vital that you understand the realities of managing a nonprofit organization. And for the most part, this experience can only come from having worked in that milieu. You need to understand the overall funding and cash-flow pressures a nonprofit faces. You need to understand that even the best-planned project faces inevitable crises that threaten the timeline or plan. You need to have a sense of what goes into executing the ideas and activities set out in the proposal.

The second is *journalistic experience*. There are many parallels between what makes a good grantmaker and a good journalist: understanding what the issue (or story) is; checking the validity of the proposal (or story) from more than one source; and maintaining a healthy skepticism that enables you to ask polite but pointed questions about the fundamental assumptions of the proposed work. Most foundation staff have to *sell* a grant to their superior or the board of directors; this takes an ability to translate what may be complex and highly technical into a brief, clear statement of support.

The third is *analytic experience*. You should be able to separate symptoms (the problem to be solved) from diagnoses (the grantseeker's solution) and, while being respectful, suggest alternative ways of addressing them if you think you have something to offer.

Broad Knowledge vs. Specific Understandings

A current trend in environmental grantmaking is to hire staff with very specific knowledge of a certain subject (such as global warming or toxics). This is in contrast to the traditional trend of foundation staff being broadly conversant with a field but not necessarily technically proficient in any one area. Which makes a better grantmaker? There is no definitive answer. Critics of the "broad knowledge" approach contend that, in this technical world, staff must be experts themselves if they are to spot solutions. Critics of the "specific knowledge" approach assert that it can lead to a narrow view of the world and, given the nature of that type of training, less ability to be flexible and integrative.

Ultimately, the type of staff person a foundation needs must reflect the institution's program interests and requirements. Personal qualities are critical, as well—probably more important than any specific technical background.

Respect for the Grantseekers

The most important part of being a good grantmaker is being respectful of grantseekers and the work they are doing. When grantseekers sit in your office, they are not just presenting a project; they are setting in front of you their dreams, hopes, and, more than likely, a big part of their livelihood. Those you are going to support are easy to work with; they will be able to pursue their plans and, with your financial assistance, are encouraged and motivated to do so.

Those you cannot support (usually the majority) are much more of a challenge. Your decision not to provide support to them, no matter how carefully explained and logically framed, is a form of rejection. How you handle this is a real test of your leadership ability. When a rejected grantee leaves your encounter (via correspondence, telephone, or an in-person visit), your goal should be to ensure that they do so with a sense that you respect them, that they got a fair and candid review, and that their work is valid and important.

My approach has been to offer applicants a candid assessment at each stage of the application process. That includes an initial opinion of which elements of their proposal strengthen their chance of support and which elements weaken those chances. It also includes pointing out what elements match the grantmaking goals of the foundation and what elements do not.

This is rarely a simple or straightforward process. Even under the best of circumstances, staff can rarely say with absolute certainty, especially in the early stages of review, whether a proposal will or will not be supported. Foundation staff are human beings and they do not like to say no to people. The desire not to disappoint can manifest itself as a tendency to offer more encouragement than may be warranted. Put simply, foundation staff can, with the best of intentions, inadvertently mislead applicants down the review path, only to surprise them with an unexpected no.

The flip side of this is the tendency for applicants to hear only those elements of reaction from the foundation staffer that they want to hear. This often begins with a reading of the foundation's guidelines that appears to be a "perfect" match for their project. It continues with meticulous analysis of correspondence and conversation with the foundation's staff in order to second-guess the chances of support. Foundation-wise applicants know how to time the asking of the key question: "What are our chances of getting a grant?" It is often an unasked question because the applicant doesn't want to hear the answer. If asked at the appropriate time, however, this question can save the grantseeker a great deal of time, labor, and anxiety.

Listening to Grantseekers

Truly listening to grantseekers is hard. For the foundation staff person it requires downshifting from the crisis management pace of the rest of office work. Simply focusing on what you are hearing can be difficult if you are mentally tidying up the previous grant request or running ahead to the next task. Understanding what a prospective grantee is saying to you is complicated by the fact that many grantseekers, by the time they are sitting in your office or have you on the telephone, will have researched and rehearsed what they think you want to hear. The most obvious example is the scripted introduction that includes all the buzzwords in your program's guidelines (words like "leadership development" or "citizen empowerment"). This is not a bad strategy, nor dishonest, if the grantseeker's project is in fact working on those issues.

The challenge for the foundation staffer is to get to the heart of the conversation. The goal, of course, is to elicit the information you need to make a sound decision. Doing this is a balancing act: giving grantseekers time to tell their story while at the same time deflecting them from conversational paths that are unproductive. There are a few simple techniques to do this well:

- Tell them how much time they have to make their case. (Imagine, as a grantseeker, the frustration of taking twenty minutes to tell the history of the organization, only to be told that you have five minutes left to describe the project.)
- Outline the goals for the session. (Is it simply to chat, or to develop an in-depth understanding of an issue or the organization, or to discuss in detail a specific request for support?)
- Set out the expected outcomes of the session. (If the project has potential, what would come next?)

While these points may seem laborious, after you've gone over them with a grantee you are usually rewarded with a sigh of relief at knowing what the session's plan and goals are.

Free Consulting

Foundation staff are in a unique position. Their role as grantmaker positions them at a confluence of ideas, individuals, issues, projects, and institutions. Most of the major grantseekers in that funding area will pass through their door at one point or another, especially if the foundation has a well-defined program.

This unique position provides—to the observant foundation person—a broad yet detailed overview of a specific area that few others may have (even those grantseekers working in the area). They also will see a wide range of approaches to executing projects and will know which ones succeeded, which ones failed, and why. This can be a real asset to the grantseeking community if the grantmaker takes the time to pass along this information to those who need it.

LEADERSHIP ROLES AND STYLES

There are two basic types of grantmaking: reactive and proactive. They reflect, primarily, where the balance of initiative is on the development of a project, from the grantee to the grantmaker.

Reactive Grantmaking

Reactive grantmaking is the traditional type. Put simply, the grantmaker sits and waits for requests to arrive in the mail or, as it is termed in the foundation business, "over the transom." Presumably this refers back to the days when publishing offices had transoms over their doors for ventilation and hopeful authors would deliver their unsolicited manuscripts that way. Reactive grantmaking, at its least organized level, epitomizes responsiveness to the grantseeking public. If the foundation has no guidelines for the submission of proposals, then it is in effect saying "I'm open to suggestions—tell me what you need." This, of course, can result in a large volume of requests. With the absence of guidelines communicating an open agenda of interests, every grantseeker will assume they fit.

Most foundations, however, have some kind of guidelines. Sometimes they are unwritten, as I learned from my nonprofit experience. My organization had, for a number of years, received significant grants from a local foundation, the major donor of which was also on my board of directors. We had always received grants for this foundation simply by sending a short letter to the donor. As this person was getting on in years, I thought it was time to start a relationship with the foundation's staff. I put together what I thought was a great proposal, submitted it, and within a few weeks received a flat rejection. My request was "outside of guidelines." When I asked why our earlier requests had been supported, but not this one, I was politely informed that the foundation had another category of grants not set out in the guidelines: "whatever a board member wants." I had simply taken the wrong route.

Most foundations do have some sort of guidelines. The degree of detail or restrictiveness depends on the degree to which the foundation wants to restrict the number and type of applications it receives. This is driven in part by how closely the foundation follows (in its own mind or as perceived by the grantseeking public) its own guidelines.

Proactive Grantmaking

The flip side of reactive grantmaking is proactive grantmaking. In its purest form, the foundation sends the message "don't call us, we'll call you." That is, they are not interested in responding directly to the needs expressed by the grantees in their proposals. Instead, proactive grantmakers seek out problems and devise strategies for funding their solution. This process is proactive in that the identification, research, and strategy are usually developed by the foundation's staff or consultants. Grantees (as well as many others) may be consulted in the process, but not necessarily.

There are both strengths and weaknesses in this process. Proactive grantmaking has great potential to address problems that go beyond the needs of any one institution. Proactive grantmaking can develop collaborative approaches to problem solving that might not evolve on their own, due to institutional competition or because nonprofits are so busy trying to solve the problems they are dedicated to that it is hard for them to find time to look at broader issues. For example, over the course of a few years I heard many leaders of small, local conservation nonprofits complain that they felt inadequate at various aspects of institutional management. I sought out a local organization that conducted management training workshops and made a grant to support a feasibility study and then a series of nonprofit management seminars developed specifically for leaders of these groups. The program was a success. Besides providing much-needed training, it gave birth to a regional association of conservation leaders and cooperative ventures in research and marketing.

A weakness of this approach is that proactive grantmaking can be unresponsive to the grantseeker's needs if driven solely by the narrow perspective of the foundation staff person's idea of what needs to be done (or if it is subject to subtle political issues that the foundation staff may not be aware of). This is a leadership risk that a proactively oriented foundation person runs. One foundation staff person undertook to stimulate a series of coalitions around environmental issues by providing funds to aid organizing and other aspects of coalition building. Because of rivalries between the groups and other problems, the coalitions failed to form.

While foundations should take these risks, they should do so in an informed and sensitive manner. Because grantseekers wish to please the foundation, they may be willing to go along with a proactive grant even if they are unenthusiastic. Finding the balance between making an unpopular but valuable leadership grant and attempting to force an unworkable change is one of the biggest challenges of grantmaking.

FOUNDATION STRENGTHS AND WEAKNESSES

Foundations play a unique role in the philanthropic community. As institutions, they have their strengths and weaknesses in how they are able to resolve problems. Understanding this is important not only to the staff who work for foundations, but also to those who seek support from them.

Flexibility vs. Continuity

A real strength of foundations is their relative ability to move quickly to respond to problems and needs as they arise. This flexibility is born primarily of a foundation's financial independence and because they, for the most part, *make grants* rather than do projects. This is an important distinction. When a nonprofit organization undertakes a project, it must first acquire resources and staff and develop the institutional infrastructure to undertake the project. This takes time. Foundations merely have to make a grant and move on to the next project. This ability can free them from institutional inertia—the tendency to continue in a certain direction even after a project is complete. It allows foundations to continuously seek out new issues and respond swiftly by providing stimulus in the form of grants for work in that new area.

For the grantees, the foundation's financial flexibility is the proverbial two-edged sword. Because nonprofits are, to a greater or lesser degree, financially dependent on foundations, they are susceptible to the vagaries of a foundation's tendency to move on to new issues. Many nonprofit CEOs have lamented Foundation X or Y's decision to fund in an area for one or two years, then rapidly shift focus to something else, leaving the organization with an issue that still needs work but no support to tackle it. It is no coincidence that many nonprofit CEOs rank "reduce financial dependence on foundations" as a high management concern.

Continuity is as important as flexibility in grantmaking. Leadership is exercised when foundations pinpoint a critical issue and fix the timelines for their commitment to it, thereby giving grantseekers a clear understanding of what they can expect in terms of funds and time.

Independence vs. Responsiveness

As noted earlier, foundations have a unique opportunity to take risks and exercise leadership in the environmental community. The degree to which they do so as experts and independent agents—versus serving just as gatherers of information and synthesizers of new programs to address them—involves a delicate balance of listening and then being able to go beyond the symptoms in a sensitive manner. For the foundation staff person, to be just a listener is to abdicate the responsibility to provide leadership based on your unique position in the foundation. To be just an expert is to lose touch with the community you are dedicated to serve. To find a healthy balance is the major challenge facing those who enter the world of foundations.

16 Six Insights

....

John C. Gordon and Joyce K. Berry

GIVEN THE PRECEDING CHAPTERS, it is clear that leadership in action has many faces and draws on many skills. This remarkable diversity of leadership qualities is the central point we wish to convey. It is also clear, however, that common themes emerge. These contributors, although representing a wide array of environmental organizations and situations, cite many similar leadership actions and characteristics. Often, though, these are described in different words and the context may obscure similarities. In this final chapter we have distilled a brief list of the common elements of environmental leadership that includes insights shared by two or more of the authors. Other insights can undoubtedly be drawn, but these seemed most important.

POINT 1: BE A LEADER *AND* A FOLLOWER

Everyone, in every environmental organization or situation, will need to both lead and follow. In every organization there are many leaders—not all, or even most, readily identifiable from an organizational chart. Charles Henry Foster, for example, concludes that leadership is not dependent on status, office, or popularity. Jay Espy shows that in a small nonprofit organization, it is vital that everyone can both lead and follow, because rapidly changing situations call for quick shifts in the leadership skills exercised. James Crowfoot says that shared power is critical to leadership especially in academic organizations because of the extreme variety of specializations and an increasingly inter-disciplinary problem-solving approach. Henry Webster stresses the

270

increasingly diffuse and participatory nature of environmental leadership (leadership through thinking and cooperation). As this trend
continues, it will become increasingly important for every leader, even
leaders pro tem, to understand and empathize with those who, for the
moment, are followers.

Leaders often are created by and confined by, at least initially, the
boundary conditions imposed by the organization. Ralph Schmidt
illustrates the structural constraints imposed by "one country, one
vote" international governance. Often the leader's biggest task is to
make clear the need to change these boundaries and structures, however, and to persevere until the change is accomplished. Thus, individual and organizational initiatives and constraints interact constantly
and effective leaders are continually aware of this tension between
themselves and their organizations.

POINT 2: THINK ABOUT CHANGE

All who will be environmental leaders must exert extraordinary effort
to think about and prepare for change. For change is now clearly the
rule, not the exception, both in the environment of environmental
leadership and in the perception and solution of environmental problems. Yesterday's burning issue becomes today's cold trail as scientific
knowledge about the environment increases. Food safety, a paramount
public environmental issue, illustrates this point. Now that a broad
public has become more concerned about pesticide residues and irra-
diation, it is clear the scientific community is much more concerned
about the human health risks of microbial contamination and toxins. It
is perhaps safe to speculate that by the time the public is aware of the
microbial risks, the scientists will have moved on. Thus the effective
environmental leader must be able to anticipate change and make it
manageable.

In the introduction we commented on the rapid changes many
environmental professions and organizations are undergoing. Just as
the real political world has outstripped the imagination of most of us,
so too will the environmental world continue to surprise us. Bill
Brown maintains that environmental excellence, including both compliance and prevention, has now become a bottom-line objective for
corporate America. Jeff Sirmon points out the sweeping changes that

the USDA Forest Service is assimilating. Different people and different leadership styles are arising there to accomplish needed change, and the very concept of "natural resource management" is changing. "Ecosystem management" and "sustainable development" are now concepts we struggle to put into practice; a short time ago they were on the fringe of the unknown.

POINT 3: DEVELOP BREADTH AND FLEXIBILITY

Environmental leaders need great breadth and flexibility—not only to anticipate and accommodate change, but because a multiplicity of disciplines is needed to understand, let alone solve, environmental problems. The complexity and scope of these problems (pollution, biodiversity, sustainable ecosystems) no longer allow us the luxury of promoting or believing in *the* environmental discipline. With grinding regularity, one is subjected to the claim that "more money for discipline X will solve (some day) environmental problem Y. According to our authors, environmental leaders know better. Nothing is quite as likely to induce humility as the need to ask the help of those specialists that only yesterday you deemed insignificant. Thus environmental leaders, while usually grounded in a single discipline or profession, look to *all* for help and maintain a healthy skepticism about the universal sufficiency of their own brand of snake oil. This means they will be, in this sense, generalists as well as specialists. It also means that they will recognize, as do most of these authors, that pure luck—and, less purely, the ability to recognize and respond to situations not of our creation—are primary attributes of environmental leaders. As Jim Lyons notes, leaders will be those who seize the opportunities created by luck and timing.

POINT 4: LEARN TO LISTEN

All agree that communication is paramount; the complexity of environmental issues and the emotion-charged atmosphere in which they are confronted make positive communication difficult. Until the discourse on an issue is fully apprehended, it is usually futile to chart a course. Leslie Carothers' examples show how anticipating and preparing for difficult issues and explaining what you are doing and why—before you do it—leads to successful communication. Specifically, environmental leaders must learn carefully and practice the first and most important communication skill: listening. Jon Jensen's suggestions for enhancing listening and communication between grantseekers and grantmakers by outlining session goals and expected outcomes can well be applied to many other situations. Carol Perry's notion of "ritual space" is another approach to lessen polarization, as is Ty Tice's advice to groups involved in conflict management to engage in "kitchen talk." Listening is especially difficult for most of us with a fairly keen sense of environmental problems and needs. Our first impulse is often not to listen but to tell. But telling doesn't work, as most accomplished public speakers remind us, unless the audience's characteristics and needs are defined with respect to a particular topic. Environmental leaders must above all understand their audience; this understanding comes only through effective listening.

POINT 5: SET AN ETHICAL EXAMPLE

Most successful environmental leaders operate from a strong ethical base and a fully formed code of personal belief and conduct. As Kent Olson makes clear in defining philanthropy, and Jack Ward Thomas in describing a land ethic, the environmental leader's ethical concerns must embrace both people and the land. No longer can we think about one without the other as we confront environmental problems and our own obligations as individuals and professionals.

Each of these authors has spoken about a deep personal commitment to the environment and a profound sense of mission. We believe, and they exemplify, that ethics is best expressed not through examination and excoriation of the conduct of others but rather by example and in workaday actions not explicitly labeled as "ethically based" or "conscience-driven."

POINT 6: BE A LIFELONG LEARNER

Leaders must be lifelong learners. Most of our authors discuss the need for continuous personal and intellectual growth. The concept of "career-long education" has progressed from a utopian concept to a practical necessity, and frequent career changes are seen to be a routine component of the informal education process. One might also say that career changes prepare one to expect change and thus prepare one for leadership. Most of these contributors have tried a variety of roles and jobs and acknowledge that the path to their current position has been anything but direct and precisely planned. We think this is an important strength. The ability to perform successfully in different organizations and different circumstances in order to achieve various goals develops the kind of breadth and flexibility that we described earlier. It also appears to cultivate a willingness to take risks, venture into areas that are not known and comfortable, and accept the fact that our knowledge and experience will always be insufficient. Many environmental professionals, for instance, note specifically their expertise in the physical and biological sciences, but their deficiencies in the social sciences. A commitment to career-long education allows leaders to reassess their strengths and weaknesses continually and develop new knowledge and skills as they and the world change. We believe this to be an especially critical attribute.

These six points—being a leader and a follower; thinking about and preparing for change; developing breadth and flexibility; acquiring communication skills; operating from a strong ethical base; committing to career-long learning—seem to define the future of environmental leadership. Leadership through thinking and cooperation, as well as honest sharing of leader and follower roles, will, we think, be more important than the diligent application of any leadership theory or the exercise of "innate" leadership talents. Anyone involved in solving environmental problems can, and must, learn leadership. Only then will we create the critical mass to solve problems that are really codetermined with the human condition and no less complex.

About the Contributors

Joyce K. Berry is former director of Career-Long Education, School of Forestry and Environmental Studies, Yale University, and is currently assistant professor, Forest Sciences Department, Colorado State University.

William Y. Brown is vice-president of Environmental Affairs, WMX Technologies, Inc., Washington, D.C.

Leslie Carothers is vice-president for Environment, Health, and Safety, United Technologies Corporation, Hartford, Connecticut.

James E. Crowfoot is professor of natural resources and urban and regional planning, School of Natural Resources, University of Michigan.

James J. Espy, Jr., is president of Maine Coast Heritage Trust, Brunswick, Maine.

Charles H. W. Foster is adjunct research fellow and lecturer at the Center for Science and International Affairs, John F. Kennedy School of Government, Harvard University.

John C. Gordon is Pinchot Professor of Forestry and Environmental Studies, School of Forestry and Environmental Studies, Yale University.

Jon M. Jensen is program officer, The George Gund Foundation, Cleveland, Ohio.

James R. Lyons is former staff assistant, U.S. House of Representatives Committee on Agriculture, and is currently assistant agriculture secretary for Natural Resources and Environment, Washington, D.C.

W. Kent Olson is director of special projects, The Conservation Fund, Washington, D.C.

Carol Rosenblum Perry is a technical editor-writer in Corvallis, Oregon.

Ralph C. Schmidt is senior advisor on forests and biodiversity, United Nations Development Program, New York.

Jeff M. Sirmon is deputy chief for International Forestry, USDA Forest Service, Washington, D.C.

Ty Tice is environmental mediator, Mediation Services, Seattle, Washington.

Jack Ward Thomas is chief research wildlife biologist, USDA Forest Service, Le Grand, Oregon.

Henry H. Webster is project director, Lake States Regional Forest Resources Assessment, St. Paul, Minnesota.

Index

●●●

Island Press Board of Directors